THE FRAMEWORK OF FICTION

SOCIO-CULTURAL APPROACHES TO THE NOVEL

The Framework of Fiction

Socio-Cultural Approaches to the Novel

J. A. BULL

M
MACMILLAN
EDUCATION

First published 1988

Published by
MACMILLAN EDUCATION LTD
Houndmills, Basingstoke, Hampshire RG21 2XS
and London
Companies and representatives
throughout the world

Printed in Hong Kong

British Library Cataloguing in Publication Data
Bull, J.A.
The framework of the novel : socio-cultural
approaches to the novel.
1. English fiction — 18th century —
History and criticism   2. English fiction
— 19th century — History and criticism
I. Title
823'009   PR851
ISBN 0-333-40674-5
ISBN 0-333-40675-3 Pbk

Contents

TO CHRISTINE, CHRISTOPHER AND STEPHEN
who kept me at it

Preface

This book arose out of a series of lectures given over the last nine years as part of the Diploma of Higher Education course at Manchester Polytechnic; as a result I felt that there was a need to gather together in one place material which was widely scattered amongst books and periodical articles, not all of them easily available to the less advanced student. Much of the element of interpretation and analysis in this book therefore owes a debt to students on that course, past and present, who in discussion helped me to sort out and knock into shape my own responses to the various theories and items of evidence cited here. I would also like to thank Tony Neville for performing a similar role in an informal way and the Research Committee of the Academic Board of Manchester Polytechnic for granting me a term's sabbatical leave in order to commit these responses to paper. Finally I would like to thank my family for putting up with the disruption to domestic routine caused by a project of this kind.

J. A. B.

1. Introduction

This is a book about one sort of literary text – the novel – and its relation to society. It outlines a certain approach to novels in general and then refers to specific texts in order to illustrate that approach. The starting assumption is that in order to understand the nature and development of the novel form it is helpful to know more than just what is between the covers of given novels on the library shelf. The approach attaches great importance to the fact that novels do not simply 'appear' or drop out of the sky but are written by men and women with definable social origins and characteristics and are read by men and women who can be defined in similar terms. Between reader and writer various other social and economic factors may intervene and the whole process of committing words to print and conveying them to readers takes place in a specific socio-cultural context at a particular period of time. To use a shorthand term, the book is about the 'socio-cultural approach' to the study of fiction.

The term 'socio-cultural approach' may seem uncouth and unnecessary to anyone who expects the study of literature to be free of the sort of jargon which is associated with the sciences or social sciences. If there needs to be a book about 'the novel and society' why not use that comparatively simple title? Alternatively, what is wrong with the phrase 'sociology of literature' which appears in the title of some recent books and higher education courses?

The issue of names is not merely a superficial one, since by careful definition it is possible to focus on what this book hopes to include and to omit. The next section therefore examines the implications behind the terms 'novel and society' and 'sociology of literature' with the aim of distinguishing them from what is implied by the approach used here. Later sections consist of an explanation of the 'socio-cultural approach', its potential and its limitations.

The Novel and Society or Vice Versa?

Some critics of literature have always held to the belief that their main task – or even their only task – is to analyse, interpret and evaluate 'the text': that is the words on the page in the work in question. In its most extreme form, for example the New Criticism that was dominant in the 1940s and 1950s, this approach regarded even information about the *author* of a given novel as marginal, slightly frivolous and distracting because it might damage the critic's ability to respond adequately to the text itself. These critics take as their motto D. H. Lawrence's advice, 'Never trust the artist, trust the tale' and reject any evidence about the society or circumstances in which the text was written. Their outlook is reflected in this comment:

> Literature by a fortunate dispensation does not reflect very accurately the convulsions of the social order. Its revolutions sometimes precede the social ones, sometimes follow them, sometimes, it would seem overlap them quite pointlessly . . . . But as soon as we begin to look closely at a particular patch of literature we are likely to see it developing according to its own principles, which have their own interest, and are likely to be at least partly fortuitous in their relations to the wars, technologies or movements of classes that are their temporal accompaniments. The dispensation is fortunate, for it is a happy instance of what we mean by freedom of the spirit. (Graham Hough, *Reflections on a Literary Revolution*, Catholic University of America Press, 1960, p. 1)

Although Graham Hough, the critic who wrote this, might now prefer not to be held to it, nevertheless it is representative of a certain view which denies any systematic relationship between literature and the society which produces it (along with the 'wars, technologies and movements of classes'). Literature is distinguished instead by a happy state of independence, here called 'the freedom of the spirit'.

However, there is another view which can be traced back to the French nineteenth-century critic Mme de Staël (1766–1817), whose approach tried to relate literature to a particular national and social setting (the *Volksgeist* – spirit of the people) and to the historical period of its production (the *Zeitgeist* – spirit of the time). Another French critic, Hippolyte Taine (1828–93) refined the idea by extending the possible influences to three: *race, moment* and *milieu* – or 'national origin', 'historical origin' and 'social setting'. It received a powerful impetus from the writings on art of Marx and Engels and of their followers who were committed to the notion that literature resembled other human activities in being adequately explained only by the social and economic relationships underlying it. Since some Marxists have also been professional literary critics it is not surprising that there have always been people prepared to argue against Hough's view quoted above and to justify their position through studies of particular texts. For these critics and for non-Marxists who have followed the same line the expression 'novel and society' implies the use of social and historical and other 'external evidence' to cast light on the text – the study and evaluation of the text as an end in itself being paramount.

Unfortunately 'novel and society' has ceased to be a satisfactory term for this tradition, since it has been given a different potential meaning by the growth of sociology as a discipline. Some social scientists have turned to fiction as a possible source of material for their own studies, as for instance does Morroe Berger. Berger's goal is not the text but the society in which the text was produced, as is indicated by the questions he sets on the first page:

> How do novelists tell about social life? How far can fiction supplant history or social science, even assuming that Engels exaggerated to make a point? How can the imagined world of the story-teller inform about the real world of experience? What good is the novel if it merely clothes sociology in narrative, incident and anecdote? (*Real and Imagined Worlds* Harvard University Press 1977, p. 1)

The implication of these rhetorical questions is that the novel can only be 'good' if it provides data for the sociologist. Berger's book is written on the premise that the novel is a reflection of society but that it is society and not the mere reflection which is deserving of study.

It is true that in discussing so-called 'popular novels' it could be argued that the most appropriate approach is to consider what they tell us about society (in Joan Rockwell's words: 'facts about the state of technology, laws, customs, social structure and institutions. Second, more subtle and less easily obtained, information about values and attitudes.' (*Fact in Fiction*, RKP, 1974, p. 4)). However, even in this case it is preferable to think in terms of a question like: 'are popular novels different from "literary novels" and is this *because* we study them in a different way?'

As an alternative to the potentially misleading 'novel and society' the title of this book might have incorporated the phrase 'sociology of literature', or more precisely, 'sociology of the novel'. Although this term has gained some currency in recent years it is open to an objection because of the *methodology* it implies: that is, our assumptions as to how a 'sociologist of literature' might go about his task. Although many social scientists themselves would distinguish the way in which they practise their discipline from the methods of the so-called 'hard sciences', such as physics and chemistry, there is still in many people's minds a notion that sociology (and even more so, social *science*) ought to be less subjective than a discipline such as literary criticism. In its fully-fledged form a 'scientific' discipline implies the gathering of quantitative, or measurable, data in order to construct a hypothesis or *theory*; this theory is then tested against further evidence and refined until it fits the data available. Obviously in the case of sociology the data are not as 'hard' as physical data, such as weight or temperature, but involve more challengeable evidence, such as population statistics or membership of given social classes; where information is gathered from questionnaires and interviews, especially, a strong element of subjective judgement is involved. Nevertheless the *aim* is still to identify data which are as accurate as possible for the purpose in hand.

It is not impossible to use numerical data in literary study. For example, we could take the publication figures for a certain eighteenth-century novel (x) and compare them with the number of the population who belonged to a certain social class at the time of publication (y). As a result, we can say *either* that (if y is greater than x) all the readers of the novel *could* have come from that social class (though they did not necessarily do so) *or* if *x* is greater than *y* that some readers of the novel must have belonged to another social group. (The numerical data do not of course tell us how much the readers enjoyed the experience!)

The term *sociometric* has been used by one writer to describe this sort of technique because it starts from a basis of social *measurement*.[1] However, it has severe limitations, even assuming the data are available and incontestable. For example it is not safe to say we can *prove* that the readers came from a given social class. Even if *x* is less than *y*, it would still be possible that some members of class *y* had not read the novel while some members of another class, *z*, had done so. Since all the readers are now dead it is not possible to assign them directly to a social class. The most we can say is that if *x* is less than *y*, it is *feasible* that all the readers came from class *y*, whereas it is obviously not feasible if *x* is greater than *y*. There are loopholes even in this highly qualified statement – one is that the number of readers is not necessarily the same as the number of *purchasers*.

Since even tentative sociometry can throw up useful suggestions it is one technique which can be employed (though not uncritically) in a socio-cultural approach. Clearly in order to look at the relationship between text and society it is necessary to have some social data and some literary data to work from. What is difficult is to identify a systematic correspondence between the two. For some kinds of critic – the Marxists – the attempt to do this is essential since their philosophy dictates that in the last analysis economic reality underlies and explains all human activity, including novel-writing and reading. The next chapter tries to assess the success of their efforts. However, those of us who are not committed Marxists are probably grateful that we have no pressing need to frame such a correspondence except in a piecemeal and speculative way. For this reason 'sociology of the novel' is probably too pretentious and pseudo-scientific to describe the kind of activity we have in mind here. In this connection it is interesting that the French critic Lucien Goldmann was careful to give his major work the tentative title, *Towards a Sociology of the Novel*.

Therefore it is not possible yet to speak with any confidence about 'the sociology of the novel' as a parallel to, say, the 'sociology of the family' or the 'sociology of the Third World'.

Certain aspects of the production and consumption of novels can be treated sociologically, or more precisely *sociometrically*: it is possible to have a sociology of the author, or a sociology of the audience. But the whole process of writing and reading has not yet been treated satisfactorily as a social phenomenon in any convincing account. The proof of this is that in all that has been published under the heading of 'sociology of literature' there are few references to concepts that non-sociologists would not easily understand; what is *called* sociology is usually a form of literary criticism.

The Approach Explained

If this book is not concerned to use fiction as an *illustration* of social concepts and there is a doubt as to whether such a discipline as the 'sociology of the novel' yet exists, what is its subject matter? Something close to the socio-cultural approach is described by Wellek and Warren in their book *The Theory of Literature* which devotes some space to what they call the *extrinsic* approaches to a text. Wellek and Warren classify these extrinsic approaches according to the aspects of human activity which they claim can affect the production and reception of the text, for example biographical, psychological, historical and sociological approaches among others. The term 'socio-cultural' seems more meaningful than 'extrinsic' to sum up these approaches. Moreover, although there are advantages in classifying the approaches, it can be done equally appropriately on the basis of a *communication model* of literature (see p. 10). A rough primary classification can be made according to the starting point used for the approach – empirical data on the one hand, or theory on the other:

(1) Involves investigations of specific circumstances surrounding texts or groups of texts. An example would be Richard Altick's writing on the eighteenth-century reading public in *The English Common Reader*.
(2) Includes overarching theories which attempt to explain literary production in terms of social determinants (e.g. Terry Eagleton's theory based on the philosophy of the

French Marxist, Louis Althusser, in his *Criticism and Ideology*.

Together with various intermediate approaches each of the above shares the goal of attempting to relate the novel to society. But whereas one starts out with *evidence* (sometimes evidence as hard as that found in branches of social science) the other is essentially abstract and theoretical in nature and can only be challenged on logical or philosophical grounds. Literary criticism can gain much support from either approach, as can be shown by the following analogy.

A geographer interested in a particular group of high peaks in a mountain range and who wanted to find out as much as possible about this natural formation could take various approaches. One method would be to initiate maps, surveys and geological studies of the peaks. This could be done in considerable detail and with much sophistication so that he ended up having a great deal of specific knowledge of a very small area. However, this approach would ignore some important aspects. By confining his attention to the very specific area he would be neglecting to study the lower peaks and the foothills adjoining so that his knowledge of the entire mountain range would be limited. (This would also imply a decision – perhaps an arbitrary one – as to which peaks qualified for his interest and which were to be excluded.) Furthermore, restricting the study to the physical nature of the peaks would omit some other dimensions: climate would be one, although wind and water both influence and are influenced by geology. Another omission would be the fauna and flora of the high peaks, particularly bearing in mind how this differed from or was similar to that for the rest of the range. Finally, this geographer would have ignored the *human significance* of the peaks – their value (if any) to the economy of the country in which they were situated and their relationship to, for example, transport routes or tourism.

In the same way, conventional textual criticism usually deals with a few selected 'great' novels, ignoring the foothills of popular fiction adjoining these peaks.[2] If, in studying the great works themselves the emphasis is on the internal structure or 'geology' of the text this neglects other data which can give us a wider perspective on the object of study. The effect is that the novel may be treated as if it were a self-contained and self-sufficient artefact that had dropped from the sky like a meteorite, with no obvious origin in time or space. The purely textual critic sees his task as studying all angles and surfaces of this unique object (as he regards it) but not taking any account of the environment which produced it or how it reached us.

These analogies can be made more relevant by considering the following pieces of evidence about some well-known nineteenth-century novels. They have a general as well as a particular significance for each text:

(1) Two distinct texts of Hardy's *Tess of the d'Urbervilles* exist, differing in literally thousands of words. One version appeared as a serial in the *Sunday Graphic*; the later one was the basis for the first publication in book form and of most modern editions.

(2) While writing *Martin Chuzzlewit* Dickens decided to 'send' the hero to America in order to stimulate sales when purchases of the monthly part-issues began to fall.

(3) Elizabeth Gaskell originally contemplated calling her novel about life in industrial Manchester, *John Barton*. Her first draft centred on the character of Mary Barton's Chartist father but she changed both the title and focus of interest as publication became an immediate possibility.

The *general* significance of this evidence is that for much fiction it is not easy to identify a complete and integral text, since even after printing it can undergo transformation. The particular significance of these items lies in the way that each illuminates different facets of this, as follows.

First, the two texts of *Tess* show how differences in *publishing media* can influence the nature of the text which is produced. Victorian reticence over sexual matters meant that the editors of some periodicals in which novels were serialised took on the role of censor to 'protect' their readers in a way which today we would regard as either laughable or outrageous. Thus in the book version of *Tess* Angel Clare carries the heroine across a muddy lane in his arms but in the serialised version he had to borrow a wheelbarrow for the purpose. A compounding factor might have been the Victorian habit of reading fiction aloud to a family audience – in other words the *mode of consumption* of a text is relevant to its form and content.

Second, the development of the plot in *Martin Chuzzlewit* demonstrates another aspect of the relationship of the nineteenth-century novelist and the reader. The practice of serial publishing meant that feedback from the readership was immediate enough and early enough to allow amendments to the original conception. Dickens's own working method, by which each serial instalment was written separately to meet a deadline, allowed him to take full advantage of this degree of response from the fiction-reading public.

Finally, in the case of Mrs Gaskell there is evidence of *political and social pressures* influencing the form of the text through the mediating role of the *publisher*. The change of emphasis from the politically motivated hero (John Barton) to the conventional romantic heroine (his daughter) was almost certainly caused by the publisher's assessment of what the middle-class reading public would 'stand for' and his trans-mission of this standard to the relatively inexperienced writer, Elizabeth Gaskell.

Even readers who insist that the main task in studying a novel is attention to the words on the page would probably agree that these are three examples of information that might be useful in coming to an overall assessment of a given novel. Given some acceptance that the approach is worth exploring further, not to supplant textual study but to complement it, it is now timely to analyse it in more detail, using a model derived from communication theory.

The Approach Analysed

Conventional literary study starts from a *static* entity – the text – although it has been shown above that the text of many novels is not quite so stable as it first appears. In contrast the socio-cultural approach assumes that there is a *dynamic* quality in the production and reception of fiction, that is that we are dealing with a *process*. This process can be described in terms of models of human communication.[3]

Anyone who doubts that writing a novel is just as much a process of communication as writing a memorandum or a newspaper should consider whether any novelist ever works without an eventual readership in mind. Although the potential size of that readership has varied and some authors because of various pressures have not been published in their own lifetime, most novelists write because they have something to say and therefore have an interest in reaching as many readers as possible. Where the overriding purpose is the collection of royalties the relationship takes on a sale-and-production form, but since readers are still implicit, we are justified in applying the same model.

The starting assumption therefore is that every novel presupposes an *author* and a *readership*, although it is worth stating at this stage that of course an author's *intended readership* is not necessarily the same as those who actually buy and consume his work. If the classical model of communication is applied to the novel it is implied that the nature of the 'message' ('text' in conventional literary terms) is partially determined by the characteristic features of the author and the readership – as well as by other elements, to be mentioned later.

In the case of the *author*, defining these characteristics is comparatively easy, since most authors of novels can be identified with certainty. Because most fiction has been written within the last two hundred years biographical information is not difficult to come by. (An impenetrable pseudonym, like B. Traven[4] is exceptional, although the use of male names by women writers such as Marianne Evans – George Eliot – is itself interesting from a socio-cultural point of view.) The sort of characteristics which are relevant include: gender; age (when the work was written); geographical origin; social class; religion.

Clearly it would be misleading to claim that such features explain completely why the novels of Jane Austen, an unmarried woman living in the Home Counties off a small legacy, differ so markedly from those of Walter Scott, a Scottish lawyer whose poetry and 'bestsellers' brought him a knighthood, wealth and international fame. However, the significance of such information has long been recognised in that only the 'purest' forms of literary study refuse to take account of such biographical details. The socio-cultural approach, however, particularly in its Marxist inflections, does not rest with attributing the uniqueness of a particular text to the individual psychology of the author, developed by circumstances. Instead it examines categories of features like the ones above, to relate a novel to the formations of the *society* in which the author's psychology has evolved – particularly the gender and class-power relationships in that society.

The characteristics of the *audience* are far less easy to define, partly because readers are so heterogeneous, partly because they are untraceable in many cases: you do not have to file birth and marriage certificates in order to read a novel. In fact the very meaning of 'read' is open to question. The *reader* is not synonymous with the *purchaser* since, apart from those who purchase books and do not read them, the borrowing of novels on a formal or informal level can mean that there are far more readers than indicated by sales figures. Furthermore, where reading aloud in a family circle is prevalent (as in the mid nineteenth century) some readers have a different degree of access to the text from others. Finally, the readership which the author has in mind for his or her work might not conform to the actual readership. Ian Fleming is said to have been surprised by the 'downmarket' appeal of the James Bond novels, while some works intended for adults, such as *Robinson Crusoe*, are now largely read by children.

So is it possible to define 'readership' at all? There are certainly reasons for including or excluding various segments of the population at any given period. For example:

(1) Before the opening of the twentieth century *literacy levels* are important in defining the potential readership for fiction, and as education is allegedly responsible for literacy it seems fair to assume that the further back we go in the previous centuries the less likely it is that readers will come from the uneducated (and therefore probably working-class) segment of society.

(2) Similarly, the *cost* of novels has tended to restrict readership to the more affluent. Accordingly we would expect reductions in price (through such devices as instalment publishing) to increase readership among the less privileged groups. Conversely we might speculate that work

which appears only in very cheap format (e.g. in our own day Mills and Boon novels) would appeal disproportionately to less well-off readers.

(3) Finally there is evidence that a particular readership was sought in statements from the author, the publisher or (though here the reasoning becomes circular) the text itself. This is evidence about the expected rather than the *actual* readership. An example would be Leslie Stephen's advice to Hardy: 'Remember the country parson's daughters. *I* have always to remember them!' In the textual histories of novels we can find examples such as the expurgations made in Lawrence's works to avoid offending their supposedly refined readers.

From the sort of sources referred to above it is possible to draw some general observations about the readership of novels. They were originally a taste of the middle classes at a time when the cultured elite regarded fiction as frivolous and scarcely literary. As literacy spread and printing costs fell with the introduction of new technology and cheaper paper, novel-reading extended both upwards and downwards in the social scale, though novels tended to cluster together in strata aimed at different social groups.

A third element which appears in the classical communication model is the *channel* of communication. The channel by which the message is transmitted should not be confused with the message itself. At different periods the channel for literature has varied in its characteristics and this has often influenced the development of different 'genres'. For example Chaucer's poetry was distributed in manuscript form to the poet's circle of friends and admirers; Shakespeare's plays were written primarily for performance by a specific group of actors in a specific theatre and it was only later that they were reckoned 'serious' enough to warrant preserving in print. In the case of the novel the technology of print was available from the beginning but the use of this technology entailed certain economic and social demands which had an influence in their turn. The capital investment associated with printing and with marketing and distribution led to the evolution of *intermediaries* between the writer and his readership, such as publishers, booksellers and literary agents. By the late nineteenth century novelists could take advantage of a system which in return for a share of the profits (calculated in different ways at different periods) cushioned them from the financial risks involved in printing, advertising, distributing and retailing books. The reverse side of this advantage was the mediation or intervention of these functions between reader and writer and the influence of this on the text.

Two examples of the working of this mediation process are the nineteenth-century development of serial and instalment publishing with its effect on the internal structure of many of Dickens's novels (for example) and in the twentieth century the commercial 'tie-ins' with film or television, which can affect the exposure or reception of a text before, during or after publication. Other examples at the present day are the marketing opportunities and pressures created by *institutions* such as literary prizes and by the Arts Council and other subsidising organisations.

A fourth element in the communication model is the *code* – the actual array of symbols which are selected from in order to compose the text or message. Since this book deals with fiction in English it might be thought that there was nothing more to say about the code than that it was the English language. However, of the many variants of English only one is usually represented in print and the *narrative* of fiction as opposed to dialogue is usually confined to this one. The monopoly of the so-called Standard, based on a written representation of the educated speech of south-eastern England, was not a foregone conclusion; until the fourteenth century several variants had equal standing in literature. Given, however, the distance between the earliest novels and the medieval period a more relevant enquiry would be: when regional variants are used in novels (e.g. Dickens's Cockneys or Lawrence's Midlanders) what determines the form and function of such representation? When do these representations occur in narrative as opposed to dialogue and how are they distributed over the range of characters and plot situations?

The last two elements in the communication model are the *literary context* of the novel and the overall social, economic and cultural context (which can be called the *social context* for short). Since no work of literature drops out of the sky unbidden and even the MS discovered hidden at the back of a drawer has been deposited there by a particular person in particular circumstances, it follows that the process of novel-writing takes place in an environment which exerts certain pressures on it and encourages certain expectations.

To consider the expectations first. The immediate context of any novel lies in the literary context out of which it springs and which causes the consumer to demand gratifications which are different from those he or she expects when picking up say a bar of chocolate or a cassette of recorded music. The expectations will be narrowed down further by the fact that it is a novel which has been picked up and not a cookery book or a dramatic text, since a novel is expected to differ in form or function from non-fictional prose or from plays. There is a historical contribution to this since fiction is now an accepted and 'serious' genre, not a new and suspect one as it was in the eighteenth century. Expectations may be further refined if the novel proclaims itself explicitly or by form and content to belong to a specific genre within the form of fiction (e.g. a historical novel, or a spy story). Furthermore at any given historical period literary *conventions* may condition the reader to welcome some features and be disturbed by others. For example the Victorian convention of the happy ending involving the marriage of the virtuous characters is as influential in its context as the convention of explicit sexual description is in the fiction of the latter half of the twentieth century.

From the perspective of the writer the expectations of the reader become *pressures*. Choice of the novel form sets up demands which can only be neglected at the risk of running counter to the reader; choice of genre within the novel form may impose further constraints. At any given historical moment it is only the exceptional novelist who will break free from the categories peculiar to that time, though some will do so partially.

Beyond the immediate literary context (what might be called the artistic constraints) lies the whole framework of society in all its political, economic, social and cultural aspects. It is the nature of the interaction of this context with the novel and with literature in general which has been the focus of the most vigorous debate. Discussion of it will therefore be postponed to the next chapter. At this stage the reader needs only to recognise the existence of *direct* and *indirect* versions of the relationship.

In *direct* terms the prevailing social context may encourage the inclusion of certain material or treatment of material into the text at the expense of other material or alternative treatments. One example is the so-called 'Condition of England' novels which were written at a time of industrial and political unrest in the 1840s and 1850s and attempted to investigate and assess its impact both factually and emotionally. The operation of this sort of influence is seen most readily in connection with certain well-defined historical events. It is less easy to demonstrate in relation to broader historical movements and shifts in power between the classes, though this has not prevented many Marxist critics, particularly in the early part of this century, from struggling to develop *reflection theories* which aim to do this, though often in a rather naïve and mechanical manner.

Because *direct* relationships are not often easy to find and may be difficult to 'prove' they are often discarded in favour of indirect ones. For example, although Jane Austen wrote at the time of the Napoleonic Wars there is no hint in her novels of the travails these produced; there seems to be a need for a theory which will explain this absence as well, unless we are to fall back on the influence of individual psychology. Often in indirect theories social circumstances are perceived as determining not so much the content of the novel as the perceptions of the novelist. One conception which facilitates this is that of *ideology*.

In many Marxist theoretical approaches (e.g. the work of Eagleton) ideology is the intervening force which shapes the text but it is more complex and less obvious than would be implied by (say) 'the writer's perspective on society'. It is certainly a product of the economic and class relations which the Marxists regard as the fundamental determining realities but it can often act as a screen or barrier ('false consciousness') which disguises to the individual the nature of these realities. Hence as many literary texts – which are written by individuals with definable class origins – will evade real events ('history') as portray them. Strictly Althusserian Marxists would claim in fact that it is not possible to escape the grip of ideology. Some critics such as Pierre Machery and

Terry Eagleton concern themselves with the identification of 'significant absences', those very evasions and omissions which arise in the text when the ideology of the novelist interacts with his or her desire to produce a work in a genre which aims at realism. Since this is a very difficult area further discussion is best left to the next chapter, which attempts to unfold the implications of various theories concerned with the social context of the novel.

To summarise: the model which has been used implies that the following elements can play a part in the process of communication through fiction:

① The author: his/her characteristics;
② The readership: its characteristics;
③ The channel: the mode of publication and consumption;
④ The immediate literary context;
⑤ The overall social context.

Clearly there can be no firm boundaries between the influence of these factors. For example the social context may, by encouraging the growth of a relatively leisured class, create a readership who have the time and money to indulge in novel-reading. There is therefore a case for assuming some sort of hierarchical relation between the various elements – as Eagleton does with the categories he identifies in *Criticism and Ideology* (see p. 50 in the next chapter). However, in order to keep the concepts relatively simple at this stage this aspect has been ignored in producing Figure 1 (opposite) which illustrates the whole process. The figure also includes one element that is frequent in communication but not always present in fiction-writing, that is *feedback*, in which the reader indicates his or her reception of the message and attitude to it. It would be present for example in the kind of serialised novels referred to above in connection with Dickens.

Organisation of this Book

The main part of this book considers how the model can be applied to a selection of novels written in English. The criteria for selection are two-fold: first, each novel illustrates how one or

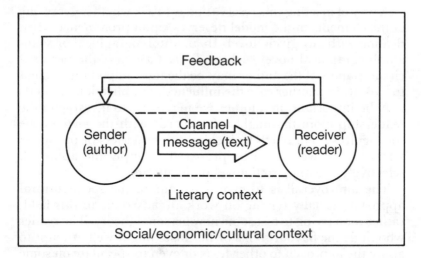

Figure 1 Novel-writing as a communication process

more of the elements in the model has a bearing on the final shape of the text and its reception. Second, the novels themselves are milestones in the development of the genre. By concentrating on this small selection of novels it is possible both to recognise the range of the form over time and also to study in a series of 'snapshots' the nature of this historical development. We can therefore relate the socio-(sulcutral) approach to the genre as a whole, as well as particular texts.

There may be a suspicion that a further motive for selecting these novels is being obscured: that they lend themselves readily to the socio-cultural approach. This raises the question of whether the approach can be used for every work of fiction, or whether the evidence has been 'bent' in some way by selecting as examples only a handful of the myriad novels published since the eighteenth century. One of the problems inherent in the socio-cultural approach is that it demands familiarity with a large number of texts. In theory it would be necessary to test every novel ever written to examine whether it can be 'explained' in terms of the model. The difficulty of doing this, of treating the model as if it were a scientific hypothesis rather than prone to subjective interpretation, is a reason for being sceptical about the term 'sociology of literature'.

A way of meeting this reservation is to ask whether every one of the elements in the model deserves equal prominence when dealing with any given novel. In an autobiographical or semi-autobiographical novel such as *David Copperfield* the personal circumstances of the author may be the most important element to look at. In another case the influence of publication methods may be important; in another we may wish to investigate the readership more thoroughly. It accords with the view of the socio-cultural approach as lacking the exactness of the social sciences that we should be prepared to apply the approach selectively, treating each novel on its merits.

The aim overall is to give a flavour of the socio-cultural approach, usually relying on work already done in this field, rather than trying to test some new personal theory. The reader who finds the flavour to his or her taste might well attempt to apply the approach to other texts or even to speculate on some theory of their own. On the basis of this strategy, the book is organised into the following chapters.

Chapter 2 develops further some of the concepts raised at the end of this chapter. It consists of a historical survey of 'over-arching' general theories of the relationship of literature to society. ('Literature' since few theorists deal only with the novel, though novels are widely used as illustrations.) While recognising that this project would easily fill a full-length book on its own, some attempt has been made, in the interests of readers who know nothing of the subject, to disentangle, compare and evaluate the main theories.

Chapter 3 describes the eighteenth-century origins of the novel, with special reference to *Robinson Crusoe*. This chapter examines critically the theory of Ian Watt on the relationship between the emergence of the novel in this period and the growing prominence of the middle classes in society, taking it as a test case for the interaction claimed between *authorship*, *social context*, *readership* and *text*.

Chapter 4 is an account of various features which underlay the publication of novels in the early nineteenth century. It analyses in detail one work of Scott, considered as a literary phenomenon of this period, and one of Jane Austen, relating her fiction to her class position.

Chapter 5 surveys the nineteenth-century heyday of the novel particularly concentrating on the *publishing channels* which contributed to the dominance of the form, such as *serialisation* and *lending libraries*. It examines in detail *Oliver Twist* and Mrs Gaskell's *Mary Barton* in order to assess the influence of these channels on the inter-relationship between authors, publishers and public.

Chapter 6 is devoted to the transition from the 'classical' nineteenth-century novel to the more flexible form of today. It therefore describes the disappearance of the standard three-volume work, the changing origins of *authors* and the influence of new groups of *readers*. The discussion of the texts in this chapter (*Tess of the D'Urbervilles*, *Sons and Lovers* and *The Rainbow*) also highlights the working of censorship, either imposed or voluntary.

Chapter 7 is about the novel today, but with particular reference to 'popular fiction' and its relationship to 'literary novels'. The chapter also examines various *economic* influences on fiction today and the location of the novel form in a new *communications context* of advertising, cinema and broadcasting. An analysis of Ian Fleming's *Thunderball* opens up the theoretical question of what is involved in the study of 'popular' novels and what repercussions this sort of study might have on our perception of the 'canon' of literary novels.

Chapter 8 concludes by attempting to pull together threads from the preceding chapters, summarising the 'state of the art' as far as the socio-cultural approach is concerned and speculating on the likely relationship in the future between this approach and traditional forms of criticism. Like the rest of this book it is intended to whet the appetite for more reading, rather than forming an attempt to have the last word on the subject.

2. Theoretical Approaches

The previous chapter identified some of the main features in a model of fiction seen as communication. Specific data relating to some of these features (such as the nature of the readership) have been gathered by scholars in a continuous process since the academic study of literature began; it provides a core of factual material which will be drawn on in relation to the texts used as examples in this book. The present chapter by contrast deals with a more subjective and controversial aspect of the socio-cultural approach; it summarises a number of theories which attempt to account for the characteristics of given novels in terms of the social composition of the society in which they were written. Since most of the theories refer to literature in general a specific application to fiction has been assumed.

Any system of belief which claims to account for the whole of human activity must by definition attempt to assign a role and value to the practice of literature. This is the case for Plato's philosophy, Christianity and Marxism. Since Marxism developed in the period when fiction was becoming the dominant literary form and is now probably the most systematic and influential system of belief – in world-wide terms, even if not in the English-speaking community – it is not surprising that it has provided the basis for many socio-cultural theories of literature. However, the academic discipline of literary criticism has also generated, in this country, a tradition which has regarded the social context of the novel as a relevant and worthwhile aspect of study. (It can be traced back to the courses on the 'life and thought' of a literary period which were introduced in the Cambridge University English School after the First World War.) These two pressures – towards explaining literary texts in the light of a global system of belief, and working outwards from a specific text towards its social context – have contributed to most of the current range of theoretical approaches. They are also responsible, however, for two, complementary, weaknesses in the theories; these are on the one hand a subordination of literary-critical purposes to some transcending social or political concern, on the other a willingness to rest content with an explanation of the social context of one particular text.

Despite these flaws, social-cultural theories form the background to much contemporary criticism of the novel and should be in the repertoire of those who study and teach it. Although no single theory has acquired a dominance (let alone universal acceptance) this does not mean that one will not do so in the future. Before examining the claims of the candidates, however, it should be decided what could reasonably be demanded of such a theory.

Theories: Potential and Limitations

A socio-cultural theory of fiction ought to provide: firstly, a plausible analysis of the social conditions within which the individual work was written. This might take the form of a generalised description of the society concerned, for example, as capitalist or feudal, but could be applied at quite a specific level (the marginalised position of the country gentry in the period of Jane Austen). Since Marxist analyses of society can be applied to any period and also claim to explain the transitions between periods they would seem to offer a great deal here, provided that, secondly, the social analysis can be extended convincingly into the literary sphere. In other words, literary conditions of production must be shown to be related in some way (however indirect) to social conditions. (In Figure 1 the 'Literary context' box was inside the 'Social context' box.) If we are trying to construct a *social* theory of the novel there is no point in developing an elaborate analysis of society (based perhaps on the profoundest academic knowledge and insights) if this is followed by a routine description of the text. It must be shown in fact how social conditions and pressures have influence on the concerns and preoccupations of the author, the readers and the mode of publication and consumption of the text.

Thirdly, at the very least the first of these relationships, that between author and society, needs to be accounted for. Despite the language used by some Marxist critics novels have never been 'produced' by 'social forces' in the abstract, without the intervention of some individual human agency; the problem is to determine correctly the quality of this intervention (for neither are authors social hermits, removed from all economic and historical pressures). Not only are we interested in, say, the social relations of Jane Austen's England, or Hampshire at the detailed level, but we also want to know how Jane Austen herself is related to these relations. Often this phase of the explanation is the most controversial since it is differently handled by the more naïve Marxist critics (for whom an author is still at bottom the mouthpiece of a class) and those who recognise convolutions and complexities in the relationship.

If the above demands are satisfactorily met the theory concerned is likely to have value in its application to a given text. However, two other stipulations might be made. The theory might be expected to have *predictive* value so that it could be used to explain the nature of certain texts not considered in the original formulation (or even unknown to the formulator – perhaps because not yet written). In chemistry once the principle behind the Table of Elements was understood the gaps in the periodic sequence could be filled in by hypothesising certain elements, which were later created artificially. A theory which only 'works' in relation to texts selected by the originator of the theory causes suspicions of 'special pleading'. Secondly, the theory, once accepted and understood, should be capable of being applied by individuals other than its originator; the fact that few theories are at the stage where the ordinary reader can apply them confidently perhaps points to their immaturity.

Some readers will object that it is unreasonable to expect literary criticism to develop as if it were a 'hard' science, in which hypotheses are constructed, modified and converted into something akin to scientific laws. They might argue that the understanding and appreciation of fiction involved demands a subjective, highly personal approach and that literary critics have no desire or responsibility for forcing a view of a particular text on others, much less encouraging others to apply that view to quite different texts. Yet once a critic starts to refer to material beyond the 'words on the page', comparisons with more factual disciplines become inviting if not inevitable. Fortunately, all the implications do not have to be resolved for us to find relevance and value in some of the theoretical approaches on offer.

Pre-twentieth-century Approaches

Attempts to correlate literature with various stages and conditions of society can be traced back at least as far as the German philosopher Johann Herder (1744–1803), the first systematic writer on literary history. In trying to explain how different types of literature came to evolve Herder resorted to biological metaphors which related the individual writer to the influence of tradition and environment:

> I was reminded of the whole course of the ages which came before him and after him. He learned and taught, he followed others, others followed him. His language, his ways of thought, his passions were ties which connected him at first with a few other poets and in the end with all others. Because he was a *man* he wrote for *men*.[1]

Despite this explicit recognition of social context, literary context and readership Herder failed to do more than speculate on their relationship to such factors as climate, landscape, race, nationality and political structures. Often he indulged in circular reasoning, explaining the nature of the text in the light of evidence drawn from the text itself. However, he popularised two vague notions which became a staple of socio-cultural criticism before the twentieth century: *Zeitgeist* (or spirit of the age) and *Volksgeist* (spirit of the people or nation).

A later critic who exploited these concepts was the formidable Mme de Staël who besides being a writer herself and presiding over a famous literary salon moved in the most influential French artistic and political circles. De Staël's *De la Littérature*, written in 1800, attempted to relate literature above all to the influence of climate. 'Southern' (i.e. Mediterranean) writers were said to react against their hot climate by producing imagery emphasising coolness ('leafy woods' and 'limpid streams' figure in their work). Northerners on the other hand, affected by a cloudy and sombre climate, were less inclined to celebrate scenes of pleasure and driven more to moods of melancholy.

From this rather naïve correlation between literature and temperature de Staël moved on to consider the influence of Protestantism on Northern Europeans, whom she claimed had been forced by their religion into observing a strict sexual morality. In England particularly the high standards expected in the relationships between men and women, especially within marriage, led to the development of eighteenth-century fiction – the novel of Fielding and Richardson – which took for its subject matter the morality of affection between the sexes. In her words:

> The main reason for the inexhaustible productivity of English writers in this genre is the condition of women in England. Relationships between men and women are conducted everywhere with a boundless sensitivity and delicacy. (*De la Littérature*, vol. 4, p. 181, my translation)

and therefore:

> The English first dared to believe that private emotions could engage men's hearts and that neither the depiction of important people or weighty affairs are necessary to capture the imagination.

Mme de Staël believed that the same strict morality which gave a secure place to women in English society encouraged English writers to regard the relationships between the sexes as a potential major theme in fiction. Although the novels which resulted were often overloaded with domestic detail this was because they aimed to appeal to English readers whose lifestyle (according to her) was based on 'regular routine and domestic affection'.

Mme de Staël's perception of the relationship between domestic morality and the novel interestingly foreshadows the theories of the twentieth-century critic Ian Watt. She also anticipates later criticism of the English novel by showing that its form was influenced by the need for it to remain suitable reading matter for women and particularly unmarried girls – whereas French novels were far less subject to sexual reticence. However, in her book these stimulating remarks remain as casual observations and are not formed into a systematic theory of socio-cultural context.

Another French critic was the first to attempt this. Hippolyte Taine wrote at a period when nineteenth-century scientific investigation and experiment was making its greatest intellectual impact. It was felt that 'scientific method' (the formation of hypotheses to explain experimental data and the testing of the hypotheses in carefully-controlled contexts so as to deduce scientific 'laws') would soon be successfully applied to all branches of human knowledge. This belief, known as 'positivism', even had reverberations on the writing of literature itself when the novelist Emile Zola (1840–1902: an admirer of Taine) asked in 1880: 'Since medicine which is an art is becoming a science, why shouldn't literature itself become a science, thanks to the experimental method?' Taine's own objective, described in the 'Introduction' to his 1872 *History of English Literature* (he was a strong Anglophile) was no less than to relate all literary texts to the societies that produced them in terms of the three key, interdependent factors of *race, moment* and *milieu*. Not only would these factors be found to explain and determine the nature of existing literature but they would also, if valid, have a predictive value: 'if these forces could be measured and deciphered, one could deduce from them, as if from a formula, the characteristics of the future civilisation.' (Wellek, *History of Literary Criticism*, vol. IV, p. 28) Taine's fundamental philosophical position is that all art (including of course fiction) is valuable in that it is a 'concrete universal'; great works of art crystallise the qualities of particular historical periods, so that the 'spirit of the age' is capable of being extrapolated from literary texts: in a great writer we find 'an exact correspondence between the public and the private manner of feeling. His mind is like the abridgement of the mind of others.' (Wellek, vol. IV, p. 38)

Taine's concept of *race*, despite its fascist connotations, seems to mean only 'national characteristics', though confusingly he distinguishes 'race' from 'nation' in some passages. Often, as in Mme de Staël, both come down to a generalised distinction between 'Northern' and 'Southern' European temperaments which is used for example to define the particular characteristics of English and French literature (and justify Taine's preference for the former). *Moment* was originally defined by Taine in a sense modelled on physics as 'the acquired impulsion' of the historical process; in his later writings its meaning is diluted to the sum of race and milieu, that is the *Zeitgeist*. The crucial term of the three is *milieu* (also modelled on scientific usage, since in zoology it referred to the habitat of an animal); the sense of this term ranges from the basic physical factors of soil and climate to the economic and social conditions supposedly related to them. For example: 'In England a political establishment of eight centuries which keeps a man erect and respectful in independence and obedience and accustoms him to strive unitedly under the authority of the law.'

Taine's efforts to be *deterministic* (i.e. to relate all literary work entirely to these three factors with no mysterious residual factor left unexplained) often lead to results which are unsatisfyingly *reductive* (reducing complex literary texts to the operation of a few mechanical causes or laws) and can be unintentionally hilarious. Because in England it rains a lot: 'the amount of inconvenience which the climate imposes upon man and the endurance it requires of him are infinite. Hence arise melancholy and the idea of duty'. (Wellek, vol. IV, p. 33) In turn these psychological characteristics are held to explain the outlook of English authors and hence the nature of their work. Although no one would now take Taine's conclusions completely seriously – there were many critics of his methods even in his own day – they do illustrate some of the pitfalls to be faced in constructing systematic theories of literature. One problem is that of *applying* the suggested social influences to the work of individual writers without invoking some idea such as 'genius' which is not explicable in terms of the theory. Taine's solution is to propose the existence of what he calls a 'master faculty', which is created in certain gifted writers as the result of the confluence of race, moment and milieu. It is the master faculty which results in the representativeness of the great writer: 'The greater the artist, the more deeply does he manifest the temper of the race.' (Wellek, vol. IV, p. 39)

Unfortunately Taine does not use the term consistently in this sense of the *typifying* quality of great art; it would have provided a useful theoretical advance if he had not also fallen back on the idea of individual genius, as in this description of Dickens:

> It is not through the accidental circumstances of his life that he belongs to history but by his talent. . . . This inner history of genius does not depend upon the history of mankind; and it is worth more. (*History of English Literature* vol. IV, 1872, p. 117)

Taine's theory demanded that he saw literary works as *representative* of particular periods and cultures and this brought him up against another problem: should *only* great works, however defined, be regarded as representative, or should that quality be sought, perhaps in a lesser degree, in mediocre or even poor novels, plays or poems? Taine's struggles with this difficulty led him to evolve a theory in which fictional characters were classified as *types* and these types arranged in a hierarchy of moral value running from the benefactors of mankind down to criminals. Unfortunately this *moral* scale of value did not coincide with Taine's own *aesthetic* judgement of the characters or the works in which they appeared, but the exercise anticipates the way in which Marxist critics developed the idea of *typicality* when they too tried to define the value of literature in terms of its social representativeness.

Taine's thinking ultimately goes back to the famous formulation of Stendhal (1783–1842) that the novel is like a mirror riding along the highway, reflecting what is there. *Reflection* theories of the novel in their simplest form reverse Stendhal's image: if by looking in the mirror we can see the outside environment, then by knowing the nature of the outside environment we should be able to ascertain what is in the mirror (i.e. the novel). However, so many factors are involved (what is the position and angling of the mirror? who are 'we'?) that Taine's theory based on the application of three imprecisely defined elements is bound to appear naïve despite the claims he makes for it.

F. R. Leavis (1895–1978)

Before considering the work of the, mainly Continental, Marxist literary theorists it is convenient here to summarise the contribution of one major non-Marxist British critic. The Cambridge scholar F. R. Leavis developed a theory of literature and society which despite his comparative isolation academically was enthusiastically adopted by many teachers of English in schools and higher education from the 1930s onwards. Considered as a theory it lacks coherence because Leavis often expressed himself in an inexplicit and non-systematic way; however it has significance because it attempted to link detailed literary-critical analysis of fiction to a wider evaluation (however wrongheaded) of social and historical change and it did so with a concern for *literature* rather than political polemic at the forefront.[2]

Leavis's argument begins with an historical contrast between the nature of society in England before and after the widespread impact of technology we call the Industrial Revolution. For him the most important feature of this revolution was the effect of machinery and mechanical methods (particularly in the most sophisticated form then known, mass production) on the nature of human work and self-expression through work. In this respect he differs from the Marxists, whose approach he always indignantly rejected, since it is the technology itself, not the control of that technology by a particular social class, which he sees as crucial. Leavis argues that in twentieth-century Western society technology has devalued work by reducing it to a meaningless routine and so deprived the individual of the capacity for artistic or craftsmanlike fulfilment which existed, for example, for those engaged in building the great medieval cathedrals. The uniformity and standardisation of products associated with mass production have in turn deformed the spiritual and aesthetic sensibilities of individuals in industrialised societies. (This view is backed up by reference to American sociological descriptions of 'Midtown', a community characterised by 'extreme mediocrity'.) Leavis believes the only hope of rescue for twentieth-century men and women, dulled and desensitised by their subservience to technology and its accompanying philosophy of materialism, is through the absorption of the superior values found in great works of art, including fiction.

For Leavis and his followers therefore the reading and criticism of serious novels has a moral role in allowing at least some individuals to recapture and possibly retransmit values which oppose the debased contemporary ones. Leavis finds these values to be most accessible in the fiction which he called 'The Great Tradition': Jane Austen, Eliot, James, Conrad and – most relevant to the present age – Lawrence. Although the capacity to write at such a level was restricted to a few, understanding of their work allowed others (though still a small elite) to absorb and safeguard the values which had been progressively threatened since industrialisation began to break up the traditional fabric of Western society.

This pre-industrial society, labelled by Leavis as 'organic', had been a rural one in which the lives of men and women were regulated by the cycle of the seasons; work, in the form of traditional craftsmanship, gave full scope to self-expression and art was typically 'folk-art' in which the members of the community participated as both artists and audience. Its artistic productions were rich with the accumulation of powerful traditions and exploited deep commonly-shared emotions in contrast to the shallow 'stock responses' and vicarious emotions of the 'mass media' and popular fiction which supplanted them.

There is space here to examine only one or two of the paradoxes in Leavis's concept of the relationship of society to art. The vanished organic society was apparently the property of all its members as was the communal art that characterised it. Yet according to Leavis its values can only be rescued through the reading of texts which are admitted to be 'difficult' (Leavis explicitly sneers at the idea 'that anyone can read a novel'). These texts yield their meaning only to an educated elite who have undertaken the specialised discipline of literary criticism. So when Leavis praises Lawrence for his emotional fidelity to 'the environment of a living tradition' we are not sure whether he is implying that Lawrence's fiction is a satisfactory *replacement* for organic popular art or simply a means of transmitting its values. Indeed is Leavis arguing that the organic community of the past is recapturable at all; and if it is, will 'post-organic' fiction like the post-Marxist 'state' simply wither away when that goal is reached?

It is much easier to conclude that Leavis values novels for aesthetic reasons rather than for their relevance to his somewhat incoherent social philosophy. The five main novelists of his 'Great Tradition' are selected for their commitment to moral discrimination (their 'seriousness') rather than for the ideas they encourage in relation to the value of any particular kind of society. Where possible Leavis tries to make a link (particularly in the case of Lawrence) between the lost organic society and the literary tradition that survives it. For example he writes in *The Common Pursuit* (Chatto and Windus, 1952): 'but for the persisting literary tradition, the history I have so inadequately sketched would have been lost, and our notions of what a popular culture might be and what relations might exist between it and a "highbrow" culture, would have been very different.' (Penguin edn., p. 192) However, he fails to explain how a literary tradition which includes such 'highbrow' writers as Henry James can contribute to our understanding of what 'a popular culture might be', since this tradition does not use the language of popular speech, neither on the whole does it describe popular life. Leavis, who so greatly laments the loss of the 'organic' culture, can hardly regard the literary work as a substitute for it – but since he values the literature it cannot be seen as a debasement of it either.

Despite Leavis's frustrating tendency to slide over these problems by falling back on assertion in place of argument (his favourite formula became 'This is so, isn't it?') his work has a twofold significance in the development of theories on the relationship between literature and society. By affirming the intrinsic value of literature Leavis counteracted a tendency of some contemporary critics to use literary works simply as a quarry for sociological evidence or in a reductive way as a proof of current Marxist doctrines. When he declared that literature was 'something in the definition of which terms of value-judgement figure essentially, and something accessible only to the reader capable of intelligent and sensitive criticism' (*The Common Pursuit*, p. 193) it defined a position that later socio-cultural critics needed to take account of, if only to refute it. In the second place, Leavis's suggestion of a historical split between 'popular' and 'highbrow' culture ('By Wordsworth's death the Industrial Revolution had done its work and the traditional culture of the people was no longer there, except vestigially') opened up the whole question of the status and definition of the literary 'canon', that is, those texts considered worthy of academic recognition and study. Admittedly Leavis and his followers were mostly concerned to deplore contemporary popular literature, in relation to the folk glories of the past, but this in itself put on the agenda for investigation a range of fiction which previous literary critics had ignored. (The work of Leavis's wife, Queenie, published in 1932 as *Fiction and the Reading Public*, was one of the first academic attempts to analyse the nature and function of popular novels.)

Leavis's insistence that novels are ultimately the product of individual human beings and that there is a measure of 'spiritual autonomy' in human affairs made him an implacable opponent of those who attempted in the 1930s to construct a reductive theory of fiction in the Marxist tradition – the origins of which must be considered next.

Marx, Engels and Literature

The usual association of Marx (1818–83) with economics should not blind us to the fact that he was a man of traditional nineteenth-century literary tastes who had himself attempted to write poetry and fiction. The sparseness of his comments on aesthetic matters no doubt arises from his preoccupation with constructing his massive philosophical and economic theory which can only be summarised here in a very simplified form.

Marxism claims to be a 'materialist' philosophy which acknowledges the supremacy of the material world. In order to sustain life mankind needs to transform the material resources of the world into food, shelter, clothing and other necessities; this activity, 'productive work', is therefore seen by Marxists as primary and other human activities as secondary to it. In all but the most primitive societies production implies a 'division of labour' which is reflected in terms of control and exploitation, that is in 'social relations' or 'class' terms. The secondary or 'superstructural' activities of art, religion and so on directly reflect and are shaped in conformity with these social relations and therefore in turn with the underlying material realities ('the base' underlying the 'superstructure'). In Marx's words:

> Conceiving, thinking, the spiritual intercourse of men, appear here as the direct efflux of men's material behaviour. The same is true of intellectual production, as it appears in the language of the politics, the laws, the morals, the religion, the metaphysics, and so on, of a people. Human beings are the producers of these concepts, ideas, and so on, that is, real, functioning men, as they are determined by a particular development of their productive forces and of the intercourse corresponding to these forces in its highest forms.
>
> (*The German Ideology* 1846, quoted in Peter Demetz, *Marx, Engels and the Poets* University of Chicago Press 1967, p. 65)

The term 'ideological' which is used in this passage is one that is employed profusely in Marxist criticism. For Marx, *ideology* referred to a way of looking at and interpreting the world which was dependent on the class position of the individual concerned. In this passage 'ideological' refers to the 'mental reflection' of the economic and material realities that ultimately determine human existence and behaviour. In an extended sense, 'ideology' is the 'false consciousness' by which individuals rationalise their relationship to the prevailing economic and social structure. Ideology is in this sense a process of illusion that enables individuals to subordinate their true interests by means of a perspective on the world that justifies and reinforces the dominance of the ruling social group. (In Raymond Williams's words, for everyone outside this group it is 'an upside-down version of reality'.) This latter sense is the one that later Marxist critics have found to be most productive and interesting.

Marx's comment above, which seems to devalue all mental activity as merely 'superstructural', would seem to encourage a 'reductive' approach to fiction, demoting it to a simple reflex of social and economic relationships with no intrinsic value or dynamic of its own. This approach was favoured by generations of 'vulgar Marxists' in Russia and elsewhere who rejected any notion of the 'autonomy' of art. However, it can be shown that both Marx and his collaborator Engels were uneasy with this simple formula and sought to elaborate it.

Marx himself found it hard to reconcile his lifelong respect for classical culture with the lack of development of Ancient Greek society which was postulated by his economic theory. In a draft preface to his *Critique of Political Economy* (not published until after his death) he concludes that it is this very immaturity which explains the appeal of Greek art:

> The Greeks were normal children. The charm of their art for us does not stand in contradiction to the undeveloped stage out of which it grew. It is rather a result, rather an inseparable connection, that the immature social condition under which it arose and only could arise can never recur.

This ambivalence of Marx on the subject of literature's relation to society is paralleled in the more frequent references to the problem by his collaborator, Friedrich Engels (1820–95). By the 1890s Engels was suggesting in correspondence that all the so-called superstructural elements could potentially have influence on the course of 'historical struggles'; he also argued that the relation between economic forces and cultural achievements could be very indirect: 'It is not so that the economic situation is *cause, active by itself alone* and all the rest only passive effect. Rather it is mutual interaction based upon economic necessity that always realises itself ultimately' (*Letter to Starkenberg*, 1894).

The progressive weakening of economic determinism in Engels' conception of literature is also evident in his observations on the form which a true 'socialist novel' should take. This is an aspect of Marxist theory which is a live issue for Marxist critics looking for criteria by which to evaluate novels written currently and in the future. One candidate for such a criterion is obviously 'truth to reality', that is an accurate description of the class basis of society. However, Engels was clearly alert to the problems posed by this demand for 'realism' (or 'socialist realism' as it came to be called when incorporated later into the official cultural programme of the Soviet Union).

Since the majority of novel readers were still bourgeois, Engels believed there was little advantage in attacking their prejudices directly (as Mrs Gaskell had also discovered). In a letter to a Mrs Kautsky, who was attempting a novel based on a thinly veiled account of Marx's life, he advised against an explicitly political approach in favour of leaving the readers to draw their own conclusions. In a later comment on Margaret Harkness's novel, *A City Girl*, on the other hand he advocated recourse to the 'typicality' which Marxist critics such as Lukács have recommended ever since: 'Realism to my mind, implies besides truth of detail, the truthful reproduction of typical characters under typical circumstances.' (quoted in Demetz, p. 132) His view here seems to be that a good socialist novel should be 'normative' – that is, represent things as they *ought* to be – since he criticises Miss Harkness for depicting the working classes as a 'passive mass' whereas: 'The rebellious reaction of the working-class against the oppressive medium which surrounds them . . . belongs to history and must therefore lay claim to a place in the domain of realism.' (ibid.)

The call to Miss Harkness to align herself more explicitly with the Marxist conception of history contrasts with the advice to Mrs Kautsky that aesthetic considerations should overshadow political ones (admittedly as a tactical device). The contradiction reflects Engels' ambivalence and that of later Marxist critics in the face of their realisation that literary appreciation does not necessarily value the same features or even the same novels as the concern to drive forward the cause of socialism. In attempting to square this circle and reconcile politics with aesthetics Engels was forced to hypothesise a subtle, covert or even unconscious tendentiousness – 'good' writers play down, hide or are even ignorant of their own sympathies. (This theory is sometimes known as 'dissociation'.)

The double standard reappears in Engels' comments on Honoré de Balzac (1799–1850). By his own admission the French novelist was a political conservative – a supporter of the pre-Revolutionary French Royal Family and therefore an ultra-reactionary in Marxist terms. Yet the revolutionary Engels finds it possible to praise his treatment of the aristocracy:

> That Balzac was compelled to go against his own class sympathies and political prejudices, that he *saw* the necessity of the downfall of his favourite nobles and described them as people deserving no better fate; and that he saw the real men of the future where, for the time being, they alone were to be

found – that I consider . . . one of the grandest features of old Balzac. (Demetz, p. 174)

Although there are undoubtedly passages in Balzac's novels which criticise the standards and behaviour of the aristocracy, by no stretch of the imagination did the French novelist sympathise with the 'real men', the republican leaders of the insurrection of 1832, with whom Engels tried to associate him. (Peter Demetz, who discusses the whole issue in more detail in his book *Marx, Engels and the Poets* (1967), comments that Balzac's view can be summarised: 'Good and evil in this world are not distributed according to a political pattern.') Swayed by Balzac's standing as one of the greatest French novelists Engels tried to recruit him as a crypto-Marxist, thus offering a model for later critics such as Lukács.

The problem of reconciling the 'great' (aesthetically worthwhile) with the 'good' (socially progressive) remained a difficulty for many later Marxists interested in literature. These later writers can be divided into three groups. In the first place there were literary enthusiasts among the political theorists and activists who developed Marx and Engels' ideas in exile or opposition and after 1917 attempted to implement them in the first Communist state. A second group comprises those critics after 1917 who worked outside the ambit of official Soviet communism, distancing themselves from or taking issue with its literary philosophy. These para-Marxists, as George Steiner has called them, have opposed orthodox Marxists in paying greater respect to the integrity of literature and suspecting any text that had a palpable political design behind it. Lukács and Goldmann fall into this category. Finally we should take note of two major British critics, Raymond Williams and Terry Eagleton, who have attempted to apply Marxist ideas in an essentially practical way which owes something to traditional literary criticism as taught in this country. (This classification ignores yet another group – the Communist writers outside Russia who followed the Moscow party line fairly closely, particularly in the 1930s. Their work is often too doctrinaire to be valuable although it is interesting to deduce from it where a strictly deterministic Marxism will lead.)

Orthodox Marxists and Socialist Realism

After Engels' death Franz Mehring (1846–1919) and G. V. Plekhanov (1857–1918) tried to systematise the occasional observations on literature contained in his work. Mehring like many activists saw literature as a secondary activity ('men must first eat, drink and have a place to live and clothes to wear before they think or write poetry') but found it worthwhile to write essays on the German writers Lessing and Schiller which not only related them to their class origins but conceded to their work a certain amount of autonomy.

Plekhanov, also torn between strict 'economic determinism' and a regard for the integrity of art, resolved the problem by elaborating a five-stage indirect relationship between the two:

   (i)   the state of productive forces;
  (ii)   the economic conditions;
 (iii)   the socio-political regime;
 (iv)   the psyche of social man;
  (v)   various ideologies reflecting the properties of this psyche.[3]

An important and politically crucial aspect of Plekhanov's work concerns the debate between the supporters of the idea of the relative autonomy or independence of art and those who saw it in an 'instrumental' way, dedicated to the service of a given cause. Although Plekhanov gives some credit to the independence of the writer he also proclaims the need for him or her to identify with 'progressive' causes. When a Marxist government was established in Russia this became a topical issue since the Communist Party found it important to distinguish writers whose work furthered the Revolution from those they felt to be subversive or counter-revolutionary.

A double perspective of this sort – a social theory of literature which evaluates the past but also prescribes for the future – can be found in the writing of A. V. Lunacharsky, the first Soviet Commissar for Education. Lunacharsky's comments on the role of economic determinism are relaxed:

> only to an extremely insignificant extent do artistic works depend directly upon the forms of production of a given

society. They depend on them through such intermediate links as the class structure of society and the class psychology which has formed as a result of class interests. (*On Literature and Art*, Progress Publishers, 1973, p. 11)

However, he is adamant on the instrumental value of literature:

> everything that aids the development and victory of the proletariat is good; everything that harms it is evil.
>
> The Marxist critic must try to find the fundamental social trend in a given work; he must find where it is heading, whether this process is arbitrary or not. And he must base his evaluation on the fundamental social and dynamic idea. (ibid. p. 11)

This view of the critic as policeman enforcing the 'party line' foreshadows the censorship of the Stalinist period in which the only approved literary form became 'socialist realism', depicting the inevitable triumph of the proletariat. By the late 1920s this concern for correctness meant that official Soviet literary scholarship had become frozen into a naïve reductionism or prostituted into an instrument of Stalin's dictatorship. It was outside the sphere of direct Soviet control that efforts were made to rethink the basic premises of Marx and Engels in order to arrive at new social models of literature.

Georg Lukács (1885–1971)

Lukács is perhaps the major Marxist literary critic least accessible to English speakers because of his thirty or so main works, mostly written in German, only a few have been translated. Although his concentration on French, German and Russian authors increases this remoteness his work is relevant here because of his specific interest in the novel and his efforts to relate Marxist thought to traditional literary culture, in a way which reflects his own chequered career.

Lukács was born into a wealthy Jewish family in Hungary (which then formed part of the Austro-Hungarian Empire); he therefore absorbed German and Slavonic as well as Hungarian literary and philosophical traditions. His first work, *A Theory of the Novel*(1920), follows Georg Hegel (1770–1831), Marx's philosophical source, in proposing the novel as the modern equivalent of the ancient epic in its potential for describing the 'totality' of a given society. When a Communist Republic was briefly set up in Hungary at the end of the First World War, Lukács was appointed its Minister of Education; on its collapse he fled first to Germany and then, after the rise of the Nazis, to exile in Russia. However, his relationship to the Stalinist government was always ambivalent and in 1956 he returned to Hungary to become Minister of Culture, only to be deported when the Russian army ousted the anti-Moscow government of Imre Nagy.

Lukács' criticism has tended to concentrate on nineteenth-century authors; it has been suggested that this was to avoid open conflict with the Party over the degree of 'correctness' shown by his contemporaries. Nevertheless his individuality emerges in praise for writers such as the conservative Sir Walter Scott whom no Party stalwart could have regarded as 'progressive' in the usual sense. Lukács judges the 'greatness' of a novelist by his adherence to the principle of 'critical realism' – that is the ability to describe with insight and honesty the society of which he is a member. The great 'critical realists' such as Scott, Balzac, Stendhal and Tolstoy (occasionally Lukács includes Dickens in his list) reflect historical reality from a progressive perspective, even though they may have consciously behaved in a reactionary way in their political and social lives. Lukács explains this paradox by borrowing a comment from a fellow Russian critic, N. A. Dobrolyubov: 'A work of art may be the expression of a certain idea, not because the author had this idea in mind while he was producing it, but because he was impressed by certain features of reality from which this idea automatically arises' (*Studies in European Realism*, Merlin Press 1964, p. 113).

Except for Leo Tolstoy (whose emergence is explained by the late development of Russian society) these 'classical' critical realists were active in the period between 1789 and 1848, when the convulsions associated with the French Revolution had destroyed (at least in Western Europe) the old aristocratic order but not yet supplanted it by a fully-fledged capitalism.

In 1848 the brutal suppression of working-class movements in many countries marked the end of this period when the bourgeoisie acted as a 'progressive' force in Marxist terms, siding with the workers against feudalism. Therefore for Lukács 1848 was a watershed, terminating the scope of the bourgeois novelist for creating a realistic analysis of society and introducing instead a period of bland escapism and concern with art for art's sake.

To illustrate this argument Lukács contrasts (to the scandal of more conventional Marxists) Balzac and Zola. Despite Balzac's reactionary politics, Lukács finds him to be deadly accurate and 'correct' in his perception of a society making the transition from feudalism to capitalism; a transition which was devastating for its victims, the peasants and working classes, but historically necessary and 'progressive' as a stage on the way to socialism. In a study of *The Peasants (Les Paysans)* Lukács analyses Balzac's depiction of the triangular conflict between the old aristocracy, the peasantry and the new middle class of financial manipulators. The novel is seen as an attack both on the transformation of the feudal landowners into a 'court nobility with dwindling socially necessary functions' and on the ethic of greed and ruthless competition displayed by their bourgeois rivals. The similarity of this 'critical realism' to Marxist analysis is summed up in Balzac's epigram: 'Tell me what you possess and I will tell you what you think.'

After 1848 (Lukács claims) novelists became increasingly isolated from the triumphant capitalist culture, with its emphasis on money-making, and their themes declined into the exotic, escapist or self-indulgent. Although a writer such as Emile Zola chose to deal with social problems and specialised in descriptions of the routine and seamy aspects of life, he was unable to penetrate to the underlying reality of class relationships. The introversion of post-1848 novelists such as Gustave Flaubert is indicated by their reluctance to participate in the political issues of the day; even Zola's championship of Dreyfus came after his period of literary production.

Lukács regarded critical realism as distinguished artistically by the employment of 'typicality', that is the idea of something standing for that which is greater and more meaningful than itself. In novels that truly reflect historical reality characters need to be 'typical', but this does not mean they are mere dummies or puppets as in so many propaganda works; men and women in the great critical realist novels are not only convincing as individuals but also by their presence point to the existence of a larger theme. In Lukács' own words:

> The typical is not to be confused with the *average* (although there are cases where this holds true) nor with the *eccentric* (though the typical does as a rule go beyond the normal). A character is typical, in this technical sense, when his inner-most being is determined by objective forces at work in society . . . . Levin [in *Anna Karenina*] was typical of the Russian landowning class at a period when everything was being 'turned upside down'. The reader learns his personal peculiarities and is sometimes tempted to consider him, not wholly wrongly, as an outsider and an eccentric – until he realises that such eccentricities are the mark of an age in transition. (*Realism in Our Time*, Harper and Row 1964, p. 122)

This doctrine of typicality allowed Lukács to approve even of those writers such as Balzac and Scott whose ideology appeared to be most conservative; it did not, however, completely absolve him from the charge of merely following conventional judgements of 'greatness' in his search for the models of 'critical realism'.

Lucien Goldmann (1913–70)

Goldmann's work on the novel is based on a *method*, which he calls 'genetic structuralism', and a *theory* of modern (i.e. post-1800) fiction. Like Lukács he sought an alternative to the sterile determinism of official Marxist literary theory but as a Romanian living in Paris and writing in French did not face the same threat of reprimand or suppression. Goldmann asserts that novels reflect what he calls the 'collective consciousness' of the social groups to which their authors belong; what we know about the novelist as an *individual* will in fact tell us less about his work than information about the group as a whole. This is because great works of art uniquely express the *world vision* of the group in a coherent way that is not consciously available to its individual members. The *world vision* resembles the 'ideology' of classical Marxism since it describes the beliefs and value system by which a class relates itself to material reality, but differs in that it is peculiar to artistic works, which alone allow the *coherent* expression of this relationship. Goldmann goes so far as to maintain that 'in the last resort' it is the group and not the individual which is the 'true author' of the work, i.e. the expression of the work is 'transindividual':

> The most important function of artistic and literary creations on the imaginary level appears to be to contribute coherence which men are frustrated in achieving in real life, exactly as on the individual level dreams, deliria and the imaginary procure the object or its substitute which the individual has never been able actually to possess. (*Method in the Sociology of Literature*, Tavistock 1976, p. 105)

Goldmann first applied his method in a study which showed how the tragedies of Racine and the philosophy of Pascal reflect the 'world vision' of the pessimistic Catholic sect called Jansenism which in turn was associated with the social group known as the *noblesse de robe* in seventeenth-century France. In Goldmann's theory world vision is related not to the *content* of a work but to its *form* or *structure*. It is the particular *tragic structure* of Racine's plays which is held to express the outlook of the Jansenists and also of the ambiguously situated and socially anxious class from which they were drawn. The literary critic and sociologist is advised to pay attention to 'correspondences' of form rather than content, since the latter may not relate to the collective world vision of a social group except in a fragmentary and unsystematic way. The world vision resembles Williams's 'structure of feeling' (see below, p. 47) since the theory holds that the function of art is not merely to reflect a consciousness based on ultimate social reality but actively to contribute to that consciousness. Goldmann claims the work of art which presents a world vision forms '*one of the most important constituent elements of this collective consciousness*, that element that enables the members of the group to become aware of what they thought, felt and did without realising objectively its signification'. (*Towards a Sociology of the Novel*, Tavistock 1975, p. 160)

In his approach to fiction Goldmann adopts an idea from Lukács' pre-Marxist writings, that the novel as a literary form intrinsically presupposes a conflict between the individual and society. The typical novel hero is idealistically seeking 'true' values in a world dominated by degraded ones. Interpreted in Marxist terms, the novel is a development of bourgeois society and its ideology of 'individualism' – the egotistical advancement of the individual in competition with others. Since this society is dominated by 'exchange values' which subordinate all relationships to the power of money only those individuals who can stand outside the 'action of the market' are able to cling to the 'authentic' or 'use values' of natural and man-made objects. The novel genre uniquely expresses the *world vision* of this group, notably creative artists who may belong in socio-economic terms to the bourgeoisie but aspire to values it rejects.

Novels usually take a biographical form, following the fortunes of a hero through time and space. However, in the traditional novel this central figure is subject to stress and conflict (is *problematised*); this process reflects both the conflict between the novelist and bourgeois society, and also the internal contradictions of the society itself, which simultaneously promotes individualism and stifles the development of individuals through the pressure of the market and the operation of exchange values. Goldmann finds confirmation for this theory in a study of the development of the French twentieth-century novel with regard especially to André Malraux and to the 'new novelist' of the 1950s, Alain Robbe-Grillet whose works (such as *Jealousy*) feature long detailed descriptions of inanimate objects.

According to Goldmann the role of the hero in the novel can be shown to diminish in correspondence with the various phases of capitalism in this century. In the 'imperialist' period when individual capitalists were being replaced by the power of large firms, cartels and monopolies (1880–1918) the hero begins to lose importance. During the period of 'crisis capitalism' (the interwar period of Depression and Communist revolution) attention shifts in such novels as Malraux's *Man's Estate* from the individual hero to the group. In the latest period, at

Goldmann's time of writing in the early 1960s, the influence of 'consumer capitalism' and benevolent state intervention in the economy has assimilated the working classes to the bourgeoisie. The resulting increase in passive consumption of material goods and the triumph of 'exchange values' has further isolated the dissident creative intellectuals. The novels which now express their world vision are typically those of writers such as Robbe-Grillet in which minute descriptions of inanimate objects predominate, since it is *things* and their possibilities for consumption and exchange which are now most significant in society after 1945.

Goldmann admits that his theory takes for granted the aesthetic worth of the novels he is studying, an important point since the theory claims that it is only 'great' works which adequately and coherently express a world vision. He claims in *Method in the Sociology of Literature*:

> I never intended to use sociological categories for the *understanding of a work*. The latter's aesthetic quality depends firstly on its richness, its meaningful coherence and upon the coherence between its universe and its form, in the strict sense of the word. In order to bring this internal meaning and coherence to light, however, I must employ *explanatory* processes which imply its insertion into a wider structure i.e. a social structure. In doing so, I in no way wish to find sociological elements in the work. The latter is nothing other than a text having, or not having, a coherent structure. (p. 103)

Goldmann's method is demonstrably circular since those texts which he describes as capable of expressing a world vision are also those which are defined as 'great' in conventional aesthetic terms; their coherence is held to stem from their expression of a world vision but this coherence was also probably a reason why we have come to regard them as 'great'.

As other writers have observed there is something over-neat and mechanistic in Goldmann's picture of the novelist passively responding to socio-economic reality, as if he were some sort of spiritualist medium through which the social group is allowed to speak. When, in the case of the novel, this group comprises the alienated writers themselves there is a flavour of redundancy about the whole explanation. It is not certain for instance that we learn more from an account of Malraux's novels in which the change from individual hero to 'group subject' is held to reflect capitalism in crisis than we do from a standard biographical interpretation under which Malraux's own personal commitment to communism leads him to portray cohesive groups of Communists in his work. Nevertheless these reservations do not detract from the view that Goldmann has given an interesting new direction to socio-cultural criticism by drawing attention to the role of structure and form as well as content.

Raymond Williams (b. 1921)

Although Williams's work (particularly after 1970) draws on the ideas of the European Marxists he owes some allegiance to the native British tradition of literary criticism, typified by Leavis, with its detailed attention to the text and respect for the intrinsic value of literature. Williams's writings on literature and society stress three elements: a theory of *cultural materialism*, the identification of *structures of feeling*, and the concept of *hegemony*; the first and second of these ideas are examined as early as *Culture and Society* (1958) while the third is first developed explicitly in his major theoretical work *Marxism and Literature* (OUP, 1977).

Williams explicitly rejects the conventional Marxist base/ superstructure model which subordinates literature and art to the 'real' world of economic production. Even Plekhanov's more elaborate and indirect formulation (see p. 37) is misleading in his view because it fails to take account of the fact that 'consciousness' plays just as important a role in social relationships as material production. Williams's alternative theory of 'cultural materialism' holds that the so-called 'superstructural' activities we call 'culture' have as good a claim to form the base on which social relations depend as have the forces of production. In fact production should be taken to include 'social production', one aspect of which is art, including imaginative literature. Williams deftly illustrates this by comparing the role of television in modern Western society to that of motor-car production; what is apparently superstructural is far more important in determining social awareness than an industry turning out what in fact are luxury goods. Nevertheless, despite rejecting the orthodox Marxist metaphor in which art is a passive 'reflection' he does not want to return to the pre- or anti-Marxist position in which literature is segregated into an independent 'aesthetic' zone, unrelated to other human activities. He attempts to resolve the problem by introducing the idea of *hegemony*, derived from the Italian Marxist Antonio Gramsci.

In Gramsci's formulation *hegemony* is the method by which a ruling social class exerts control over other social groups other than by crude political or economic pressures; it is in effect a 'hearts and minds' method, although it is rarely understood as a conscious 'strategy' even by members of the ruling class themselves. Hegemony works through concepts which are regarded as self-evident and are therefore never questioned or even considered as available for questioning. In this way it masks from all classes but the rulers the conditions of their existence and their true self-interest. Hegemony differs from *ideology* in being less a formal, articulated system of meanings than what Williams calls a 'saturation of the whole process of living' for which the usual description is simply 'commonsense':

> It thus constitutes a sense of reality for most people in the society, a sense of absolute because experienced reality beyond which it is very difficult for most members of the society to move, in most areas of their lives. (*Marxism and Literature*, p. 110)

Through the operation of *hegemony*, which may be expressed in economic, political or cultural institutions and forms, the capitalist ruling class in Western societies acquires the *consent* which allows it to govern without physical repression. (For example the 'class interest' of the ruling group may be expressed in hegemonic terms as 'the national interest'.)

In culture, *hegemony*, according to Williams, weaves its spell through a number of categories seen as self-evident but in fact actively working to ratify the existing social order: these include traditions – the literary canon of work considered worthy of preservation and study is an example – institutions, educational or cultural, and formations, by which Williams denotes 'conscious movements and tendencies (literary, artistic, philosophical or scientific)'. At a more detailed level hegemony expresses itself through the development of conventions, genres and forms within the accepted tradition. Williams's examples here are tantalisingly sparse but one he does identify is the fictional convention relating to narrative and direct speech in novels. This ranges from the integrity of style, based on a 'real or assumed social identity' found in Jane Austen to 'the break or even formal contrast between narrated and spoken language (as in George Eliot or Hardy)'. (*Marxism and Literature*, p. 178)

The above example suggests that hegemony is supple and dynamic, changing over time to accommodate new material realities and reconciling contradictions. At any one time it operates through three categories: the *dominant* (most powerful and accepted version), the *residual* (including elements inherited from the past which are still active in constructing present notions of social reality) and the *emergent* (corresponding either to a new phase of the dominant or to that which is in opposition to it). With the emergent category Williams particularly associates the *structure of feeling*, a term which he prefers to employ rather than 'ideology' or 'world vision' in relation to particular authors, since it lays stress on the quality of 'felt' or 'lived' experience, as dictated of course by the prevalent hegemony, rather than mere passive reflection of some superior reality.

Because *structures of feeling* are associated with the emergent they often appear as private and idiosyncratic; in a chemical analogy Williams describes them as holding social experiences *in solution* as opposed to having been *precipitated* and therefore available to all members of that society. Because this quality is characteristic of art and literature it often results in these activities being misleadingly relegated or quarantined in a separate category of the 'aesthetic'. One *structure of feeling* which Williams identifies is that of those novelists of the 1840s such as Dickens and Mrs Gaskell who were the first to respond to the momentous economic, social and cultural implications of industrialisation. In their work he finds sympathetic observation and a largely successful attempt at imaginative identification with the new world of the industrial working class. However, their 'feeling' is modified by their own middle-class origins, resulting in fear of becoming too much involved. 'Sympathy was transformed not into action but withdrawal.' (*Culture and Society*, p. 119)

For Williams the value of literature lies in its ability to disturb the existing hegemony. He expresses this belief in a lecture given in 1983 (although somewhat confusingly he reverts to the term 'ideology'):

> Literature is not just a carrier of ideology, as in most forms of reflection theory. It is inescapably ideological, but its specific relative autonomy is that it is a form of writing, a form of practice in which ideology both exists and is or can be internally distanced and questioned. Thus the value of literature is precisely that it is one of the areas where the grip of ideology is or can be loosened because although it cannot escape ideological construction, the point about its literariness is that it is a continual questioning of it internally. (*Writing in Society* Verso 1984, p. 208)

Unfortunately Williams does not satisfactorily prove his claim that 'literariness' entails the ability to escape from ideology; he is content to reassert his argument against the artificial segregation of literary works into the category of the 'aesthetic'. In *Marxism and Literature* he calls for a new 'sociology of culture' which would merge work on the economics of publishing and the composition of the reading public (for example) into what is normally seen as the province of literary criticism. However his argument soon becomes bedevilled by the familiar problem of the reconciliation of 'value' as traditionally conceived with notions of social significance – a problem which is explored but not really solved.

Because it rejects the base/superstructure model Williams's attempt at reshaping and humanising Marxist theory throws great weight on the 'structure of feeling' but it is not clear that this concept is well-defined or powerful enough to provide the mediation between text and society that Williams demands of it. Nevertheless he commands admiration for his belief in

literature as more than mere social reflection and his effort to
relate it 'to the lives of the majority of our own people'.
(*Marxism and Literature*, p. 2)

Terry Eagleton (b. 1943)

After Williams (whose relationship to Marxism is ambiguous
as we have seen) Eagleton is the most prolific and incisive
Marxist critic writing in Britain, although some readers may
find his rigorously systematic approach somewhat blunted by
a highly condensed and metaphorical style and an implicit
reliance on the difficult ideas of the French Marxist philosopher,
Althusser. These are most persuasively argued in his *Criticism
and Ideology* (NLB, 1976).

Unlike Williams, with whom he worked at Cambridge and
who he warmly though not uncritically quotes in his own
work, Eagleton has no wish to turn the conventional base/
superstructure account upside down. Instead he tries to elaborate
it by expanding the role of ideology. As maintained by Althusser,
ideology is an all-pervasive presence, not only distorting reality
in the interest of the ruling group but, because it appears to us
in the guise of concrete experience, conditioning all attempts to
penetrate and unmask it. For Althusser the unveiling of ideology
can only be achieved by the application of a rigorous and
'scientific' Marxist theory but Eagleton believes that it can also
be done in a unique way through the study of literary texts.

This apparently eccentric notion is based on the perception
that imaginative writing by definition makes no claim to be
dealing *directly* with reality. Unlike the writing of (say) history,
the writing of novels has no 'determinate object'; characters,
incidents and emotions are not related to any 'primary reality'
but form 'ends in themselves' or as Eagleton puts it are 'pseudo-
real'. What is represented in fiction must therefore be ideology
itself, since the choice of what goes into a given novel (into
which theoretically *anything* can go) must be determined by the
ideological constitution of the society in which the novel was
written, the author and the 'aesthetic' of that society in conjunction. Eagleton suggests that the process by which these
ideological 'formations' give rise to a literary text is similar to

the way in which a theatre director 'produces' a performance of a play from a written script. Just as different directors will produce radically different interpretations of the same script so that an audience cannot identify with certainty a definitive 'play' at all, so the literary text in general is a 'production' of ideology, leading to radically different final forms. However, by studying the process of 'production' we are privileged to glimpse from outside the operation of an ideology otherwise inaccessible to us.

In order to examine the 'production of the ideological' and to discover its relation to ideology and beyond that to 'history' Eagleton advocates the method of the French Althusserian critic, Pierre Machery. Machery claims that all literary works are characterised by internal contradictions and that what is significant about a given text are those very 'dissonances' and 'absences': 'Ideology is present in the text in the form of eloquent silences.' In this light each text is seen as having a kind of Freudian 'Unconscious' which it is the task of the Marxist literary critic to penetrate and awaken, whereas conventional or 'bourgeois' criticism is content to analyse as 'flaws' or 'defects' those inconsistencies or gaps left after the 'production of the ideological'. (See *Criticism and Ideology*, pp. 89–97)

This concept of the function of criticism implies a detailed theory which relates literary work to ideology and society. Eagleton proposes a number of categories, the 'conjuncture' of which underlies a literary text. In much simplified form these are given below:

(1) The *General Mode of Production* of society (GMP): this is the particular mode of production which underlies the 'social formation' of a given society (e.g. land-owning feudalism or industrial capitalism).

(2) The *Literary Mode of Production* (LMP): in any society there are a number of ways in which 'literature' is transmitted from 'author' to 'audience' but one mode is usually *dominant*. (In a capitalist society the LMP for fiction is speculative publishing though this does not preclude writers reading their novels aloud to an audience.) The LMP implies certain social relations: for example the relationship of the 'producer' to his 'patron',

or the relationship of the 'independent' author to the commercial publisher.

In a suggestive example Eagleton shows how the Victorian circulating library system (described in more detail in Chapter 5) as the dominant nineteenth-century LMP determined the *selection* of authors for publication (because the libraries had a monopoly on purchasing new fiction), the *pace* of production (three-deckers had to be produced at the rate of one a year to allow the writers even a subsistence salary) and the format of the *text* (the required length could only be achieved by multiple plots, long digressions and padding).

(3) The *General Ideology* (GI): is the dominant ideology produced by that GMP. In capitalist society it is the hegemonic bourgeois ideology which brings about in individuals those 'misperceptions of the real' which enable the society to function.

There is a set of complex interactions between GI and LMP. One example Eagleton gives is the *language* of literary composition itself which takes a form determined by ideological needs (e.g. the adoption of a vernacular language – English rather than Latin – at a particular point of cultural development). In addition, the idea of 'literature' itself, in the form of a canon of accepted texts available for study and criticism within the educational system, has an ideological function in sustaining a particular concept of 'culture' and 'education' through the apparatus of publishing houses, bookshops, literary journals and academic Departments of English. Finally GI can directly interfere with LMP through direct or indirect censorship.

(4) *Authorial Ideology* (AuI): is the author's 'specific mode of biographical insertion into GI' which is influenced ('overdetermined') by a number of factors: social class, sex, nationality, geographical origin and so on.

AuI has a relationship to GI which can take the form of correspondence ('homology'), partial 'disjunction' or complete contradiction. The author may belong to a social class that predisposes him to conflict with the prevailing GI but the conjunction of the other factors may return him to conformity with it, as in the case of many working-class writers under capitalism. Alternatively a woman writer in a male-dominated society may come into conflict with GI despite conforming to it by social class. AuI is therefore distinct from GI but the text does not merely reflect AuI (as 'vulgar' or 'reductive' Marxism would claim); the text is the product of an aesthetic 'working' of a GI that has itself been 'worked' by the authorial-biographical factors – so that it becomes, as Eagleton puts it, 'ideology raised to the second power'.

(5) Finally there is *Aesthetic Ideology* (AI): this is a specific 'region' or aspect of GI which concerns itself with the expectations and conventions of a given society in matters of literary tradition, genres, forms, stylistic devices, etc. It is AI which for example assigns a distinctive status to the novel as a genre or demands that novels have a 'happy ending' or are supplied with a recognisable hero.

The relationship between LMP, AI, AuI and GI is complex as would be expected from so many variables. Readers who would like more detail should turn to *Criticism and Ideology* (pp. 60–2) where Eagleton maintains, for example, that the novel could only be developed at a particular stage of evolution of an LMP, and also gives a lengthy analysis of nineteenth-century culture which shows how Victorian bourgeois ideology was transmitted by a group of writers whose own lower-middle-class origins brought them partly into conflict with it.

Eagleton's theory contains a rejection of the view that some texts somehow 'transcend' the conditions of their production and acquire a kind of universal status; he claims the texts we value most are precisely those that relate most revealingly to those conditions. 'Great' works survive because of the 'aesthetic producibility' of the 'concrete ideological conjunctures in which they inhere'. Accordingly Marxists do not need to hold that 'great' literature is confined to that which corresponds to or expresses the Marxist version of reality. Often it is the most reactionary ideological 'conjunctures' which throw up the 'aesthetic problem' that in turn 'produces' the stimulating, relevant text as opposed to the mere contemporary potboiler.

However, Eagleton's concept of the critic as an 'ideological detective' raises problems of principle and method. While he concedes that not all texts are equally valuable there is still the question 'Valuable for whom?' Would two critics both trained in materialist methods and accepting Eagleton's categories come to the same conclusions about the relative merits of, say, Thomas Hardy and Anthony Trollope? If the answer is 'They should', does this mean Eagleton's 'materialist criticism' is a mere mechanical application of dry theoretical principles? If the answer is 'No, they shouldn't', is the method any more than a rationalisation of those impressions and intuitions that Eagleton condemns in bourgeois critics? Is it merely another – politically 'clean' – way of exalting Charles Dickens and Joseph Conrad over second-rate authors such as Wilkie Collins or Arthur Conan Doyle?

If, on the other hand, 'materialist criticism' and the unmasking and analysis of the 'ideological' is seen as an activity in its own right, is there any need to restrict its application to 'great' works? Although Eagleton remarks that the average love-story in a teenage magazine is inferior because 'the withered ideological matrix within which it moves simply precludes that transformative textual production of such myths which might alone "redeem" them' (*Criticism and Ideology* p. 185), once we start regarding the canon of literature as itself an ideological construct there is no reason for not examining the power and recurrence even of 'withered ideological matrices'.

In effect, to do this would be to expand the subject matter of literary criticism to include popular fiction and the mass media, as Eagleton himself advocates in his later work, suggesting that the now blurred discipline of literary criticism be replaced by a revival of the ancient discipline of *rhetoric*, which concerns itself not with the features and status of texts, but with their *effect*. In this respect he is close to the concern of the final group of theorists to be described, *reception theory*.

Reception Theory

Marxists seek to explain literature and fiction in terms of a systematised view of society. Their theorising tends to be author-oriented, describing a text in terms of the 'ideology' under which it was produced. *Reception theories* make the *reader* their starting point and attempt to examine the expectations which readers may have of a particular text, the effects which the text may have on the readers and the *uses* to which the act of reading may be put.

An early attempt to assess the response of readers to a particular author was made by the German cultural sociologist Leo Lowenthal. Recognising a disproportionate interest by middle-class Germans in Feodor Dostoievski in the period after the First World War, Lowenthal tried to link the values which the Germans found in this writer (as attested by the comments of critics and reviewers) with their apathy in the face of Hitler's rise to power. Lowenthal suggests that Dostoievski was felt to represent passivity, expressed in ideas of duty and suffering, a distrust of efforts to change society and a semi-magical belief in the ability to reconcile or transcend opposites. It is not suggested that Dostoievski's novels necessarily uphold these values but that they were used to reinforce and symbolise the concept that 'The middle class cannot question the existing organisation as a whole' with its corollary of passive resignation before fascism. (*Literature, Popular Culture and Society*, Pacific Books, 1961, pp. 151–156)

Lowenthal's study was restricted to *written* observations on Dostoievski and therefore oriented towards professional writers and critics rather than the common reader. Only questionnaire techniques could analyse the attitudes of the latter and then only of course with living subjects. Robert Holub's *Reception Theory* (1984) describes some studies in which ordinary readers were asked to comment on texts, but the techniques are more suited to poetry than prose because of the more manageable length of the former. Perhaps the most obvious use of the questionnaire technique is with popular novels where the readers' reaction to a whole genre rather than to single novels can be explored. (As for example in Janice Radway's *Reading the Romance* – see Chapter 7).

Another approach is to analyse changes in the response to the 'great' novels over the period of their history. Eagleton has done this in skeleton form for Hardy, showing how contemporary critics could not cope with Hardy's unconventionality; Hardy became popular as an 'anthropologist' of rural Wessex, but then fell out of favour and was dismissed as nihilistic. After a period of neglect in the 1920s and 1930s his fiction was rediscovered and reinterpreted as propaganda for the lost, allegedly 'organic' rural community. A more elaborate, non-Marxist historical theory is that of the *horizon of expectation*, offered by Hans-Robert Jauss (reception theory has become almost a national speciality of German literary critics).

Like Raymond Williams Jauss criticises the orthodox Marxists for seeing literature as tamely dependent on the economic base and therefore (ironically) ignoring its 'revolutionary' implications. Whereas Marxists limit their interest to the social position of the reader Jauss stresses the aspect of *dialogue* or *interaction* in the reception of literature. Each reader comes to a novel with a framework of expectations and criteria drawn from his previous reading of fiction; this framework therefore varies at different points in history. However, the reception of the new text itself alters the existing framework or 'horizon of expectation'. It does this by satisfying, refuting, disappointing or surpassing the expectations, so that the framework itself is 'varied, corrected, altered or just reproduced' (in Jauss's words). Jauss dismisses as 'culinary art' those texts which merely reinforce existing horizons; the great works are those that go beyond them. One task of criticism is therefore to write literary history which reconstructs the 'horizons' as they existed in the past in order to understand the way the work would have been received by the contemporary reader and assess its impact in modifying that horizon.

As a lively example of the way in which a horizon functions Jauss gives an account of the prosecution of Flaubert in 1857 for the allegedly immoral influence of his novel *Madame Bovary*. In the course of the trial the prosecuting counsel cited the passage in which Emma Bovary is shown contemplating adultery for the first time:

'I've a lover!, a lover,' she said to herself again and again, revelling in the thought as if she had attained a second puberty. At last she would know the delights of love, the feverish joys of which she had despaired. She was entering a marvellous world where all was passion, ecstasy, delirium.

(*Madame Bovary* Penguin edn, p. 175)

The prosecution attributed to Flaubert himself the enthusiasm for adultery which the defence counsel argued was only meant to be expressed by the heroine. The confusion arose because Flaubert's innovation of *style indirect libre* (free indirect style) represented the attitudes and emotions of characters as if they were narrative. Under the contemporary 'horizon of expectation' narrative was limited to expressing the point of view of the *author*. A new 'horizon of expectation' had to be established under which the inner mind of a character could be presented as objectively as her physical movements but it could still be left ambiguous as to how those inner thoughts should be judged. The court were so disturbed by the implications of the latter idea that they acquitted Flaubert but condemned the literary technique which had registered such a convulsive effect on the bourgeois nervous system.

Jauss's approach tends to regard literature as being 'socially formative', in direct opposition to those Marxists who see it as a mere reflection of the society in which it was written. His 'horizon of expectation' idea is a very useful one, particularly as it can be applied to the author as well as the reader. The author, writing with certain potential readers in mind, is under pressure to conform to their aesthetic, social and moral expectations. This is the situation described by Darko Suvin, in an essay which is treated in greater detail in Chapter 5:

> These normative structures are then refracted (and partly refashioned) through the more or less adequate 'structure of feeling' in the literary work – which of course can also anticipate not yet realised possibilities of human relationships, not only conforming to existing values and desires but also partly defining new desires, formulating and thus stimulating new horizons of expectation. (See 'The Social Addressees of Victorian Fiction' *Literature and History vol. 8:1* Spring 1982, p. 12)

The idea of 'expectation' also figures in the theory of the 'implied reader' associated with the work of Wolfgang Iser, Professor of English Literature at Constanz University in South Germany. Iser builds on a philosophical and psychological basis which stresses the reader's role in 'producing' the final text. Since the direct merging of the experience of writer and reader is not possible (in the absence of telepathy) the reader ultimately is responsible for the task of assembling the meaning of a text on the basis of 'perspectives' supplied by the author (i.e. it is not entirely arbitrary). This concept of the reader as 'producer of meaning' is termed the 'implied reader' and is to be distinguished from the 'intended reader' (or reader as the *addressee* of the author).

Nevertheless Iser seems to resurrect the idea of the 'intended reader' when he talks about the *repertoire* of a novel. This term corresponds roughly to the dominant thought-system of a given period. Although the text *implies* or assumes the existence of this thought-system the reader's role is to respond to *challenges* to it which are provoked by contradictions or 'negations' in the text, since in Iser's view: 'The field of action in a literary work tends to be on or just beyond the fringes of the particular thought-system prevalent at the time.' Reference to a 'repertoire' suggests *some* overlap between the values of reader and author; unless the reader accepts or adheres to these conventional values even partially there is no benefit to him from the therapeutic effect of having them challenged. Conversely if the challenge is too radical, that is if the distance between the values of reader and writer is too great, the work is likely to be dismissed as revolutionary claptrap.

Like Jauss, Iser maintains that the artistic works with greatest impact are those that seem to conform to existing norms but in essence mount a challenge to them. This idea is similar in effect (though not presented from the same political perspective) to Eagleton's suggestion that the greatest challenge to bourgeois norms through literature comes from those writers who are *within* but not *of* bourgeois society – the lower middle classes (Eliot, Dickens) and foreigners (James, Conrad). It is also reminiscent of Lukács' attempt to enlist Balzac and Scott as progressive authors, despite their 'reactionary' political records, using the concept of 'dissociation'. In all such cases there must be enough overlap between the 'thought-system' of the author and the readers to allow that system to be subversively attacked from within. By contrast what Jauss calls 'culinary art' is that which is content tamely to meet expectations, a quality which Iser ascribes also to certain genres of popular fiction, repeating accusations of 'stereotyping' and complacency made by the Leavises:

> there are some texts which offer nothing but a harmonious world purified of all contradiction and deliberately excluding anything that might disturb the illusion once established, and these are the texts we generally do not like to classify as literary. Women's magazines and the brasher forms of detective story might be cited as examples.
>
> (*The Act of Reading*, RKP 1978, p. 73)

The issue of popular fiction is taken up in more detail in Chaper 7. At this point it is enough to register that most of the socio-cultural critics feel the need to justify a distinction between 'popular' and 'literary' in terms that emphasise the greater power of the latter to disturb conventions of style and thought, though the Marxists take this further by relating this power to the class origins of the author. For example Eagleton claims in relation to nineteenth-century England: 'Only writers with an ambivalent class relation to the society could, it seemed, be open to the contradictions from which major literary art was produced'. (*Criticism and Ideology* p. 125)

As with the other approaches described in this chapter the reader or student is free to decide whether reception theory provides a useful context for examining fiction of the past or present. The purpose of the chapter has been to introduce terminology and to identify principles and issues; the more text-based chapters that follow allow the application of the various approaches to be examined in practice.

3. The Novel New: Defoe and Richardson

The novel, as its name indicates, was regarded as a new phenomenon in its time. The sort of extended prose fiction which became popular in England in the mid eighteenth century was sufficiently different from anything which had preceded it for contemporary commentators including the novelists themselves to remark on the fact. For example, in 1741 Samuel Richardson told Aaron Hill that his first work, *Pamela*, might possibly 'introduce a new species of writing'.

Admittedly some modern literary historians have made valiant attempts to exhume pre-eighteenth-century texts which might conceivably be described as novels or to find parallels to the novel in classical or Far Eastern cultures. However, the view has tended to prevail that the beginning of modern fiction can be dated fairly precisely to the early eighteenth century. Even the author of a book on the novel 'before Richardson' admits that the publication of *Pamela* constituted a literary breakthrough (for which Defoe's narratives had provided the 'crucial preparation'),[1] while Walter Allen in his standard history *The English Novel* (1954) suggests that critics who want to trace the form back to Elizabethan or medieval archetypes have fallen into the error of assuming that 'the words fiction and novel are interchangeable'.

Since this is not a book about the aesthetic definition of the novel form there is no need to unravel Walter Allen's distinction. For our purpose it is sufficient to recognise that the literary culture of eighteenth-century England gave birth to a form of extended prose narrative, describing imaginary but plausible characters and incidents in a well-formed structure which was

distinctive enough from previous literary texts to attract
contemporary comment (of a semi-sociological as well as a
literary kind). Not surprisingly later literary critics felt equally
prompted to comment on and try to explain this phenomenon.
In doing so they have drawn on evidence from historians and
economists about the overall social context of the period in
which the genre was launched. Despite flaws in the arguments advanced by Ian Watt and others there is considerable
evidence to support the view that the new genre was written
for a readership drawn from a particular socio-economic
group (the middle classes) by writers who were often though
not exclusively from that same group. It is an idea which
deserves a full and rigorous examination since it has tended to
thread through all the descriptions of the development of the
genre.

Examining the theory involves making reference to three
novelists who are generally regarded as the leading eighteenth-
century exponents of the art form. They are, with the dates of
their major works:

Daniel Defoe	*Robinson Crusoe*	1719
(1660?–1731)	*Moll Flanders*	1722
Samuel Richardson	*Pamela*	1740–1
(1689–1731)	*Clarissa*	1747–8
	Sir Charles Grandison	1753–4
Henry Fielding	*Joseph Andrews*	1742
(1707–54)	*Tom Jones*	1749
	Amelia	1751

Of course selection of these three from amongst a great
number of less well-known names can itself be regarded as a
way of biasing the evidence. (Some people would say that
Sterne and Smollett have as good a claim to be in the list.)
However, as most of the debate on the theory has been in terms
of these writers, the argument will be allowed to occupy this
ground in the present chapter. In particular one text – Defoe's
Robinson Crusoe – will be considered in detail for the light it can
throw on the issue.

A Middle-class Art Form?

In defence of his own version of the socio-cultural approach the Marxist critic David Craig has considered the possibility of what he calls 'laws of literary development'. Accepting that at the time of writing (1970) it was too early to speak of 'fully-fledged laws, thoroughly verified and with a predictive value', he nevertheless puts forward a number of what he calls 'axioms', admitting that to test their validity would require a long programme of work by a team of scholars, including historians and mass-media experts as well as literary critics. The first of these axioms (and the most relevant to this chapter) runs: 'The rise of a genre is likely to occur along with the rise of a class (e.g. in average wealth, in the proportion of the population belonging to it).' (See *Marxists on Literature*, Penguin 1975, pp. 134–160)

Any student of the novel who is at all sympathetic to the socio-cultural approach is likely to be interested in whether this idea can be applied to the development of fiction. Craig had the advantage of writing in the knowledge that the correlation between genre and social class had already been attempted thirteen years before by Ian Watt, in *The Rise of the Novel*. Despite a hostile treatment from some quarters since 1957, Watt's attempt to relate the rise of the novel to the increased power of the middle classes after the Glorious Revolution of 1688 has remained influential. Terry Eagleton, for example, begins his 1982 book on Richardson (*The Rape of Clarissa*, Basil Blackwell, 1982) by remarking on the appropriateness of the novelist's birthdate in 1689, only one year after the historical watershed. Watt's theory therefore needs to be considered in detail both for its own sake and for what light it throws on the plausibility of socio-cultural theories in general.

The Revolution of 1688 was called 'Glorious' by those who supported the claim of Parliament to sovereignty in raising taxes and making laws, in opposition to the 'absolute monarchy' which was, or was held to be, the objective of the Stuart kings. The House of Commons, whose power had been eroded under Charles II and which had been affronted by the conversion of his son James to Catholicism, connived at James's overthrow and then welcomed the Dutch prince, William of Orange, as his successor; in so doing they were averting the possibility of absolutist rule by securing for themselves powers which in other European countries had passed to the monarchy. Since by definition the Commons represented interests other than the great aristocratic landlords their victory has been held to inaugurate a transfer of political authority to what in the nineteenth century came to be known as the middle classes.

Many historians believe that this political and constitutional shift of power accompanied an economic shift away from the traditional forms of wealth based on the ownership of land to one derived from trade. The development of the joint-stock company as a mechanism to encourage financial investment, the expansion of opportunities for overseas trade following the 'discoveries' of the previous century, and the growth of colonies in America and elsewhere added enormously to the scope and influence of what were known at the time as the 'mercantile' or 'merchant' classes. By the mid-eighteenth century, this group whose source of wealth was the capital accumulated through trade and the production of goods at home or abroad was sufficiently distinctive and sufficiently powerful economically to pose a threat to the landowning aristocracy, who up to this time had formed the governing class.[2]

In *The Rise of the Novel* Watt bases his argument on assumptions about the ideology of this group. What distinguished them ideologically was the value they set on the *individual*, which could take several forms: in the economic sphere, the amassing of individual wealth; in the social sphere, the seeking of a higher social status through individual mobility; in the religious sphere, the individual's direct relationship with God and his responsibility for his own salvation. Such an ideology could only arise according to Watt in a society marked by 'an economic and political organisation which allows its members a very wide range of choices in their actions' and is also shaking itself free of 'the allegiance to past modes of thought and action denoted by the word "tradition" – a force that is always social not individual'. (*The Rise of the Novel* p. 66) Individualism was associated with two particular trends: the development of modern industrial capitalism and the spread of the Puritan form of Protestantism which came to be known as Dissent in the eighteenth century and Non-conformism in the nineteenth. As the middle classes were in the forefront of both developments one might expect them to be champions of individualism. Watt's original achievement was to show how this ideology was reflected in the aesthetic of a new genre, the novel.

The Rise of the Novel describes in some detail how fiction contrasts with previous literary forms in its concern for truth to individual experience and its lack of deference to tradition (for example in the form of approved models of structure). From the beginning the novel writers were concerned with the behaviour of specific individuals in specific circumstances and as a consequence they made use of plots which were original, whereas Shakespeare's by contrast had been based on traditional sources (e.g. histories or folk-tales). A minor but symptomatic feature of the desire for plausibility was the naming of characters in the early novels. Moll Flanders, Clarissa Harlowe and even Robinson Crusoe (truth is stranger than fiction!) are particular and lifelike, whereas previous writers had used names allegorically to suggest qualities or types (Malvolio and Mr Badman). Having established the *particularity* of fiction Watt goes on to illustrate how the *content* of the leading trio of early novelists reflects the orientation of the new middle classes towards the independence of each individual.

Watt's argument has been treated to searching criticism, most notably in Diana Spearman's *The Novel and Society* (RKP 1966). Spearman attacks a number of propositions that must be shown to be valid if Watt's theory is to be credible. These are that:

(1) The political, economic and social power of the middle classes increased after 1688, leading to the dominance of their ideology of 'economic individualism' and its reflection in fiction. (In terms of the model given in Chapter 1 it provided the *social context* which supported a literary context in which the new genre was able to develop.)

(2) The authors of the earliest novels were members of or closely associated with the new middle class described above and therefore the novels reflect the values of that class.

(3) The readers of the novels also belonged to this social group and shared its ideology. Clearly the 'fit' between

writers and readers does not have to be exact but according to Watt the instant and overwhelming success of the new genre suggests a community of interest and feeling that had suddenly been tapped for the first time.

Spearman finds serious flaws in all the above three propositions which we will now look at separately.

Social Context

It is possible to bring evidence to show that the shift of power to the middle classes was nothing like as drastic by the mid eighteenth century as Watt suggests. (In the end the argument reduces to a dispute about statistics and definitions.) Spearman quotes historians to prove that the House of Lords still retained a considerable political role and that it provided most members of the cabinet. Even in the Commons, she claims, the middle classes did not form the largest group, being outnumbered by the squirearchy, or non-aristocratic landowners, and they were restricted in their attainment of the franchise (i.e. the right to vote for the Commons). Admittedly the City of London was a powerful force and was a base of the middle classes but it had been such a force long before 1688. In summary she quotes J. H. Plumb to the effect that even after 1688 'social and political life was dominated by the aristocracy'. (*The Novel and Society* p. 22)

Against Spearman's scepticism it can be pointed out that the holder of the crucial new post of Prime Minister was usually a member of the Commons and that the middle classes were vocal in that body out of all proportion to their numbers. Alan Swingewood, who has attempted to reconcile the views of Watt and Spearman, notes that although the aristocracy may have managed to constrain the new rising class politically for some time after 1688 it was within the context of a society 'increasingly geared towards profit, capital accumulation and rational accountability'. (*The Novel and Revolution*, Macmillan 1975 p. 34) He argues that the impetus for cultural developments in the eighteenth century derived from the very tension between the classes: 'In the fiction of Richardson middle class manners and an acute sensitivity to problems of social status embody artistically the bourgeois class's struggle for hegemony' (ibid. p. 35).

The distinction between the bare facts of social or economic status (as quantified in statistics such as the number of Members of Parliament from a given background) and actual social influence is also stressed by David Craig who rejects Spearman's argument by referring to the subjective psychological aspects of the changing social pattern:

> In politics [Diana Spearman] implies, the old fundamentals remain little changed. This is not the view of the leading authorities, who see the later seventeenth century as a political watershed. As for the nation's work, of course corn and wool still bulked largest in our trading but (even according to her own figures) manufactures were *expanding faster*, and here as so often what counts culturally is the thrust of the new factor, which begins to change people's sense of the possibilities open to them. (*Marxists on Literature*, p. 155)

Although there is an ironic side to a Marxist discounting hard economic data in favour of 'what counts culturally', Terry Eagleton also maintains that in some less than tangible way English society had altered in 'feel' after 1688:

> The sway of feudalist aristocracy in England had been decisively overthrown: although the aristocracy retained social and political dominance, with many of its familiar institutions surviving intact, the economic directions of the society had been irreversibly altered. (*The Rape of Clarissa*, Basil Blackwell 1982, p. 1)

For Eagleton it is the penetration of the cultural and ethical sphere by middle-class values that is crucial, since it reforms the prevailing *hegemony*:

> any revolutionary class, in addition to seizing political power must secure *cultural* hegemony over its opponents. To seal its victory such a class must do more than break the political, military and juridical strength of its oppressors . . .

it must also challenge and oust them in the realms of religion, philosophy, art, morality, language and manners. (Ibid.)

Although the Revolution of 1688 was 'bloodless' this transformation of values had begun. In a way reminiscent of Williams's view of the way in which culture affects consciousness as much as the material world Eagleton claims that Richardson's novels, for example, were a direct contribution to it:

> It would be easy and relatively unoriginal, to show how Richardson's novels are among other things great allegories of class warfare, narratives of alliance and antagonism between a predatory nobility and a pious bourgeoisie . . . . For Richardson's novels are not mere images of conflicts fought out on another terrain, representations of a history which happens elsewhere; they are themselves a material part of those struggles, pitched standards around which battle is joined, instruments which help to constitute social interests rather than lenses that reflect them. These novels are an agent, rather than a mere account, of the English bourgeoisie's attempt to wrest a degree of ideological hegemony from the aristocracy in the decades which follow the political settlement of 1688. (Ibid., p. 4)

Writers

Moving from economic and political realities to the more subjective area of values demands that we prove a relationship between the early novel writers and the middle-class values they are held to be representing (or even shaping, in Eagleton's formulation).

If we restrict ourselves to the three leading writers who are at the centre of Watt's theory we see a variety of life-styles. Richardson corresponds most closely to the stereotype which Watt puts forward; although his father was a mere joiner, by the time he came to write his first novel *Pamela*, at the surprisingly mature age of 51, he had risen sufficiently in social status to enable him to absorb the self-satisfied middle-class ideology, declaring that tradesmen 'are infinitely of more consequence, and deserve more to be incourag'd than any other degree or rank of people'. (See *The Rape of Clarissa* p. 3) Beginning as a printer's apprentice he had acquired the lucrative and highly-prized position of Printer to the House of Commons, and therefore became in effect a businessman with thirty or forty of his own employees, rather than merely a highly skilled artisan. Furthermore his trade had brought him into contact with the professional literary world since he occasionally acted as a publisher would today (dealing directly with authors) and of course came into frequent contact with the 'booksellers' who were the equivalent of publishers at the time. (*Pamela* was written as a result of a request to him from two booksellers to produce a manual of model letters for 'those country readers who were unable to indite for themselves'.)

Defoe's career was more chequered. The son of a London butcher who was wealthy enough to send him to a Dissenting Academy (a boarding school run for Nonconformists), he was himself intended for the Nonconformist ministry. Having recognised in himself qualities which would have made him unsuited to this profession and at the same time developed a flair for commercial undertakings he set himself up as a merchant in the City. On at least three separate occasions he rose to positions of considerable wealth which encouraged him in fantasies of becoming a 'gentleman' (changing his name from Foe to the more aristocratic sounding Defoe) only to find that an inclination towards unwise speculation led him into debt and commercial ruin. As a businessman and expert on overseas trade Defoe made himself useful as an adviser to the new government of William of Orange after 1688; his ideological identification with the new political order led him to become a propagandist for it, bringing in payment for pamphlets that helped sustain him in times of financial embarrassment. After the transition to a Tory government (representing the old feudal interests) under Queen Anne Defoe switched sides for a while but this was for mercenary reasons and fear for his own security. His later career, in which he worked clandestinely for the 'Whig' faction (the supporters of the 1688 settlement) while overtly writing on behalf of the Tories, shows no evidence that he lost his identification with and respect for the values of the trading classes and their Nonconformist religious faith. Even his aspiration to the status of gentleman reflected this, since in his view 'gentility' did not necessarily relate to birth but to qualities which could be cultivated by 'breeding' and were therefore theoretically available to all. He stated in his *Compleat English Tradesman* (1726):

> a gentleman-tradesman is not so much a nonsense as some people would persuade us to reckon it . . . the wealth of our tradesmen is already so great; 'tis very probable a few years will show us still a greater race of trade-bred gentlemen than ever England yet had.

It is difficult to agree therefore with Spearman's rejection of middle-class status for Defoe despite the far from respectable course of his career at times, which included spells in Newgate prison and in the pillory. She is on surer ground in denying the 'bourgeois' theory of the novel with regard to Fielding, who came from a Somerset family of small landowners and whose political satire and invective on behalf of the Tories eventually brought him its reward in the form of a post as Justice of the Peace for Middlesex. Even Watt finds difficulty in relating Fielding's literary work to the 'realism' which he sees as the hallmark of the new middle-class genre. Swingewood prefers to see Fielding as representing a politically-conscious reaction to the rise of the middle-class mentality, stressing against it the values associated with the organic (and feudally organised) rural community. The difference between the ideologies of Richardson and Fielding comes out most starkly in their treatment of sex; whereas Fielding's hero, Tom Jones, is portrayed as 'healthily' promiscuous (in the image of the young aristocratic male of the time) – though not insensitive to the appeal of romantic love – Richardson's concept of sex is based on the Puritan ideal of 'delicacy' which advocated chastity before and fidelity within marriage. The historian Christopher Hill has correlated this in turn with the conditions of the original small capitalist family business in which the wife was treated as a valued helpmate and partner to the man. (See *Clarissa Harlowe and Her Times* in J. Carroll (ed.) *Richardson: Twentieth Century Views*, Prentice Hall 1969 pp. 115–118).

Much of the theme of *Tom Jones* turns on aristocratic notions involving 'birth' and 'honour', which reflect Fielding's conservative belief in the need for stratification in society: 'Men are superior to each other . . . by title, by birth, by rank in profession and by age.' Given this, it is hard to see Fielding as an exponent of a new bourgeois art form. What we can say is that he succumbed enough to the prevailing literary climate to exploit the new genre to express values diametrically opposed to those of writers like Richardson with whom it was becoming associated – two of his works are direct parodies of Richardson and by implication attacks on Richardson's values. Watt points out that Fielding made a strong effort to create a 'respectable' ancestry for the novel by relating it to the classical precedent of the 'epic'; would he have felt the need to adopt the form of fiction at all if it had not been used so successfully in the service of the middle-class ideology he despised?

Readers

The third aspect of the debate on 'the rise of the novel' concerns the nature of the original readers. Since readers leave no fingerprints indicating class or other characteristics on what they read we are even more dependent on conjecture here. Watt's argument, supported by Mark Shinagel (in *Daniel Defoe and Middle Class Gentility*, Harvard University Press 1968), is that even in the eighteenth century the book-buying public were still a tiny minority, to be numbered only in tens of thousands: the biggest market was not for 'imaginative' literature but for political and religious books and pamphlets. However, this public probably expanded during the century. It is estimated that the number of new books published showed a fourfold increase between 1666 and 1802. (*The Rise of the Novel*, p. 40) The expansion was restricted by a number of factors: the cost of books was high in relation to current incomes – *Robinson Crusoe* which was later to become a 'cottage classic' originally sold for five shillings (25p) at a time when the average income for a skilled working man would not have exceeded £1 a week; literacy was limited – arising from poverty and lack of educational provision; and there were restrictions on two crucial physical requirements for reading – light and privacy. On the other hand the growth of a new intermediate class of tradesmen, shopkeepers, richer farmers and clerks provided a new group of potential readers, with enough disposable income to spend on books. The invention and development of circulating libraries (described in more detail in the next chapter but dating from at least 1720) reduced the cost of reading to that of a borrowing fee and at least one important category of new readers – women – may have come about because of the increasing leisure time which they acquired as certain traditional domestic activities such as weaving and spinning came to be transferred outside the home.

The resulting increased appetite for reading matter was partially satisfied by the new literary form of fiction, which in turn may have been encouraged by the decline of the system under which authors had been subsidised by powerful aristocratic patrons or by political factions. The end of patronage led to the rise of the 'bookseller' (closer to today's concept of the 'publisher') who had to be attuned to public taste in his role as middleman between author and readership. This probably assisted the shift towards fiction from the traditional genre of poetry favoured by the aristocracy. As Shinagel says:

> Previously, an author had sought to flatter a wealthy or powerful patron which meant he wrote for a cultivated taste common only to a small coterie of aristocrats and wits. Now, the situation was significantly reversed. The public rather than the patron determined the kind of literature it wanted . . . . If the aristocracy and refined readers favoured poetry and classical models, the unsophisticated middle-class readers were naturally inclined towards prose and unadorned prose at that. If the heroic couplet was the vogue around 1700, the novel was to become established as the new vogue by about 1750. (*Defoe and Middle Class Gentility*, p. 117)

In her attack on Watt's theory Diana Spearman emphasises the proportion of this new reading public who would have been at the 'lower' end of the social range and so less inclined to share solid middle-class values. It is true, as both Watt and Shinagel point out, that servants, who often had access to the discarded reading matter of their masters or mistresses, may have formed a significant group of readers. However, this does not imply they were the only readers for these novels or even the majority group, any more than does Defoe's own celebrated comment on his readership: 'Down in the kitchen, honest Dick and Doll/ Are studying Colonel Jack and Flanders Moll.' (Spearman, p. 32) When Spearman quotes a contemporary comment that 'There is not an old woman that can go the price of it but buys *The Life and Adventures of Robinson Crusoe*' (ibid. p. 32) she ignores the fact that the asking price of five shillings must have restricted severely the number of old women who could in fact 'go the price'.

Although the readership for Defoe and his successors may have extended below the class with most investment in the new middle-class ideology the very values presented in the novels suggest an overlap between the concerns of writer and reader that forces us to go back to Craig's formulation about the rise of a class and the rise of a genre. It is now appropriate to see how these values emerge in a specific case.

'Robinson Crusoe'

A novel might fairly be described as presenting middle-class values if the values of its author are middle class and are explicitly presented in the text or if the characters are middle class (or have adopted middle-class values) and are treated in a way that encourages sympathy or admiration. In eighteenth-century England such values imply: firstly, a social outlook or ideology which attaches greater importance to the production of wealth through trade or manufacturing than through the ownership of land; secondly, a concern sometimes amounting to an obsession with the earning, spending and saving of money (and the book-keeping techniques associated with this activity); thirdly, an adherence to Protestant forms of religion which can be traced back to Puritanism and which stress, among other things, the individual's personal responsibility for his own salvation.

R. H. Tawney, whose *Religion and the Rise of Capitalism* (1926) traces the emergence of this socio-economic-religious

complex of characteristics has described its typical representative in these terms:

> the Puritan flings himself into practical activities with the
> daemonic energy of one who, all doubts allayed, is conscious
> that he is a sealed and chosen vessel. Once engaged in affairs,
> he brings to them both the qualities and the limitations of his
> creed, in all their remorseless logic. Called by God to labour
> in his vineyard, he has within himself a principle at once of
> energy and of order, which makes him irresistible both in war
> and in the struggles of commerce. Convinced that character
> is all and circumstances nothing, he sees in the poverty of
> those who fall by the way, not a misfortune to be pitied and
> relieved, but a moral failing to be condemned, and in riches,
> not an object of suspicion – though like other gifts they may
> be abused – but the blessing which rewards the triumph of
> energy and will. Tempered by self-examination, self-discipline,
> self-control, he is the practical ascetic, whose victories are
> won not in the cloister, but on the battlefield, in the counting-
> house, and in the market. (Penguin edn., 1964, p. 229)

Any reader of *Robinson Crusoe* will perceive resemblances between
what Tawney here describes as the Puritan 'temper' – whose
social 'home' came to be in the middle and commercial or manufacturing classes – and certain themes in Defoe's novel which
can be detailed here, leaving aside for the moment the question of
whether they are presented consistently and without ambiguity.

At the beginning of the novel Crusoe describes himself explicitly as belonging to 'the middle station' of life. (It is worth remem-
bering that although Watt and others freely use the term 'middle
classes' Defoe's own contemporaries preferred – as Spearman
rightly points out – phrases such as 'middle station', 'middle
orders' or 'middle ranks'.) Crusoe's father had accumulated for
himself 'a good estate' through trade and he warns young
Robinson against going to sea, which he regards as fit only for
those who are desperately seeking fortune or have enough money
to risk in ambitious enterprises. In contrast Robinson's position
was favourable enough not to squander:

> mine was the middle state, or what might be called the upper

station of low life which he had found by long experience was the best state in the world, the most suited to human happiness, not exposed to the miseries and hardships, the labour and sufferings of the mechanic part of mankind and not embarrassed with the pride, luxury, ambition and envy of the upper part of mankind. He told me I might judge of the happiness of this state by this one thing viz. that this was the state of life which all other people envied; that kings have frequently lamented the miserable consequences of being born to great things, and wished they had been placed in the middle of the two extremes, between the mean and the great. (Penguin edn, p. 28)

Although the term 'middle class' did not come into use until the nineteenth century this account of society, with its three distinct strata, suggests there was more consciousness of their social position among the 'middle orders' than Spearman is prepared to give credit for. Her argument is that in eighteenth-century England 'no-one thought it was either necessary or particularly virtuous for a man to remain in the station in which he was born'. (*Novel and Society*, p. 37) However, the advice of Crusoe senior with its emphasis on 'our' class is based on precisely the idea that it is unnatural for Robinson to seek his fortune at sea and so miss the benefits, and perhaps also the responsibilities, of the middle station.

When he does launch himself into a career of adventure Crusoe's attitudes and behaviour strikingly parallel those of Tawney's Puritan 'man of action'. What most impresses us and encourages our involvement in the action of the novel is the sheer energy and commitment of Crusoe in transforming a dangerous wilderness into a functioning habitat. This physical resourcefulness (and the mental resilience that accompanies it) recurs in the heroes of nineteenth-century imitations such as *The Swiss Family Robinson* and *Coral Island* and contrasts revealingly with twentieth-century versions of the 'castaway' story such as Golding's *Lord of the Flies* where the psychological pressures on the individuals involved come to the fore. By comparison with our modern pessimistic myth-making *Crusoe* is emphatically a 'success story' in which the hero overcomes the challenge of the natural environment and of inferior species, unhampered by more than transient evidence of mental stress.

The quest for material success to which the Puritan or Non-conformist businessman applied his energy and resourcefulness could, however, entail a neglect or a devaluation of human relationships. Tawney shows that the characteristics of the Puritan religion could be adapted readily to the pursuit of wealth through trade and industry: 'By a kind of happy, pre-established harmony, such as a later age discovered between the needs of society and the self-interest of the individual, success in business is in itself almost a sign of spiritual grace, for it is a proof that a man has laboured faithfully in his vocation.' (Tawney, p. 244) The so-called Protestant Ethic demanded a commitment to work which paralleled the Puritan commitment to God's service; the same ascetic 'temper' that forced the individual to ignore even family ties in his religious calling ('It is an irrational act, and therefore not fit for a rational creature, to love any one farther than reason will allow us . . . . It very often taketh up men's minds so as to hinder their love to God' as one of Tawney's seventeenth-century sources put it) could be applied to and even justified in the everyday practice of trade and money-making. There are many examples in *Crusoe* of what Tawney calls 'the shrewd, calculating commercialism which tries all human relations by pecuniary standards' (p. 247) but three stand out: Crusoe's initial decision to cut himself off from home and caring family in the pursuit of wealth; his treatment of the Moorish boy Xury who befriends and helps him but whom he then sells into slavery; and the superficial account he gives of his marriage, made 'not either to my dis-advantage or dissatisfaction'. As Watt remarks, neither sexual relationships nor the enforced deprivation of them play much part in the narrative.

At first sight it would seem that Crusoe's situation of isolation makes it difficult for Defoe to show the operation of the mercan-tile outlook which Watt labels 'economic individualism'. The lack of other human beings on the island prevents any develop-ment of the 'division of labour' necessary in an advanced economy; there is no opportunity for trade or exchange and our involvement in the novel seems to depend on our identifying with Crusoe as he struggles to acquire primitive and pre-capitalist skills, such as agriculture. On the other hand it might be argued that the novel gains a dimension of irony from the way in which Crusoe's mental 'set' persists in such unpromising circumstances. In contrast to Golding's castaway schoolboys a psychology derived from a particular social context does not break down in alien surroundings. Hence Defoe treats us to the delicious paradox in Crusoe's attitude to the money he finds in the wrecked ship:

> I smiled to myself at the sight of this money. 'O drug!' said I aloud, 'what art thou good for? Thou art not worth to me, no, not the taking off of the ground; one of those knives is worth all this heap; I have no manner of use for thee; e'en remain where thou art and go to the bottom as a creature whose life is not worth saving.' However upon second thoughts I took it away. (p. 75)

There is some dispute about the extent to which the original punctuation of this passage increased the ironic effect but it surely acquires sufficient impact from the words 'second thoughts' which point to the kind of mental stock-taking which features frequently in the novel, and which is related to the 'book-keeping' mentality which the sociologist Max Weber associated with the 'Protestant Ethic'. The deliberate balancing of Debit and Credit is most explicit in the passage where Crusoe sums up his situation on the island under the headings 'Good' and 'Evil' in a tabular form reminiscent of a ledger. There are other occasions, however, in which an account is 'rendered' – for example the outcome of the battle against the cannibals is somewhat cold-bloodedly given in this form ('3 killed at our first shot from the tree/2 killed at the next shot' etc.).

The habit of reflection and systematic self-examination links this 'book-keeping' mentality with the religious demands of Puritanism. Although a frantic industriousness marked the Puritan's daily existence it had to be tempered by 'self-examination', as Tawney suggests. One vehicle for this was the 'journal', another kind of 'account-book', which was used to record not only worldly events but also the triumphs and defeats of spirituality. The narrative of *Robinson Crusoe* incorporates such a 'Journal' but in one sense the whole novel forms a kind of 'confessional autobiography' (to use Watt's term), based on the autobiographical memoirs which were characteristic of the introspective tendencies of Puritanism.

Other ways in which Crusoe's behaviour reflects Puritan orthodoxy include his habit of referring to the Bible for guidance in times of crisis (the Puritans stressed the significance of Bible reading for the individual who was expected to seek the Word of God directly without the intervention of a priest) and his search for religious meaning in commonplace events. The sense of God as Divine Providence is very powerful in the novel not only in the interchangeable use of the terms but also in such passages as this:

> Another reflection was of great use to me, and doubtless would be so to anyone that should fall into such distress as mine was; and this was to compare my present condition with what I at first expected it should be; nay with what it certainly would have been, if the good providence of God had not wonderfully ordered the ship to be cast up nearer to the shore, where I not only could come at her but could bring what I got out of her to the shore for my relief and comfort; without which, I had wanted for tools to work, weapons for defence, or gunpowder and shot for getting my food. (p. 141)

One final aspect of the Puritan version of Christianity which Crusoe obviously adheres to is the idea of the Christian as 'steward' of the material resources of the world on God's behalf and accountable for the use and expansion of those resources through work. Crusoe's commitment to unremitting labour reflects the way in which the virtue of industriousness and even material accumulation became progressively incorporated into the ideals of Puritans and Dissenters.

Some critics have made the point that there are inconsistencies and paradoxes in Defoe's presentation of the middle-class Puritan complex of values through the story of Crusoe. It has already been mentioned that the hero's solitude on the island excludes any possibility of the trade on which the mercantile life-style was based. There are also ways in which the novel fails to support conventional Dissenting morality: for example Crusoe's disobedience to his father's instructions brings not punishment and retribution (although he sometimes sees his situation in this light) but eventually profit and success. Another odd aspect of the novel is Crusoe's tolerance towards Catholicism in the shape of the Spaniards.

However, even these criticisms do not necessarily undermine the thesis that there exists a coherent set of beliefs in the novel, with which the reader is expected to sympathise and which can be associated with a definite social group to which Defoe himself belonged. One rejoinder arises from Lukács' distinction between the 'typical' and the 'average'; a totally consistent Puritan hero would have been a stereotype without interest. It is also possible to attribute inconsistencies in *Crusoe* to the emerging conflict within middle-class ideology between economic and spiritual values which eventually resulted in the triumph of the former at the expense of the latter. Watt even claims that this process ('secularisation') was a crucial factor not only in *Crusoe* but in the development of fiction in general, which it allowed to break free from the mould of religious parable or allegory in which such works as *Pilgrim's Progress* had remained stuck. (See *The Rise of the Novel* pp. 92–95)

A Long Note on Richardson

Defoe's status in the history of the novel has not gone unchallenged. In the nineteenth century Leslie Stephen classified him as a mere reporter or journalist and wrote that 'the merit of Defoe's narratives bears a direct proportion to the intrinsic merit of a plain statement of facts'. Although this sneer undervalues the strength which early fiction drew from such 'real life' accounts as that of Alexander Selkirk (on whom Crusoe was based) and which distinguished it sharply from such forerunners as the 'romance' it is certainly true that *Crusoe* does not conform closely to what we would expect of a novel today: the structure is crude, the main character lacks psychological depth and there is little in the way of interaction between other characters, who scarcely exist apart from the castaway himself.

In order to test with more typical material the 'rise of the novel' theory we might do better to turn to Samuel Richardson. Unfortunately anyone who does not have several weeks of study time available is unlikely to do full justice to Richardson;

Pamela runs to two volumes in the Everyman edition, while *Clarissa* totals over two thousand pages (it was originally published in seven volumes) making it probably the longest novel in the language. The minuteness of observation which Watt regards as a hallmark of the new genre results in such a distended narrative that it is surprising that prospective novelists were not discouraged altogether if they took Richardson as a model. (The habit of the booksellers in paying novelists to some extent by quantity of words may have been an incentive, however.) This final section therefore refers to Richardson's novels in a highly condensed form, attempting to relate them to the debate over middle-class values and origins. An additional reason for discussing them, even superficially, is that they raise two other issues of interest to the socio-cultural approach: the role of women in the development of the novel and the significance of the epistolary form and its relationship to that role.

We have seen that Richardson can be described as unequivocally middle class in income, social position and outlook. It should be easy therefore, if we believe that there is a relationship between text and social framework, to demonstrate that his novels express a sympathy for this class position. Both *Pamela* and *Clarissa* are accounts of seductions, though with differing results. In both cases the seductions are perpetrated by aristocrats on women who are not aristocratic in their origins. This is obvious in the case of Pamela, a servant girl who successfully resists the advances of Mr B, her 'gentlemanly' employer, until she is in a position to secure her social advancement by formally marrying him. In some ways Pamela's psychology resembles the mercenary tough-minded outlook of Defoe's heroes from the commercial classes. As readers, it is not always easy for us to be certain of whether we are to see her as a threatened maiden or as a determined schemer and this ambiguity operates at the level both of male-female relationships and of class. Eagleton points out the paradox created for such women in a male-dominated society: 'The contradiction of patriarchy is that Pamela is forced to treat herself as a sexual object in order to avoid becoming one for others'. His analysis shows how her behaviour results from Richardson's determination to make her also representative of social mobility:

Pamela is both realist character and bearer of Richardson's ideological project of integration with the gentry; so it is not her fault so to speak, if she is sometimes forced by those textual exigencies to act suspiciously. If she faints or fails to escape at convenient moments, it is because she is, as Mr B himself heavily hints, part of a comic romance, whose social logic must not be imperilled by her complete plausibility. Pamela's 'guilt' is that she is no free agent but the function of an historical *plot* which the bourgeoisie have been long hatching. (*The Rape of Clarissa*, p. 35)

Clarissa Harlowe on the other hand comes from a wealthy family but it is one that Richardson takes pains to establish is not of ancient origin and is both sensitive to and ambitious for its social position. Lovelace, her seducer, says disparagingly: 'For her FAMILY, that was not known to its country [i.e. the immediate neighbourhood] a century ago; and I hate all but her.' (Everyman edn. vol. II, p. 270)

The resistance of the Harlowe family to Lovelace as a suitor, which leads to him becoming a seducer, originates with Clarissa's brother James, who looks unfavourably on such a marriage because it would block his plans to expand his estates by incorporating property which Clarissa is due to inherit; the expansion would secure James a place in the peerage and so promote the nouveau-riche Harlowes ('sprung up from a dunghill' in Lovelace's terse description) to the level of the older landed gentry. Eagleton claims that in terms of historical development this apparent 'clash of interests' between older aristocracy and newly rich is an illusory one; the destiny of the two social groups was eventually to lie not in conflict but alliance. The novel in fact dramatises a significant moment in *ideological* change:

Lovelace is a reactionary throwback, an old-style libertine or Restoration relic who resists a proper 'embourgeoisement'; the future of the English aristocracy lies not with him but with the impeccably middle-class Sir Charles Grandison. The death of Clarissa is the mechanism of his downfall, and in that sense the triumph of bourgeois patriarchy. Yet the death, as we have seen, is a two-edged sword: it cannot cut

down Lovelace without mutilating the Harlowes too. No
Harlowe-like critique of Lovelace is fully possible, for it was
they who forced their daughter into his arms in the first
place. It is for this reason, not on account of an undue
specialisation of class crisis to virginity, that the novel has
finally nowhere to turn but to Clarissa herself. Her dying
encompasses both aristocracy and bourgeoisie, revealing
their true unity of interest. Lovelace . . . represents a cynical
Hobbesian deflation of middle-class sentimental hypocrisy;
but having used him to discredit that ideology, the novel will
then use Clarissa in turn to discredit him. (p. 89)

On this reading Clarissa's resistance and death are against the
grain historically; her deathbed forgiveness of Lovelace 'reflects
something of the bourgeoisie's impulse to make peace with the
traditional ruling class' but also 'frustrates it, since, given her
death, no actual alliance will ensue' (ibid., p. 90).

Clarissa's heroic (and fatal) defence of her virginity in this
novel has been exposed as paradoxical by Eagleton and others.
The *value* of chastity – which became an increasing preoccupation in fiction after Richardson – could be expressed in crude
financial terms as is almost explicit in the deliberations of the
Harlowe family. Chastity was a crucial element in the growing
concern with the legal dimensions of marriage, particularly the
'marriage settlement' by which an ambitious family could
improve its social position through their daughter's choice of
husband – but only if her virginity was assured. In an essay on
the social context of *Clarissa* the historian Christopher Hill
suggests that by the early eighteenth century marriage was
increasingly becoming an instrument in the expansion of
material wealth, in combination with a series of legal constraints
which ensured the succession of the property through future
generations:

the father became in effect life tenant of the estate. The eldest
son came to occupy a unique position of authority; and the
estate, the family property, acquired greater importance
than the individual owner.
   The new legal devices themselves sprang from 'profound
changes . . . in the attitude to the family and the land.' These

changes were related to the necessity of adapting landowner-
ship to a society in which standards of expenditure were
increasingly set by those whose wealth derived from sources
other than land and in which taxation fell heavily on landowners . . . . They were the consequence of the political
compromises of 1660 and 1688, by which the landed class
had been left in possession of its property but deprived of
power to check the development of capitalism. ('Clarissa
Harlowe and her Times', p. 102)

In *Clarissa* the institution of marriage therefore forms the
battlefield for a clash of class-related 'codes' – the cynical and
dissolute but socially self-confident aristocratic code represented
by Lovelace and that of the ambitious, money-minded Harlowes.
Clarissa, the tragic victim of the clash, understands this well
when she asks in relation to her seducer: 'whether the value
some of my friends put upon the riches they possess (throwing
perhaps contempt on upon every other advantage and even
discrediting *their own* pretensions to family, in order to depreciate
his) might not provoke him to like contempts' (Everyman edn,
vol. I, p. 403).

Space is too short to examine fully Hill's further suggestion
that *Clarissa*, regarded as an attack on the implications of the
'property marriage', is also an expression of the original Puritan
ideal, which had held marriage to be based on mutual affection.
The heroine's, and therefore Richardson's, clinging to an inner
purity despite the pressures of the market morality of the
property marriage system (and despite Lovelace's eventual
'success' in physically raping her) illuminates contradictions
within the middle-class value system which spring from the
conflict between its 'mercantile' and its Puritan origins.
'Clarissa's standards, high Puritan standards, were not of this
world; they could only be realised in the after-life. They are a
criticism of this world's standards.' (Hill, p. 117) Eagleton's
reading also, which is highly sympathetic to Clarissa, is forced
to admit to a contradiction between the alleged ideology of the
middle-class Richardson and his literary production: 'It is not
only that Clarissa exposes a rift between bourgeois pieties and
practice; it is also that those pieties themselves, once submitted
to the pressures of fictional form, begin to crack open.' (*The*

Rape of Clarissa, p. 77) Here we see Eagleton applying his idea
that the act of literary production *exposes* ideology while Hill on
the other hand is forced to resort to the concept of an unprovable
split between Richardson's conscious and unconscious intention:

> His *conscious* desire in writing the novel was to assert the
> bourgeois and Puritan conception of marriage against the
> feudal-cavalier standards of Lovelace and the Harlowe
> emphasis on concentration of property. But the contradictions
> of subordination in equality which were inherent in the
> Puritan view of women were too strong for him. (Hill, p. 119)

However the socio-cultural critic attempts to explain it he must
admit that *Clarissa* and *Pamela* illustrate the naïvety of a
straightforward reflectionist theory of society and fiction more
strikingly than *Crusoe* does.

While the heroines of *Pamela* and *Clarissa* are undeniably
caught up in the advance of a middle-class value system
(whatever its contradictions) in the teeth of aristocratic resistance
they also represent a tendency for the novel to appeal to the
concerns of women readers. (Richardson eventually became
the focus of an admiring circle of women as the result of his
literary conquests.) This appeal may have been reinforced by
Richardson's practice of casting the whole narrative in the form
of a series of letters which express the private thoughts and
emotions of his characters.

The fact that at the age of 51, with no previous literary work
to his credit, Richardson was encouraged to write *Pamela* on
the basis of a series of 'model letters' suggests an existing
market for this so-called 'epistolary' format. Collections of
letters which were transparently or covertly fictitious had been
published since the early seventeenth century and between one
and two hundred of these collections date from the early part of
Richardson's own century. Ruth Perry in *Women, Letters and
the Novel* (1980) has speculated that the adoption of this format
for the early novel can be related to the role of women in the
development of fiction. Whereas female poets and dramatists
were exceptional, fiction writing seemed to attract women from
the beginning. Perry cites a list of 72 examples of fiction
produced before Richardson, out of which 54 are by women.

Readership was similarly 'skewed'; in a list of subscribers to an early epistolary novel 123 out of 309 names belong to women – admittedly not a majority but probably far different from the proportions for the 'high-status' genre of poetry. There are many contemporary allusions also to the popularity of novel-reading among women.

The appeal of the new genre to women can be related to the social upheavals already described. For women in general the eighteenth century was a period of increasing economic dependence on their husbands as they were progressively excluded from various traditional occupations. (The development of the word 'spinster' from denoting a particular trade to the – now slightly derogatory – sense of an 'unmarried woman' illustrates this.) Economic specialisation increasingly removed from the home or transferred to servants many activities which had been the province of married women and their unmarried daughters. The newly expanded middle class was significantly one in which women were spared both the need for incessant labour and the time-consuming rituals of aristocratic rank. Perry quotes a historian who comments:

> For many women marriage became the sole preoccupation, and the preparation was rather in the direction of accomplishments which would please a man than those which were really helpful to both . . . . The education which girls received suffered in consequence. Deportment – the proper carriage of the body . . . dancing and music became all-important . . . housework in too many cases became something beneath them; while, as vigorous sports were something in which no lady shared, their health deteriorated and fainting fits became somewhat common. (*Women, Letters and the Novel*, p. 38)

In this context it is not surprising that fiction was seized on as a way of filling leisure time. The function of the novel as a distraction is clear in Lady Montagu Worsley's comment on what she herself chose to read: 'I doubt not that at least the greater part of these are trash, lumber, etc. However they will serve to pass away the idle time.' (*The Rise of the Novel*, p. 48) Not only did many 'idle' women read novels but a few attempted to write them. Perry claims the 'epistolary' format made it easier for women to do this since it provided a 'bridge' between 'real-life' letters and the previously uncharted (for women) waters of literary composition. As a format it demanded a simple, personal style which was within the grasp of women, who mostly lacked a formal classical education and therefore also familiarity with the forms, conventions and problems of the traditional literary genres.

The status of women writers of course remained in question until well into the nineteenth century as is shown by the furtiveness of Jane Austen's composition and the adoption of male pseudonyms by the Brontës and George Eliot. (It was common for publishers to require the signature of the authoress's husband on contracts.) The epistolary format, however, gave women an *entrée* into this male-dominated world and – because it implied a frank and emotionally-charged approach, with the emphasis on sentiment rather than narrative – it appealed to that ideology which enforced idleness was cultivating in the 'ladies of leisure' of the newly affluent classes. Deprived of economic usefulness, they developed an idealisation of the married state, a delight in romantic love and the intrigue which accompanied it and a half-suppressed sexual fantasising which the new genre was able to serve. The upright Colonel Morden in *Clarissa* claimed in relation to women: 'their early learning, which chiefly consisted in inflaming novels and idle and improbable romances, contributed to enervate and weaken their minds'. This popular concept of female susceptibility to fiction which persisted into the nineteenth century and was satirised in the portraits of Catherine Morland and Madame Bovary may have owed its origins to the attractions of the epistolary form:

> The experience of long-distance correspondence made it possible for the reading audience to imagine carrying on an emotional life at some remove or to maintain a one-sided relationship in the imagination rather than to live it out in the social world. This new kind of literature encouraged readers to dream themselves into the lives they found in books, lives of characters for whom reading and writing were their most significant acts. (Perry, *Women, Letters and the Novel*, p. 166)

In Perry's view the nature of the conventional novel heroine also owes much to this format and the lives of those who were attracted to it:

> The epistolary mode also made plausible a new kind of heroine – literate, isolated, unhappy – who symbolised in a purer form the dilemmas of the current culture than the heroes of earlier romances and epics. Such heroines, who poured out their hearts on paper, valued their individual happiness above social approval and assumed that this happiness was not to be found in work or religion but in a perfect sexual union whose institutional form was marriage. These were assumptions which however widely adopted by middle-class English society, belonged particularly to the women of that class, for the economic and social reorganisation which took place in England in the course of the seventeenth century had abridged many of their functions. (ibid., p. 166)

4. Scott and Jane Austen: Varieties of Conservative Ideology

The previous chapter considered how the socio-cultural approach might throw light on the birth of the novel and its relationship to the economy and social structure of the time. This chapter switches the focus to developments in production, distribution and readership of fiction which laid the foundations for the establishment of the novel as the dominant literary genre of the nineteenth century. The concentration is partly on the *literary context* in terms of publishing methods and economics, but also on a specific illustration in the form of Sir Walter Scott's *Waverley*. Scott's outstanding literary success and influence cannot be ignored in terms of the status and development of fiction as a whole. His work reveals the operation of an ideology whose influence survives to some degree today. A second example of the relationship between social class position and fiction can be seen in the novels of Scott's contemporary, Jane Austen, whose work seems so radically different in form and content.

Fiction Becomes a Commercial Product

One of the rare contemporary estimates of the size of the reading public before the nineteenth century was the politician Edmund Burke's guess in 1790 that it numbered about 80,000. (See Altick, *English Common Reader*, p. 49) The remark, which has not been located in Burke's own writings, was attributed to him in a periodical of 1832 and typifies the flimsiness of the evidence available for judging the impact of the new novel genre before 1800; quite apart from whether Burke had any qualifications for making such an estimate it is certain that a great many of those potential readers would have been largely interested in non-fiction. The highest sales for reading matter in the eighteenth century were achieved by religious works and political pamphlets, for example Swift's *Conduct of the Allies* (1711) which sold 11,000 copies and Price's *Observation on the Nature of Civil Liberty* (1776) which sold 60,000 over a period of a few months. Compared with these topical successes the sales of even the more celebrated novels were steady rather than spectacular. (It should be remembered that the total population of the United Kingdom at the time was seven to eight million – of whom the vast majority were illiterate.) Single editions even of Richardson and Fielding rarely exceeded 4,000 copies and in a year might run to four or five editions totalling 9,000 copies. The available contemporary evidence suggests that a first printing of a novel rarely exceeded 500.

In *The English Common Reader* (from which these figures are taken) Richard Altick suggests a clear reason for these small editions: novels were still relatively very expensive, costing (until about 1780) between 2s. (10p) and 3s. (15p) a volume (i.e. for each of the two, three or, in the case of *Clarissa*, seven volumes in which the complete work was published). This was at a time when clerks in a merchant's office earned about £1 a week, shop assistants 4s. (20p) plus board, and craftsmen in London (the highest paid) between 15s. (75p) and £1. Pamphlets at between 6d. and 2s. 6d. (2½p and 12½p) must have seemed to offer a better economic bargain since they could often be over fifty pages long; as Altick points out the 'man in the lower bracket of the white-neckcloth class' who wished to purchase a three-volume novel would have had to sacrifice most of the cost of a new pair of breeches, or a month's supply of tea and sugar. A woman in one of the London trades in the 1770s would have had to spend the equivalent of a week's work.

Nevertheless, as usually happens when there is an evident growing demand, market changes took place which allowed some of the difficulties to be circumvented and the demand to be met – at least partially. Eighteenth-century publishers were apparently content with a policy of small editions of high-priced new books which put them out of reach of anyone below the tradesman level. Three main methods of circumventing this policy were developed of which two were to become almost essential to the publication of fiction in the following century, while the third has remained an important factor in the book trade up to our own day.

Firstly, fiction could be brought to the public more cheaply in *serial* form, either as free-standing instalments or included in an inexpensive periodical. The practice of instalment publishing became a vogue in the mid eighteenth century, for historical works and editions of the Bible, but the idea of 6d. (2½p) or 1s. (5p) instalments was one which nineteenth-century novel publishers were later able to exploit. The history of the publication of fiction in magazines, in the form of serials, is an even longer one, stretching back to the publication of Laurence Sterne's *Sir Launcelot Greaves* in 1760–1.

As with instalment publishing, the circulating library was an eighteenth-century invention that reached its most developed form in the nineteenth century when it became the dominant form of distribution for fiction. The original non-profit-making 'proprietary' libraries had aimed to build up collections of non-fiction for serious readers, based on 'reading clubs'; they charged quite high fees and disdained 'light reading' such as novels. By contrast the commercial circulating libraries began as a sideline offered by retailers such as grocers, tobacconists and haberdashers and regarded the new genre as their staple. In the eighteenth century even the highest annual subscription to such libraries was only a guinea (£1.05) while non-subscribers were allowed to borrow at a flat rate of 1s. (5p) per volume. The popularity of these libraries caused consternation among the literary and social establishment, who were suspicious both of the quality of the works they purveyed and of their success in encouraging the reading habit among the middle classes. Anthony Absolute's comment in Sheridan's *The Rivals* ('Madam, a circulating library in a town is as an evergreen tree of diabolical knowledge! It blossoms through the year! And depend on it . . . they who are so fond of handling the leaves, will long for the fruit at last') bears out in exaggerated form Altick's observation that: 'people who, for social or economic reasons, opposed the expansion of the reading public found it handy to conceal their true purposes by harping on the common reader's notorious preference for the novel.' (*English Common Reader*, p. 65)

A third way of providing for this preference arose when publishers recognised the existence of a readership who were prepared to wait for a reprinted version of a successful work rather than fork out for a first edition. This two-tier system, in which the reprint sold at a lower price, survives in our hardback/ paperback division of today. Up to the end of the eighteenth century cheap reprints had been discouraged by the common law principle that copyright belonged in perpetuity to the original publisher. However in 1775 the *Donaldson v. Beckett* case resulted in a limitation of the copyright period (at first to 28 years), which had become necessary because the law was being constantly infringed by 'pirate' editions. It became common practice for publishers to offer cheap reprints of the classics; Bell's Poetry and Editions of Shakespeare were followed by Cook's sixpenny editions, which included reprints of early novels. (This was the medium in which Hazlitt as a schoolboy read *Tom Jones*.) The readership for these cut-price editions was expanded even further by second-hand sales. A nineteenth-century observer commented: 'You never see on a stall one of Cook's books but it is soiled by honest usage, its odour . . . speaks of the thousand thumbs that have turned over its pages with delight.' (*English Common Reader*, p. 261)

The Scott Phenomenon

Despite these attempts to bring it down, the price of novels remained obstinately high – especially for new works. Ironically, Sir Walter Scott's phenomenal popularity which might have succeeded in turning the novel into a cheap mass medium overnight was instrumental in eventually taking fiction beyond the reach of the individual buyer. *Waverley* (his first novel after his considerable success as a poet) sold 1,000 copies in the first five weeks of publication in 1814 and another 6,000 in the next six months. It established the historical novel as a distinctive genre and encouraged many imitators. However, it must have reached all but the most affluent readers through reprints (such as the 11,000 copies of Scott's *Collected Romances* printed between 1820 and 1829) or through the medium of circulating libraries since it cost 6s. (30p) for each of its three volumes. Its success did not encourage Scott's publishers to reduce their prices to meet an assured market. They set a price of 30s. (£1.50) for the three-volume set of *Ivanhoe* (in 1820 when Scott's market appeal was incontestable) and one-and-a-half guineas (31s. 6d., or £1.57½p) for *Kenilworth* in 1821 – a significant figure since it very quickly became the standard for a three-volume novel and remained so until the 1890s.

The three-volume novel or three-decker which developed into the staple of the Victorian fiction industry will be considered in more detail in the next chapter. It is worth noting at this point that it never became a 'mass-produced' article; Scott's novels were unusual in the large editions they went through. Even taking into account sales to circulating libraries 1,250 copies was a much more representative quantity for new fiction in volume form. Later in the century *Pickwick Papers*, which was first published in monthly instalments, was to sell up to 40,000 copies per instalment; by comparison the outstanding feature of Scott's popularity was not the sheer volume of sales but the way in which it permeated the literary culture of the period, giving a new authority and legitimacy to the previously undervalued genre of the novel. At least some of this was due to publishing and marketing practices associated more readily with the most commercialised forms of fiction up to our own day.

The contemporary impact is typified by a letter written by Maria Edgeworth, the Irish originator of the 'regional' novel which Scott was consciously trying to imitate in his use of Scottish settings. The letter is addressed to 'The Author of *Waverley*' since Scott's responsibility for the first novel in the series was disguised; though it soon became an open secret that *Waverley* was written by the man whose sensational success as a poet had only recently been outshone by Byron. The reference to reading aloud to a family audience suggests one reason for the rapidity with which Scott's reputation spread:

> We have this moment finished *Waverley*. It was read aloud to this large family, and I wish the author could have witnessed the impression it made – the strong hold it seized of the

feelings both of the young and old – the admiration raised by
the beautiful descriptions of nature – by the new and bold
delineations of character – the perfect manner in which every
character is sustained in every change of situation from first
to last, without effort, without the affectation of making the
persons speak in character – the ingenuity with which each
person introduced in the drama is made useful and necessary
to the end – the admirable art with which the story is
constructed and with which the author keeps his own secrets
till the proper moment when they should be revealed, whilst
in the meantime, with the skill of Shakespeare, the mind is
prepared by unseen degrees for all the changes of feeling and
fortune, so that nothing however extraordinary shocks us as
improbable and the interest is kept up to the last moment.
(quoted in *Scott: the Critical Heritage* ed. J. O. Hayden, RKP
1970, p. 75)

The comparison with Shakespeare (and an even more extra-
vagant one with Homer) became commonplace amongst an
increasingly devoted public. Scott could not put a foot wrong –
at least until he forsook the Scottish themes of the earlier
Waverley Novels. The praise was not confined to less sophisticated readers either; he was reviewed with enthusiasm in the
highly-respected and influential *Edinburgh Quarterly* (it was
the first time that this periodical had deigned to notice a mere
novelist) and his contemporary Jane Austen wrote: 'Sir Walter
Scott has no business to write novels, especially good ones. It is
not fair. He has fame and profit enough as a poet and should not
be taking bread out of other people's mouths.' (*Letters* ed. R. W.
Chapman, p. 101)

James Hillhouse, who has charted the course of Scott's
success, finds little contemporary dissent from this view, apart
from Coleridge, Carlyle and the liberal or radical periodicals
which objected to Scott's Tory politics. After Scott's death it
came to be agreed that the non-Scottish novels, such as *Ivanhoe*,
showed a falling-off in quality but the *Waverleys* were enthusiastically praised by Dickens, George Eliot, Thackeray and
Trollope among others. It was not until the 1870s that a critic
first hinted that Scott might survive chiefly as a writer for
juveniles. Despite or perhaps because of this changing image

his novels still sold in huge quantities in cheaper reprinted editions in the 1880s and 1890s.

Obviously the actual themes of the novels had a part to play in raising Scott's reputation so high that Katherine Tillotson specifically refers to the 'legacy of Scott' in her account of the fiction of the 1840s. (*Novels of the 1840s*, Oxford 1961, p. 140) John Henry Raleigh in his article 'What Scott meant to the Victorians' (1963), lists the vital ingredients as: the comparatively realistic descriptions (as opposed to the grotesqueries of the preceding Gothick writers); the extension of the novel genre to the immediate past; the inclusion of characters drawn from the upper and lower as well as the middle classes; and finally the massive apparatus of informative notes and appendices which allowed the novels to function as guidebook and encyclopaedia to a country perhaps still seen as exotic by English readers. Nevertheless other factors can also be identified which relate not so much to the content of Scott's novels as to the way in which they were marketed and received.

The Scott Industry

Scott's orientation towards the reading public is obvious from his own comments and behaviour, beginning with the deliberate mystification over the authorship of *Waverley*, which he lost no opportunity to exploit (on one occasion even managing to review his own work). In his view – as publicly expressed – novels were not to be taken too seriously; although they 'sometimes instruct the youthful mind by strains of generous sentiment and tales of fictitious woe' in many cases they were 'a mere elegance, a luxury contrived for the amusement of the polished life'. This patronising dismissal of the genre – shared by many other commentators of the time – was combined with the modesty of a technician, providing the public with what it wants: 'I care not who knows it. I write for general amusement, and though I will never aim at popularity by what I think unworthy means, I will not, on the other hand, be pertinacious in the defence of my own errors against the voice of the public.' (*Fortunes of Nigel* 1822) In 1819 Scott's sense of what was acceptable for 'general amusement' told him that the Scottish settings which he had milked for five years and which had encouraged many imitators needed to be given a rest. When he turned to the portrayal of English medieval history in *Ivanhoe* it was with the self-consciousness of a businessman investing in a new product: 'Novelty is what this giddy time demands imperiously, and I certainly studied as much as I could to get out of the old beaten track, leaving those who like to keep to the road I have rutted pretty well.' (*Journal* ed. Tait p. 222)

Despite these self-deprecating remarks Scott's 'product' would scarcely have appeared to contemporary readers as a cheap and ephemeral one. There was the high price at which the novels sold and which turned new fiction into a luxury item for nearly a century. There was the status conferred by reviews in the 'heavy' quarterlies which had previously treated poetry and drama as the sole serious literary forms. (Although this may have been undercut by Lockhart's remark in the *Quarterly* that 'novel readers who remain in our time exclusively readers of novels would have been in the immense majority of cases readers of exactly nothing at all had they lived a hundred years ago.') There was the dignity implied by the dense apparatus of footnotes and addenda which helped to stimulate the sale of historical source material after the success of each novel; for example, old Scottish tracts and memoirs after *Waverley*. Finally there was the prestigious Collected Edition of 1829 which made the impact of a modern 'classic': 'bold and titled uniformly, complete with general and individual prefaces, introductions, postscripts, dedications, glossaries, along with historical appendices and notes', an image of cultivated taste and scholarship as well as amusement.[1]

The confidence of the nineteenth century in the *Waverley* novels as a superior and consistent product must have been reinforced by the nature of Scott's themes and content. The supposed indelicacy of Fielding and even Richardson meant that until the mid century Scott was considered the novelist best able to match up to the exacting standards of Victorian morality. He was constantly praised for his wholesomeness which made him suitable for family reading; a history of literature described the novels in 1853 as 'lacking the sentiment which banishes most works of prose fiction from the libraries of the young' while a periodical published in the notoriously straitlaced city of Boston, Massachusetts, called them 'full of instruction and moral uses' and *The North American Review*, which circulated chiefly among Evangelical church members, regarded Scott as acceptable to the 'graver part of the community'. Hillhouse sums up:

> The Waverley novels, if one is to believe these critics, practically by themselves opened pious, middle-class households to the novel. Scott was not only thrilling, he was pure, he was inspiring, he inculcated the noblest ideals and if he did not preach and instruct, he did not at least say any thing subversive of natural or revealed religion. (*The Waverley Novels and their Critics*, University of Minneapolis 1936, p. 90)

One last thread in the Scott phenomenon was provided by the promotional and 'spin-off' activities which preceded, accompanied or followed the publication of the novels. The publication of *Kenilworth* for example was preceded by factual articles on the history and architecture of the Kenilworth Castle in the *Literary Gazette*. This periodical claimed that its reviews of the novels were done from unbound 'sheets', rushed from Edinburgh to London so as to precede publication – and given the routinely idolatrous attitude of the *Gazette* – to stimulate the public to hurry out and borrow or purchase them. Lockhart's biography, published in 1838, stoked up the flames of Scott worship, as did the flow of tourists to the scenes portrayed in the novels. The tide of curiosity and reverence also washed around Abbotsford, the mock-gothic mansion the funding of which was one reason for Scott's prolific output (the other being the collapse of the publishing firm of Constable in which he was a partner and whose debts he felt an obligation to repay). Abbotsford stood in the midst of a recognisable Scott country – no similar shrine had existed for Defoe, Richardson or Fielding – and it was the tangible embodiment of years of literary success which had begun with the publication of *Waverley* in 1814.

Waverley: History and Ideology

It is commonly held that with *Waverley* (subtitled ' 'Tis Sixty Years Since') Scott founded the historical novel. It was to become a prolific genre in its own right in the nineteenth century. Apart from direct imitators such as Harrison Ainsworth, whose novels declined into children's reading even more quickly than Scott's, many serious novelists set at least one novel in the past. It is also possible to argue, however, that Scott's pioneering effort played an important role in the legitimation of the novel. History added weight and dignity to what was previously a rather suspect literary form. In addition for the first time the recall of the past had come to have a far-ranging popular significance.

The case for this has been put by Georg Lukács for whom Scott is, as Balzac was to Engels, a political reactionary whose fiction somehow transcends his class origins. According to Lukács the period of the French Revolution and the rise and fall of Napoleon was the first time in Western Europe in which for the middle and lower classes the past came to be seen as more than a meaningless flow of events. A sense of history as something to be grasped, understood or even cherished was implicit in the idea of 'nationhood' which the Revolution and the political upheavals associated with it had awakened in many parts of Europe.

Paradoxically, Lukács sees Scott's literary strength in the device of the colourless and mediocre heroes who are often regarded as the weak link in the novels. Heroes such as Edward Waverley, Lukács suggests, are presented as passive victims at the mercy of conflicting forces which must be reconciled in the interests of the peaceful development of the British nation-state.

In the novel *Waverley* the opposing forces are those of Jacobitism (Catholic Stuart legitimacy, supported by the feudal clan system) on the one hand, and the modernising, Hanoverian nation-state on the other. Waverley, the central character, acts as the symbol of the resolution of the conflict; he draws back from the romantic feudalism of Fergus McIvor and his sister in favour of the gentlemanly code of Colonel Talbot (representing the modernising influences) but retains his emotional investment in Scotland through his marriage to Rose Bradwardine and his succession to the Bradwardine estate.

This treatment of the hero as a relatively inactive 'centre' round which great historical forces swirl and press allows Scott, according to Lukács, to present his novels as vast canvases on which the 'social-historical' types (dear to this critic's theory) can be portrayed and shown to interact. These 'types' are not the great characters of history, such as Prince Charles Edward of *Waverley*, but ordinary men and women; through an account of their behaviour Scott is able to show the human greatness which is liberated by some all-embracing national disturbance – such as the rebellion of 1745. Lukács' view of Scott has therefore been called a 'dualist' one; he sees Scott's class loyalties leading him to approve of the outcome of past historical conflict but also to count the cost in human terms of the transition to 'modern' society, illustrated most notably in the offer of the Highlander Evan Dhu in *Waverley* to sacrifice himself on behalf of his chief, Fergus McIvor. In examining this destructive as well as creative historical process, Scott evokes our sympathy, against the grain of his own conservative political leanings, for 'serfs and free peasants, the fortunes of society's outlaws, the smugglers, robbers, professional soldiers, deserters and so on'. Lukács sums up:

> Scott sees and portrays the complex and intricate path which led to England's [sic] national greatness and to the formation of the national character. As a sober, conservative petty aristocrat he naturally affirms the result and the necessity of this result is the ground on which he stands. But Scott's artistic world-view by no means stops here. Scott sees the endless field of ruin, wrecked existences, wrecked or wasted heroic, human endeavour, broken social formations etc., which were the necessary precondition of the end-result.
> (*The Historical Novel*, p. 58)

This passage – sensitive to the effect of the novels in some respects – also reveals some of the woolliness underlying Lukács' interpretation of Scott's world-view. Lukács ignores the national distinctiveness of the various parts of the United Kingdom: Scott's main concern was not *England's* national greatness, unless 'England' and 'Britain' are already assumed to be synonymous. Neither was Scott by birth a 'petty aristocrat' since his father's, and his own, occupation of Writer to the Signet (a kind of lawyer) put him firmly among the professional classes by origin – whatever pretensions might later have been encouraged by the conferment of the baronetcy and the purchase of Abbotsford. Nevertheless Lukács' reading does open the way for a socio-cultural interpretation of Scott in terms of the formation of the modern British nation-state.

The incorporation and subordination of Scotland and 'Scottishness' into the United Kingdom proceeded rapidly after the defeat of the Jacobites in 1745. It was symbolised in 1822 by an event which Scott himself stage-managed: on a visit to Edinburgh in 1822, immediately after his coronation, the new King George IV ostentatiously wore the Highland tartan which had been banned to the Highlanders themselves for a generation after 1745. The event was a promotion of the superficial symbolism of 'Scottishness' in the wake of the suppression of that very Highland culture to which it rightly belonged. Cleansed of their political and cultural associations with Jacobite resistance, the tartans, Highland clan-names and weaponry could be used to provide a bogus legitimation for a Scotland which was – both Lowland and Highland – submerged into the United Kingdom.

Scott's participation in this process, to which his novels directly contributed since the industrial expansion of the town of Stirling was partly based on the production of tartans, encouraged by the success of the *Waverleys*, explains an ambiguity often noticed in his fiction; a nostalgia for the Highland culture of the past (although he himself was not a Highlander) is combined with an enthusiasm for the new Britain in which the middle and professional classes were to figure more strongly. This conflict of pressures is symbolised in the career of Edward Waverley itself; Scott's subtle and artistic handling of it made this first of his novels an ideal vehicle for legitimating in ideological terms the post-1745 settlement in the eyes of his chiefly English and Lowland Scots readership.

Although Waverley's English origin allows him to function in the novel as a 'historical tourist' who observes and is impressed by the social and cultural peculiarities of the Highlands he is not an ordinary representative of the English ruling caste. His childhood has been influenced from one direction by the affection of Sir Everard, his uncle and guardian, whose commitment to the cause of Stuart legitimacy excludes him from public life, and from the other by his estranged father, Richard, whose career has taken the opposite turn: his involvement in Parliament on behalf of the Hanoverian successors to the Stuarts has supplanted all family ties – except in the matter of his son's material advancement. When Edward Waverley is secured a military commission at his father's instigation this seems to seal his commitment to the post-Stuart regime. However, the young man's childhood upbringing and reading has instilled in him a Romanticism, parallel to Scott's own immersion in old Scottish ballads and legends:

> From such legends our hero would steal away to indulge the fancies they excited. In the corner of the large and sombre library, with no other light than was afforded by the decaying brands on its ponderous and ample hearth, he would exercise for hours that internal sorcery, by which past or imaginary events are presented in action, as it were, to the eye of the muser. (Penguin edn, p. 53)

Scott's emphasis on Waverley's romantic and self-indulgent reading has led many critics to interpret the novel as a novel of 'education' or 'growing up', in which Waverley is initially bewitched by the glamorous aspects of Jacobitism, but learns to settle in the end for the 'unheroic' virtues (as Donald Davie puts it). An important scene in this reading is the one in which Flora McIvor, the sister of the Gaelic chieftain Fergus, makes her first appearance, in a setting worthy of the 'internal sorcery' of the previous passage:

> Here, like one of these lovely forms which decorate the landscape of Poussin, Waverley found Flora gazing at the waterfall. Two paces further back stood Cathleen, holding a small Scottish harp, the use of which had been taught to Flora by Rory Dall, one of the last harpers of the Western Highlands. The sun, now stooping in the West, gave a rich and varied tinge to all the objects which surrounded Waverley and seemed to add more than human brilliancy to the full expressive darkness of Flora's eye. (p. 176)

In the introductory chapter of the novel Scott had specifically warned his public against expecting *Waverley* to conform to the features of the 'Sentimental Tale', one of which was the 'heroine with a profusion of auburn hair and a harp'. The appearance of just such a derided figure highlights the fact that it is an *appearance* – not so much to the reader, but to Waverley's youthful and impressionable mind. It soon emerges in fact that both Flora and her brother, who have lived in France and added a cosmopolitan sophistication to their Gaelic authenticity, are in the business of manipulating the naïve Waverley by aesthetic as well as emotional means into support for the powerful but ultimately (in Scott's presentation) hollow and corrupted myth of Jacobitism. The contemporary reader (and the modern one) who was aware of the historical outcome of 1745 and the illusory and forlorn nature of the Jacobite cause has licence from this point on to read the novel as a study of the balance in Waverley's mind between 'sound and unsound judgement'. The very choice of name for the hero supports the idea of a movement between two attracting influences.

Critics who hold this view of the novel have pointed out that Scott deliberately introduces characters and factors which complicate Waverley's growing awareness of where his true allegiances lie. There are the differing inflections of Jacobitism represented by Fergus and his subordinate Evan Maccombich Dhu: in one case a political position, in the other a blind fierce feudal loyalty. There is the element of violence on both sides: Callum Beg against the Cameronian fanatic Gilfillan. Above all Scott introduces the Baron Bradwardine and his daughter Rose – Jacobites but not Highlanders – as representatives of the way in which the past can survive innocuously into the present. According to this reading Waverley undergoes a real maturation towards the position which Scott himself, despite his romantic affection for the Jacobites, saw as necessary and realistic: support for a government of law and order, protecting property and the domestic security of the upper and middle classes.

Waverley's growing disillusionment with Jacobitism is presented in a number of crucial scenes. After his capture of Colonel Talbot he finds himself warming to the superior behaviour and humanity of his enemy. When Waverley himself shows humanity by rescuing a dying man, the action of kindness appals the Highlanders and exposes their brutal fatalism: 'it will be a thousand men's fate before night' (p. 329). Equally indicative of the distance between Waverley's cultural values and their own is the way in which they immediately withdraw criticism when they discover that the rescued soldier is the son of a tenant of the Englishman's uncle: 'as apprehending that the sufferer was one of his *following*, they unanimously allowed that Waverley's conduct was that of a kind and considerate chieftain, who merited the attachment of his people.' (p. 329) Finally the reader, though not at first Waverley himself, is let into the secret of 'Bonnie Prince Charlie's' cynicism about his followers, 'adroitly using the few words of Gaelic he possessed and affecting a great desire to learn it more thoroughly', but using French to convey to his companion his weariness with his chosen role: 'que mon métier de prince errant est ennuyant, parfois. Mais, courage! c'est le grand jeu, après tout' (p. 403).

Given Scott's own conservative view that the troubles of the past have resulted in a satisfactory present, there is no other logical outcome for the novel but that Waverley should surrender his attachment to the doomed Jacobite cause after the retreat from England. In order that the switch of loyalty should not appear too cynical Scott removes his hero from the sequence of historical events at this point. Moreover as the influence of Fergus and Flora wanes, Scott deftly reintroduces Rose Bradwardine and reveals that she has secretly been his helper during the period of his imprisonment. The stage is then set for the final episodes of reconciliation in which Colonel Talbot generously repays Waverley's kindness by reinstating the Baron Bradwardine and facilitating a match between Waverley and Rose. The title of the last chapter, 'Dolce Domum', sums up the role for which Waverley is now securely headed – the domestic security of a conventional and law-abiding English gentleman – which was foreshadowed by Flora McIvor's sardonic prediction: 'I will tell you where he will be at home, my dear, and in his place – in the quiet circle of domestic happiness, lettered indolence and elegant enjoyments, of Waverley-Honour' (p. 370).

Nevertheless certain strains and contradictions arise from the way in which Scott diverts the course of the novel into a story of personal development. It is difficult for the reader to avoid a comparison between Waverley's ability to turn himself into a passive observer of the events after Culloden and the plight of the rebels who are unable to escape retribution so easily. In particular, the most striking impression of the last chapters is Evan Dhu's behaviour at the trial in Carlisle. The ferocious feudal loyalty with which the clansman offers to stand in for his condemned chief, although anachronistic, works against any dismissal of Jacobitism as mere self-indulgent romanticism.

Moreover this heroism is not the whole story as any acquaintance with the events following Culloden (such as are described in the book of that name by John Prebble) will show.

One 'significant absence' in the novel is the final battle of Culloden itself and another is the series of brutal reprisals and persecutions that followed the defeat of the Highlanders and underlay the incorporation of their feudal society into the same social and political system as the rest of the United Kingdom. Elaine Jordan has pointed out that when Fergus McIvor 'forbids' Waverley to see his public execution, this also allows Scott to spare the reader the details of the ghastly process of hanging, drawing and quartering which was prescribed for 'traitors' – and which is as Fergus wryly points out one of the 'benefits' which the superior English have bestowed on the Scots.[2] In the same way the wholesale retribution and eviction associated with the arrival of the victorious English army is condensed into the 'figure of old Baron Bradwardine stuck in a hole to be rescued by Waverley' a pathetic figure, indeed, but scarcely a representative one when set against the barbaric historical behaviour of the Duke of Cumberland, the English commander ('Laws? I'll make a brigade give the laws!') (*Culloden*, Penguin edn, p. 155)

In the light of the account of atrocities which John Prebble gives in *Culloden* the conciliatory conduct of Colonel Talbot (one of Cumberland's leading officers) also appears implausible or at the least unrepresentative. We understand therefore Scott's anxiety to move away from the broad historical canvas as the Jacobite fortunes recede – with the somewhat insincere words: 'It is not our purpose to intrude on the province of history' – and to restrict the later chapters of his story to the psychological development of Waverley. In the interests of an ideology which stresses the 'progress' made by Scotland since 1745, Scott has to

screen off from the reader the cruelties documented in the condemned Highlands which had continued, in the form of the
'Clearances', up to his own day.

Scott, who was deeply influenced by the vigorous Lowland
Scots culture centred on Edinburgh in the late eighteenth century
(the culture of Adam Smith and David Hume), probably supported the ideas of those Scottish historians who saw history as a
progressive development from primitive culture to the present.[3]
He writes in the Postscript to *Waverley*: 'like those who drift down
the stream of a deep and smooth river, we are not aware of the
progress we have made, until we fix our eye on the now distant
point from which we have been drifted.' (p. 492) In *Waverley*, and
other Scott novels, the Scotland of the early nineteenth century,
benefiting from the 'gradual influx of wealth and extension of
commerce' is allowed the luxury of looking back to a period
romanticised by the glow of a 'lingering though hopeless attachment to the house of Stuart'. The past was seen as in some ways
admirable – for the simple heroism of the clansmen and the
antiquity of their culture – but regretfully it had to be laid aside in
favour of the process of regeneration symbolised by figures like
Waverley. This relegation of the past to the realm of 'the
romantic' obviously struck chords with both the Scots and
English reading public, though later commentators have seen it
otherwise: as 'the great source of the paralysing ideology of defeat
in Scotland' (Hugh McDiarmid) or 'a sickness from which
Scotland, and the Highlands in particular never recovered. It is a
sickness of the emotions and its symptoms can be seen on the
labels of whisky bottles' (John Prebble).

Jane Austen: the Regeneration of the Gentry

It would be difficult to find two contemporary novelists differing
more greatly than Sir Walter Scott and Jane Austen. Whereas
the former attempted narratives on an epic scale, involving the
destinies of nations, the latter confined herself to her 'little bit
of ivory', depicting small networks of friends and relations in
a secluded homogeneous community, from which events of
national significance seem remote. While Scott was fêted,
baroneted and elevated to the European (if not universal)

literary pantheon, Austen's success and influence in her own day were negligible. Scott earned many thousands of pounds from his writing; Austen never gained even a modest income from hers, the profits from which scarcely exceeded £700 by the time of her death. While Scott became the pride of his publishers, Austen's publishers had so little faith in their author that her novels were brought out on a commission basis: the publisher taking 10 per cent of all profits while the author stood the risk of an overall loss.

On the surface both authors had similar origins: both were the children of middle-class professional parents, Scott of a lawyer, Austen of a clergyman. The particular nature of Austen's class background and its implications have been examined by Terry Lovell, in an essay which expresses dissatisfaction with the standard 'middle-class origins' theory of the novel because of its inability to discriminate between different groups within the middle class and also because of its neglect of gender differences.[4] According to Lovell the particular social niche of Austen's family – professional but with strong links to the country gentry whom they served – explains the intense concern with moral standards for which critics like Leavis have found her novels so notable. In Lovell's view, Austen's perception of a threat to the minor gentry, with which she associates herself, is displaced onto the *moral* plane; her novels reflect a conservative ideology in which the inadequacies of a class are seen in terms of individual failings, redeemable by the successful passing of a series of moral ordeals.

In the late eighteenth century an unmarried woman above a certain social level was entirely dependent on relatives for social status and support, unless she had wealth of her own. Jane Austen's father needed to supplement his income from the produce of the glebe, or church agricultural holding. Nevertheless the Austen family enjoyed a relationship with the landowning classes through their wealthy kinsmen, the Leigh-Perrots, and through the Knight family who owned the Steventon living and had actually adopted one of Jane's brothers, for the purpose of ensuring the succession to their considerable lands. (This is the situation of Frank Churchill in *Emma*, who also took the name of his wealthy patron.) Jane's mother, widowed shortly before the major novels were published, was left only £210 a year for herself and her unmarried daughters to live on; the heroines of the novels by contrast seem to regard about £2000 to £4000 as an adequate income and Emma is richer still. Nevertheless the power of patronage assisted the rise of Jane's brothers in the navy and in the church, from which in turn they contributed to their mother's meagre income. The Austens' connections with wealth located them in what Lovell calls a 'subaltern section of the dominant gentry class' rather than an independent grouping and this is characteristic of many families of the period, including those portrayed in her novels, where the younger sons entered the church, law or military services, but retained their relationship with the landowning class.

The gentry at this period was itself dividing into two camps. The very large landowners (outside the ambit of Austen's novels, but represented by an off-stage character, Mrs Churchill in *Emma*) were actively expanding their lands through marriage and purchase and were equally actively injecting capital in order to modernise and commercialise agricultural methods. While such landlords provided large-scale funds for projects such as drainage, their tenant farmers contributed minor capital and the application of their growing technical expertise. In the shadow of this increasingly capitalised sector, the traditional, usually minor, gentry had nothing to fall back on but their age-old allegiance to their 'estates' and their paternalistic values in relation to their employees and tenants. Lovell's argument is that Jane Austen interprets, through the ideology of her fiction, the threat to this class as a threat arising from the failings of its individual members. Only by assuring the moral qualities of its members could its leadership be guaranteed and the whole class regenerated and reinstated.

Emma can be used as an illustration of Lovell's thesis. The novel is set in a restricted local community ('three or four families in a country village') of which the Woodhouses form the apex. Within this little closed world a few 'favoured' couples and families are almost incestuous in their social contact, while a system of filters and barriers prevents their circle being greatly enlarged. (The discussions over who is eligible for the social gatherings in the book are symptomatic.) Much of the humour and irony in *Emma* arises from this application of a system of finely graded social distinctions – though often the humour is at the expense of Emma for applying them either too enthusiastically – her attitude to the newly-rich Coles – or not rigorously enough – her misperception of Harriet Smith's social niche. Nevertheless there is no possibility that Emma's social world could broaden to include either the rich Mrs Churchill, who exercises her power from two hundred miles away, or Robert Martin, Knightley's tenant farmer, of whom Emma snobbishly, but surely realistically, says: ' a farmer can need none of my help, and is therefore in one sense as much above my notice as in every other he is below it.' (Penguin edn. p. 59) Nor is mere financial wealth the only criterion, as is shown by Emma's suspicion of the parvenu Mrs Elton, from mercantile Bristol, with 'no name, no blood, no alliance'. (p. 196)

Oversensitive as Emma is, her concern for social discrimination reflects a general need among the gentry to monitor society against threats from without or subversion from within. This was a time when, as we have seen in the case of *Clarissa*, the landowning families used many legal devices to prevent the sale or breaking-up of their property; the most common being *entail*, under which land was settled in advance on a chain of heirs so that there was no current absolute owner who could dispose of it through marriage or sale. In Austen's novels, similarly, our sympathies are directed to those characters who show a sense of responsibility towards the estates they own; Mr Knightley, like the other heroes, is concerned to manage his property properly and to carry out 'improvements', though not on so large a scale as to change it out of recognition.

In the case of the heroines the correct class responsibility involves making a suitable marriage – on which of course the plots of all the novels are based. Marriage must, obviously, be a matter of compatibility but it has wider implications as well since it offers a prospect of stability and happiness for the whole family from which the bride comes. Lovell quotes the historian G. E. Mingay to the effect that because of their power to effect alliances with other families 'daughters were the key to family connection and influence'. (Lovell p. 29) *Emma* differs slightly from the other novels because of the heroine's personal fortune, but it is still notable that Mr Woodhouse's wishes in the matter are the decisive factor. The *strict settlement* made at the time of the marriage by lawyers from both families arranged such things as the *jointure* (income for the wife should her husband die first), marriage portions for daughters and allowances for younger sons.

Jane Austen's distinctive contribution to this ideology, based on the significance of marriage as a crucial element in the network of gentry families, was to invest it with a moral element. Since marriage is so important those – or at least the women – who come to it must undergo a process of re-education before they are worthy of the position of influence which a 'good' marriage provides. The process is a very searching one in Emma's case, since she starts with flaws which her creator herself publicised: 'a heroine whom no-one but myself will much like'. The novel recounts a series of misconceptions on Emma's part: over Harriet Smith's status and qualities; over Mr Elton's intentions; over Frank Churchill; and of course over her own feelings towards Mr Knightley. Each recognition of the faults in her own judgement brings her closer to a realisation that life is more complex and other people less able to be manipulated than she had imagined. The series culminates in the episode where she recognises the superiority of Mr Knightley's moral discrimination – his rebuke of her for her sarcasm towards Miss Bates on the Box Hill outing. The sting of the rebuke is sharpened by Emma's realisation of how much she values Mr Knightley's opinion of herself: 'How could she have been so brutal, so cruel to Miss Bates! – How could she have exposed herself to such ill opinion in any one she valued! And how suffer him to leave her without saying one word of gratitude, of concurrence, of common kindness!' (Penguin edn, p. 369). From this moment on, Jane Austen implies, Emma's self-knowledge grows and there is no question, despite the trials still to come, but that she and Mr Knightley will end up as marriage partners.

In the world of the Austen novels all the heroines – though not all as flawed as Emma – are redeemed because they pass what Lovell calls a 'series of moral and discriminatory tasks set for them'. Sometimes characters are shown attempting but failing to pass these hurdles; Frank Churchill falls into this category. Other characters, the innately 'ill-natured', are clearly irredeemable from the start (Mrs Elton). Yet others are basically 'good-natured' (in Lovell's phrase) but lack the complexity of character which will enable them to surmount the hurdles set for the heroines; Miss Bates is an example here, as are many minor characters in the novels. The goals each category can achieve vary according to their starting point; whereas the ill-natured and those who have failed the moral ordeals can achieve at the most a neutral social respectability, the way is open for the protagonists of the novels to achieve a self-knowledge that qualifies them as the social and moral leaders of their class.

Jane Austen's class position, then, can be held to determine her attachment to an ideal of individual moral integrity, which she saw as the way in which her class could be regenerated, in a period when it was under pressure. It is her sex, however, that explains the focus of her novels on marriage as a way of exercising this moral worth; the women in her novels can only take the role of leaders if they find a suitable marriage partner who is both compatible and adequately wealthy. By contrast the helplessness of the single woman, especially if she is poor and unattractive, is made starkly clear – in the cases of Miss Bates and Jane Fairfax for example. It is true that in discussion with Harriet, Emma pours scorn on the idea that spinsterhood need be a problem for a wealthy heiress:

> A single woman, with a very narrow income, must be a ridiculous, disagreeable, old maid! the proper sport of boys and girls; but a single woman of good fortune is always respectable, and may be as sensible and pleasant as anybody else. And the distinction is not quite so much against the candour and common sense of the world as appears at first; for a very narrow income has a tendency to contract the mind, and sour the temper. (p. 109)

The argument here is plausible, despite Emma's snobbery. Yet the whole course of the novel runs counter to the idea of 'singleness' as a satisfactory state. Emma's self-blindness – already becoming evident to us – and her dogmatism tempt us to read ironically the passage in which she claims to look on a single future for herself with equanimity:

I do not perceive why I should be more in want of employment at forty or fifty than one-and-twenty. Woman's usual occupations of eye and hand will be as open to me then, as they are now. . . . And as for objects of interest, objects for the affections, which is in truth the greater point of inferiority, the want of which is really the great evil to be avoided in *not* marrying, I shall be very well off, with all the children of a sister I love so much, to care about. (p. 110)

If there is a hollow ring to this, since the whole direction of the novel implies that Emma's life would have been the poorer without marriage, it must have been combined with a painful irony for Jane Austen herself as she wrote it. Austen's own life was closer to the devalued, meagre lives of Miss Bates and Jane Fairfax (in her governess role) than to Emma's. This may explain why she does not extend more than routine sympathy to such socially stranded individuals, preferring to focus on the eligible heroine; or could it be that the lifeline which the involvement with fiction provided was sufficient for her not to see herself in this to-be-pitied category? The paradox is, as Lovell remarks, that: 'Jane Austen endorsed the narrow view of women in the conservative ideology of her novels while simultaneously denying it by the act of writing them.' (Lovell p. 35)

5. The Novelist in the Market Place: Dickens and Mrs Gaskell

The years of the mid to late nineteenth century are normally regarded as the high-water mark of the novel form. A genre which had struggled to establish itself as a serious literary expression, in the face of scorn and suspicion, now acquired a predominance in both popular and artistic terms. The nineteenth century is also the period of the overwhelming dominance of the three-volume novel which set a standard for fiction in length, price and quality until its sudden capitulation to economic pressures in the 1890s. Because in the nineteenth century socio-cultural evidence becomes so much more prolific and reliable there is a problem in a general book of this kind as to what material is most relevant. To help the reader the evidence has been organised under the categories used in the 'communication model' of fiction set out in the first chapter. The propositions are then developed in relation to two novels, *Oliver Twist* and *Mary Barton*.

The Social Context

The emerging mercantile class of the eighteenth century became the capitalist middle class and their 'white-collar' subordinates of the lower-middle class in the eighteenth century. It lost much of its wilder Puritan fervour, though remaining largely Nonconformist in religion, but retained the respect for self-reliance and sobriety that had characterised Puritanism; its most notable attribute was a concern for money-making. Bourgeois values centred on the idea of individual self-improvement, both material and spiritual, leading to an ideal state of respectability based on a domestic security dominated by the male breadwinner. These values were eventually to permeate every sector of society and influence the economy, government, the law and the national culture generally. Eric Hobsbawm has described the members of this class as:

> a formidable army, all the more so as they became increasingly conscious of themselves as a *class* rather than a 'middle-rank' bridging the gap between the upper and lower orders. . . . They were self-made men or at least men of modest origins who owed little to birth, family or formal higher education. . . . They were rich and getting richer by the year. They were above all imbued with the ferocious and dynamic self-confidence of those whose own careers proved to them that divine providence, science and history have combined to present the earth to them on a platter. (*The Age of Revolution*, p. 222)

Many historians regard the hegemony of this class as confirmed after 1848 with the failure of the political revolutions in Europe and of associated social movements such as Chartism in Great Britain. From this date the middle class and working class who had combined against the power of the aristocracy on such issues as parliamentary reform increasingly recognised their separate interests and developed opposing values in the fields of politics, economics and culture. For the new middle classes:

> The ideal of an individualist society, a private family unit supplying all its material and moral needs on the basis of a private business suited them because they were men who no longer needed traditions. Their efforts had raised them out of the rut. They were in a sense their own reward, the content of life, and if that was not enough, there was always the money, the comfortable house increasingly removed from the smoke of mill and counting house, the devoted and modest wife, the family circle, the enjoyment of travel, art, science and literature. . . . The successful middle class and those who aspired to emulate them were satisfied. Not so the labouring poor –

in the nature of things the majority – whose traditional world and way of life the Industrial Revolution destroyed, without automatically substituting anything else.[1]

The Industrial Revolution – the rapid development of new technologies and the economic investment required to implement them – was the basis for this social revolution and it had its own part to play in forming the middle-class ethos. In Hobsbawm's words: 'There was an order in the universe but it was no longer an order of the past. There was only one God, whose name was steam and spoke in the name of Malthus, McCulloch and anyone who employed machinery.' (*The Age of Revolution*, p. 223) Fiction often supported these values, since the middle-class emphasis on home life, particularly as far as women were concerned, encouraged the activity of reading novels which in turn reinforced the domestic ideal.

> The image of the cosy hearth, round which the family gathered regularly, was repeated endlessly in poems and magazine articles. . . . Such was the dominance of the cult of home that domestic virtue extended to literature and the fine arts. Novels and plays had to be such as a father could read aloud to his wife and daughters without embarrassment.[2]

The novel was felt to have a role in drawing together the secure domestic circle, but only if it did not import troubling influences or ideas from outside.

Literary Context

As the novel became an established art-form it increasingly subdivided into distinct *genres*, that is, forms of fiction each with their own characteristic content and conventions of treatment. Each genre provided a tradition and a model which authors could either imitate or react against. Some of these forms succeeded each other in time; for example the 'silver fork' novels of the early 1800s had begun to die out by the 1840s while others co-existed, such as the historical novels popularised by Scott and the 'Newgate' novels about criminals. Although major writers such as Charles Dickens transcended the limitations of the conventions traces of their influence can often be found in their works.

One such example is *Oliver Twist* which owes something to the 'Newgate' genre, named after the notorious London prison, and held (though sometimes wrongly) to romanticise crime and criminals. The 'Newgate' novel created a stir in the 1830s with the works of Edward Bulwer and Harrison Ainsworth; Bulwer's *Paul Clifford* has some parallels to *Oliver Twist* – its hero who is of respectable parentage but warped by being brought up in poor surroundings is arrested for an act of pickpocketing committed by someone else – but is much more overtly an attack on the criminalising effect of poor environment. The genre drew strong criticism and a parody from William Makepeace Thackeray. It was Thackeray's insistence that 'rogues' should not be treated sympathetically that forced Dickens to defend himself in the preface to the third edition of his own novel. To Thackeray's comment: 'in the name of common sense, let us not expend our sympathies on cutthroats, and other such prodigies of evil!' (made in his novel *Catherine*) Dickens retorted:

> It appeared to me that to draw a knot of such associates in crime as really did exist; to paint them in all their deformity, in all their wretchedness, in all the squalid misery of their lives . . . it appeared to me that to do this, would be to attempt a something which was needed, and which would be a service to society. And therefore I did it as I best could. (*Oliver Twist* Penguin edn., p. 34)

Mrs Gaskell's *Mary Barton* on the other hand belongs with a group of novels that attempt to deal with the 'Condition of England' question, as first defined by Thomas Carlyle in an essay of 1839 on Chartism: 'Is the Condition of the English working people wrong; so wrong that rational working men cannot, will not, and even should not rest quiet under it?' (*Selected Writings*, Penguin, 1971, p. 152) In the case of *Mary Barton* the influence of genre is less easy to show since of these novels (Raymond Williams calls them 'Industrial Novels' in *Culture and Society*) only Disraeli's *Sybil* was published earlier, in 1845. There is perhaps less in common between these two works than between either of them and the non-fiction, but highly poetic language, of Carlyle to whom Kathleen Tillotson thinks the 'serious' or 'prophetic' novel owes a considerable debt.[3]

Readership

It is not difficult to show that the *potential* readership for fiction was increasing steadily throughout the nineteenth century. Mere literacy figures, which were often based on the ability to sign a name in a church register, do not tell us much about the actual ability to interpret the written word or discriminate between those who could cope with Dickens and those whose fiction reading was confined to the penny-serials or the sub-Newgate productions of the so-called 'Salisbury Square' novelists. Nevertheless some expansion of the total market must be indicated by the difference between Burke's estimate of 80,000 potential readers out of a population of seven million in 1790 and the fact that by 1840 those nominally literate included 67 per cent of males and 51 per cent of females out of a population which had by now increased to sixteen million.

The expanding market can to some extent be gauged by considering the sales of the leading 'bestsellers', not forgetting that many of the cheapest and most popular publications must have gone unrecorded, and also the figures for sales would not have included the kind of multiple readership implied by borrowing from libraries or friends or by listening to family readings. Nevertheless the figure of 40,000 copies for each of the instalments in which *Pickwick Papers*, Dickens's earliest novel, appeared in 1836 compares well both with Burke's figure of 80,000 serious readers and with the sales of Scott.

The first systematic attempt to measure the potential readership for nineteenth-century novels was made in 1980 by Darko Suvin in an essay on 'The Social Addressees of Victorian Fiction'. Suvin's figures are intended to illustrate the number and class-composition of the *addressees* the nineteenth-century novelist would be entitled to expect; they define his or her *horizon of expectation*. Suvin's article attempts to identify these addressees by examining the income of various social groups in relation to the price of novels in order to determine who would have been able to afford them. He does not claim to be able to quantify other *receivers* of fiction such as casual borrowers, purchasers of second-hand copies and others whom the authors could not reasonably be expected to have in mind as their 'target audience'.

Suvin's article deals primarily with the second half of the century: the period from 1867 to 1900. However, there is some justification for summarising it here, as background to the century as a whole, since the price of a three-volume novel remained constant throughout the century – though cheaper reprints were more common in the later period – while real incomes actually rose slightly. Altick's evidence is that the average annual income of a lower-middle class family rose from £90 in 1851 to £110 in 1881. (*English Common Reader* p. 306) It is probably true to say therefore that Suvin's proposition of a very restricted, mainly affluent, readership for new full-length fiction or even for first cheap reprints holds even more true for the earlier part of the century.

Suvin's conclusion is that there is little truth in Altick's thesis that the expansion of the market was so rapid that by the 1890s new, good-quality fiction was available to all classes. He excludes from the potential reading public those earning below the minimum level to maintain a healthy physical existence, who, except in cases of great voluntary sacrifice, would have had no spare money to spend on fiction, although they may have had access to the discarded books of masters or employers. Using contemporary evidence from R. Dudley Baxter (*National Income: United Kingdom*) Suvin estimates this group as comprising between one-half and two-thirds of the population in 1867. (In the 'hungry' 1840s it must have been at least as great a proportion.) Even with a nominal literacy rate as high as 70 per cent, which had been reached by 1860, this underprivileged group would have been prevented from reading fiction by lack of money, lack of leisure time and other consequences of poverty such as lack of privacy, poor lighting and bad eyesight.

Suvin also uses figures for the national annual expenditure on books and newspapers in 1880 to calculate that the average working-class family at that time would have been likely to spend only three or four shillings a year (15–20p) on reading material of any kind. Since most of this sum probably went on newspapers, magazines or factual and educational works, Suvin concludes that even late in the century the working classes could be left out of account as potential addressees of new volume-length fiction: 'They were moving in different circuits of discourse: those of cheap serialised fiction, of non-fiction, of Sunday papers and of the submerged, informal oral tradition.' ('The Social Addressees of Victorian Fiction' *Literature and History* Spring 1982, p. 21)

By contrast, volume-length fiction reached perhaps only 5–15 per cent of British families, with a further 10–15 per cent buying cheap instalment parts and reprints. A third group relied for their reading matter on the commercial circulating libraries and later on the public lending libraries, the earliest of which were established in 1850; however, this group would of course have overlapped with the other two. In any case it was scarcely large: Suvin estimates that commercial libraries, with their guinea-a-year subscription, were used by only 0.6 per cent of the population (250,000 readers) even by the end of the century, and public libraries attracted only 5 per cent or so of the population in reach of them. It follows that the addressees of Victorian fiction and the resulting *horizon of expectation* were overwhelmingly middle class.

Suvin divides this potential readership for fiction into three 'clusters'. The first comprised those one-and-a-half to two million readers, with an income of between £100 and £5,000 a year who had the money to buy fiction or to subscribe to libraries such as Mudie's. The group included the richer bourgeoisie, professional men (e.g. barristers, clergymen, doctors of medicine) and senior clerks – or rather it included them and their families, for it was often the female members of the household who were the most enthusiastic novel-readers. Inside this group, Suvin suggests, values and expectations were determined by a small 'hegemonic' core comprising no more than 2 or 3 per cent of the total population. This consensus of values was enforced partly by the intervention of publishers, periodical editors and library proprietors who in ways we shall examine below made it their task to see that the published texts did not offend the expectations of their readers.

Outside this group (Suvin sees them as concentric rings) was a *subsidiary* group of between 1.1 and 1.7 million members, together with their families, whose consumption of fiction was mostly through reprints and later through free public libraries. Their income ranged from £100 to £300 (often regarded as the boundary of the middle class in Victorian England) and they comprised such occupations as middle and junior clerks, and the so-called 'unacknowledged' professionals – elementary schoolteachers, nurses and certain grades of engineers. They were subsidiary in the sense that as purchasers of reprinted fiction they were neither the primary addressees of the novelists nor were they taken into account by publishers and editors, but their values would probably have been 'hegemonically' formed by those they regarded as their betters.

A third or *parasitic* cluster of 500,000 to 1 million members were the domestic servants (90 per cent of them women) who did not spend money on books but might have had the opportunity to read fiction discarded or handed-down by the hegemonic group on which they were largely dependent.

The operation of the strong middle-class hegemony meant that even where working-class groups featured as part of the readership for fiction their horizon of expectations was based on that of their middle class. As Suvin summarises in a quotation:

> Throughout the period [of 1830–1914] the dominating ideas – and the reactions against them – were those based on middle-class idealism, middle-class prosperity, the whole system reaching its height in the sixties and seventies. . . . And in the main the literature of the period is literature about the middle class, by the middle class, even that written by the most violent critics of the edifice. (p. 26: the quotation is from Edith C. Batho and Bonamy Dobrée *The Victorians and After*, 1962)

Mode of Consumption

It has been mentioned in this chapter and the preceding one that privacy is one condition conducive to reading. However, this should not be taken to mean that fiction was always read alone and in silence. It is true that many eighteenth-century pictures and engravings exist – as George Steiner has pointed out – which characterise reading as a solitary and privileged act:

> A man sitting alone in his personal library reading is at once the product and begetter of a particular social and moral order. It is a *bourgeois* order founded on certain hierarchies of literacy, of purchasing power, of leisure, and of caste. (*On Difficulty*, p. 189)

However, the reading of fiction was often a communal activity in the nineteenth century. Sometimes this took place in a group assembled for the purpose and the reading public may have been expanded in this way to an extent that we can never measure. For example, Kathleen Tillotson refers to an illiterate charlady becoming familiar with *Dombey and Son* read aloud to a group of Dickens enthusiasts. (*Novels of the 1840s*, p. 21) Primarily, however, reading aloud was to the family group and there are many accounts of Victorian parents reading to a family circle even when the children were well able to read for themselves. The reading of Scott for example could take this form as Maria Edgeworth testifies (see pp. 91–2) and Ruskin the art critic and social commentator enjoyed the same tradition in his family. Altick describes how:

> Ruskin's father was a devotee of Scott and as a child Ruskin himself knew the Waverley novels and Pope's *Iliad* better than any other book except the Bible. After tea, it was the father's custom to read aloud to his wife and son, and the choice of authors in these sessions was as broad as one could find in any cultured nineteenth-century household. (*English Common Reader*, p. 116)

This semi-public mode of consumption had two effects on the style and content of the novels which were subjected to it. Some novelists aware of the fact that they would be read aloud may have been encouraged to play up the semi-dramatic elements in their work. This element is attested in Dickens by his practice in later years of giving his own 'performed' readings of the text, including the frenzied rendition of the death of Nancy which is said to have killed him. Secondly, since the family reading

circle often included adolescent girls, the novelist was under
pressure not to embarrass the paterfamilias who was 'delivering
the text' by including material which Victorian standards
classified as 'indelicate'. The very limited freedom of the
British novel on matters of sex was reinforced by the influence
of the circulating library and as often happens in matters of
implicit censorship it is difficult to assign the responsibility
between the readers, who had certain expectations, and the
writers, publishers and library proprietors who perhaps interpreted those expectations too cautiously. Nevertheless whether
the public got what they wanted or only what was thought good
for them, it would have created a scandal at any time up to the
1890s if a British novel had included a passage as free as this
one from Balzac's *Les Chouans*:

> The so-called naval officer . . .watched captivated for the
> repeated movement of the eyelids, the seductive rise and fall
> of the breathing. Sometimes his thoughts led him to look for a
> relation between the expression of the eyes and the almost
> imperceptible curving of the lips. (Penguin translation, p. 149)

Publishing Methods

In the previous chapter we saw how Scott's success established
the high price of 31s. 6d. for the standard three-volume novel
that made it a luxury commodity even for the middle classes.
By the end of the century purchases by individuals of three-
volume first editions were regarded as so abnormal and eccentric that a cartoon mocked the 'man who bought himself a
three-decker'. Although the length and literary prestige of the
three-decker set a standard for all novels, it was at least as
common for readers to encounter fiction in *serial* form, either as
monthly part-issue instalments or incorporated into a monthly
or weekly magazine; though such works would often, of course,
eventually appear in three-volume form.

Under the *part-issue* system novels were published in shilling
monthly 'numbers' over a year or more, so reducing the
standard 31s. 6d. price of the three-decker to as little as £1 and
of course spreading the outlay. The method had been developed

in the previous century for reprints – Hazlitt reminisces: 'The sixpenny numbers of this work regularly contrived to leave off just in the middle of a sentence, and in the nick of a story, where Tom Jones discovers Square behind the blanket' (Tillotson, *Novels of the 1840s*, p. 26) – and for expensive non-fiction, such as that containing illustrations. The latter practice indirectly gave birth to the part-issue system for *new* fiction when in 1835 the publishers Chapman and Hall planned a series of 'cockney sporting prints' by the artist Seymour, accompanied by text by the young journalist Charles Dickens. The death of the original artist and the fact that Dickens knew little about field sports and asked for a wider brief altered the ratio between illustrations and text and thus produced the first new novel in instalment form, *Pickwick Papers*.

Eight of Dickens's novels were published in this format, consisting of eighteen monthly parts of thirty-two pages with two illustrations and a final 'double number' selling at two shillings. It was also adopted by Ainsworth, Marryat, Thackeray and Trollope among others, and in a modified form by George Eliot. The medium was attractive to readers because of its cheapness and perhaps because of its 'cliffhanger' characteristics; it appealed to the publishers, who found it provided a high circulation, a way of spreading production costs, subsidy from advertisers and independence from the circulating libraries; and it appealed to writers, who gained from an increase in income – sometimes paid while they were still writing – and the opportunity for a more immediate relationship with the reading public.

Despite its massive early success the part-issue method was largely superseded during the course of the century by serialisation in magazines and eventually in newspapers. By the 1840s the fiction serial which had its origins in the eighteenth century was a regular ingredient in the more expensive half-crown monthly magazines such as *Bentley's Miscellany* in which *Oliver Twist* was published in 1838. A distinctive nineteenth-century development was the extension of the practice to very cheap weekly papers selling to the growing working-class and lower-middle-class reading public for as little as a penny (1d.). Much of this fiction was reprinted material but Suvin may be wrong when he discounts the readers of the penny serials on the ground that they were not consumers of original fiction. Certainly Dickens was capitalising on the phenomenon when he founded his twopenny weekly, *Household Words*, in 1850; it published Mrs Gaskell, Reade, Bulwer and Collins apart from Dickens himself.

Apart from the greater strain on the authors of producing weekly rather than monthly instalments, magazine serialisation implied the possible intervention of a further outside influence, the editor. Kathleen Tillotson gives two examples of this: one political, Charles Kingley's *Yeast* which *Fraser's Magazine* asked the author to curtail when subscriptions were cancelled by offended readers, and one aesthetic: Dickens himself as editor put pressure on Mrs Gaskell to supply more exciting endings for her novels. (Tillotson, p. 32)

One further aspect of magazine serialisation on which more research needs to be done is what has been called *intertextuality*; Andrew Blake has shown for example how in the 1860s the fiction published in *Blackwood's Magazine* directly paralleled the social and political themes of its editorials and non-fiction ingredients.[4]

Although serial publication was both popular and influential the standard for novels in structure content was still dictated by the three-volume format, in which many successful serialised novels were reprinted. The 'three-decker' usually reached the consumer through a lending library and until the establishment of free public libraries (a slow process dating from the 1850s) this meant a commercial circulating library.

Mudie's Protectorate

Although the circulating libraries which originated in the eighteenth century had several Victorian successors none were as important as W.H. Smith's and Mudie's. In terms of influence, social prestige and sheer psychological significance to novelists, readers and publishers no nineteenth-century library matched what Carlyle once called the 'Mudie Mountain'.

Charles Edward Mudie, of Nonconformist Scottish parentage, began lending books from his stationer's shop in Bloomsbury in 1842 and by 1852 had done sufficiently well to move his Select

Library to a larger site on the corner of New Oxford Street which it occupied until its closure in 1937. Here stood the magnificent pillared lending hall which had the grandeur of a great public institution but which was founded on two commercially acute notions: the attractiveness of the guinea annual subscription which allowed the reader to borrow and then exchange a volume of a novel costing half as much again to buy and the guarantee of respectability contained in the title: 'Mudie's *Select* Library'. Mudie's freely expressed policy of choosing his stock to match rather than extend contemporary middle-class taste has caused his biographer Guinevere Griest to refer to his 'protectorate' over the nineteenth-century novel.

It was Mudie's which allowed the Victorian reader to become a book-borrower rather than a buyer and thus in various subtle ways affected the behaviour not only of the readers but also of publishers and writers. Mudie's dominance over the library market is indicated at least for the latter part of the century by a letter to the publisher Bentley indicating that 125 copies of a Bentley novel had been sent to Mudie and 57 to the remaining libraries put together. As a *social* event, borrowing from Mudie soon acquired its own particular cachet, as Mudie's biographer describes:

> Nothing could be more reminiscent of Victorian society than the picture of it drawing up in carriages – victorias, phaetons or dogcarts – at Mudie's door, sweeping in upon the counters and shelves and emerging again, followed by flunkeys carrying loads of the newest books. Majestic 'three-volumers'. . . . It was almost as much of an afternoon duty as a drive in Rotten Row. (Guinevere L. Griest, *Mudie's Circulating Library and the Victorian Novel* David and Charles 1970 p. 85)

For some of Mudie's visitors the social aspect of borrowing may even have been the primary one – were those loads of books necessarily even read? – but the practice of borrowing itself was founded on economic realism. It is not surprising that borrowers flocked to Mudie's Great Ionic Hall during the years of his ascendancy (roughly from 1850 to 1890) when the one-and-a-half guinea cover price on the prestigious three-decker had prompted even Gladstone to complain in the Commons in 1852 that there was no article 'for which the public are called on to pay a price so high in comparison with the actual cost of production as books'. (Griest, p. 216) When a guinea subscription could secure any exchangeable volume in stock it made sense even to the more affluent to patronise the Select Libraries. The attraction extended to readers in the provinces, or those overseas or too infirm to pay a personal visit; Mudie's sent them boxes of books by post, providing for colonial subscribers a cultural lifeline to the 'Mother Country'. The prevalence of borrowing is therefore explained by the cost of the three-volume novel, though in turn the supremacy of the 'three-decker' as a literary format is explained by the preference of the libraries for it. This was a symbiotic relationship in which each institution profited from the other for fifty years.

'Three Compact and Indiwidual Wollumes'

The description given in *David Copperfield* of the small, squat 'post-octavo' format with its wide margins and well-spaced lines of print fits the vast majority of novels which Mudie lent out. Between 1853 and 1862 alone his stock increased by 960,000 volumes – of which half were fiction – and by the end of the century he was said to stock seven-and-a-half million volumes available for borrowing. The 'three-decker', which took its nickname from the 'three-deck' naval warship, represented a stabilisation of book prices at a level at which most individuals could not buy new fiction and encouraged the development of alternatives such as part-issue or periodical serialisation. Why was this?

Although apparently economically illogical the high price of new fiction met several needs in a complex web of pressures and demands that survived until it dissolved almost overnight in the early 1890s. Clearly by deterring individual purchasers the high price of the three-decker made the circulating library not only possible but necessary. However, the system also gave the *reader* some advantages. Borrowing enabled him (or more likely her) to sample a greater variety of authors at a fixed cost and there was the added reassurance provided by Mudie's policy of 'selection'. Bookshelves would not become cluttered since the system compelled each volume to be exchanged when it had been read. If a family paid more than one subscription the three volumes of a given novel could be borrowed together and the physical format allowed all three to be in use at the same time; for example, mother finishing volume three as the younger daughter began volume one.

For the *publisher* the chief value of the system was the guaranteed market that library sales provided. Once a library had agreed to take a quota of a certain title its publishing costs could be regarded as covered, meaning that later sales, for example from a one-volume reprint brought out after the book had proved its worth in the library list, were mostly profit. In 1876 Trollope gave some figures to illustrate the economics. (See Griest, p. 59) The cost of printing, binding and paper for 600 copies was £200. If Mudie took 550 of these at his usual heavily discounted price of 15s. (75p) this brought in £412 10s., and provided a profit of £212 10s. to be shared between publisher and author. Since until late in the century the royalty system was rare and publishers bought a writer's copyright outright the potential for the publisher's profit was enormous. Another advantage was that most of the publicity costs were borne by the libraries and in fact the presence of the novel in a 'select' library soon came to be regarded as evidence of its worth.

To the *writer* the guaranteed market seemed to offer more security, particularly to unknown or less popular authors. The publisher, knowing Mudie or Smith could be contracted to take a fixed number of copies, was able – or at any rate claimed he was – to take risks he might not have considered otherwise. In the 1890s when the three-decker came under attack from all sides this was one of the few convincing arguments presented in its favour. The publisher William Heinemann for instance claimed that the disappearance of the form would drive to destitution 'a considerable number of quite worthy and not un-useful writers', a somewhat hypocritical complaint from a man who had rushed in more quickly than others to profit from the new single-volume novel which was replacing it. (See Griest pp. 182 and 185)

Finally the continuing value of the three-decker to the *libraries* is evident in the financial success of Mudie's, which in 1864 became a limited liability company with a capital of £100,000, supported by 50,000 subscribers and employing over 250 workers. Mudie's main rival, Smith's, had its origins in a rare failure of financial acumen, when Mudie declined to open branches on railway stations to serve travellers. The energetic William H. Smith who pioneered the station bookstalls then started his own lending service on the back of his already considerable success with the 'yellow-backed' cheap reprints which came to be called 'railway novels'. Not only did the scale of operations of Mudie and Smith, the 'twin tyrants of literature', enable them to buy novels at a bulk discount, while protecting the nominal 31s. 6d. price as a discouragement to individual purchasers, but they gleaned a further profit by selling off second-hand those novels that had outlived their popularity with borrowers. It was only the libraries' own growing disenchantment with the three-decker at the end of the century that led to a collapse of the system under which a potential thirty-seven million readers were forced to wait until the lucky quarter of a million Mudie and Smith subscribers had enjoyed their nine month run.

The three-decker was for all these reasons endowed with a prestige which remained with it for most of the century. There are many stories of publishers discouraging their authors from using anything but the three-volume length and of the low status of novels in one volume – the traditional format for cheap reprints. When, for example, *Wuthering Heights* was published in 1847 as a two-volume novel it was bound together with Anne Brontë's *Agnes Grey* so as to form a three-volume set: the title page of the last volume read 'Agnes Grey/ A Novel/ by/ Acton Bell/ Volume III'. The system depended of course on the willingness of publishers to comply with the delay mentioned above and postpone issuing a cheaper edition until the libraries had had their 'first bite'; just as today a paperback edition follows the hardback after a twelve-month interval. Even when a novel first appeared in a serialised format there was normally a three-volume edition in prospect at some stage.

Dickens's *Great Expectations* first appeared in serial form in *All The Year Round* (the successor to *Household Words*) but its explicit division into the three 'stages' of Pip's expectations is obviously designed in advance to reflect the three-decker format.

After the three-decker had had its 'run' in the libraries the final stage of publication might be a single-volume reprint in two phases: at 6s. (30p) and then as a popular 3s. 6d. (17½p) or 2s. (10p) edition, the latter being the famous 'yellow-back' or 'railway novel' which expanding train travel had made so necessary as a way of passing the time. The extent to which a publisher could squeeze so many editions out of the same work was of course related to the library circulation of the original three-decker which provided him with a valuable index to the novel's popularity. The following chapter, which charts the end of the three-decker (and with it the borrowing system for fiction), documents some less attractive side-effects of the system. Two of them need to be introduced here.

Firstly, the sheer bulk of the three-decker compelled novelists to adopt a length and structure that came to be regarded as almost indispensable in nineteenth-century fiction. Many authors, like Reardon in Gissing's *New Grub Street*, found it a 'procrustean bed' on which they had to stretch what was really only long enough for one or two volumes. (One critic referred to the three-decker as a perversely composed sandwich in which two slices of meat concealed a second volume which was 'a great slab of ill-baked and insipid bread' (see Griest, p. 206).) Those authors who overcame the problem did so by developing or inventing techniques which we have come to regard as 'standard' for the novel of the period: multiple plots (contrasting or parallel), a profusion of incidental description and detail, the use of summaries to guide the reader (who might not have an earlier volume on hand) and authorial digression and commentary. In turn the existence of a cluster of plots meant a complicated dénouement in which all the threads had to be systematically unravelled. Above all, when the three-volume format was used imaginatively this implied a tripartite division of the story, often with a crisis to round off each of the first two volumes. George Eliot said of *The Mill on the Floss*: 'The three volumes will certainly have the advantage of being very various while they have the psychological unity that springs from their being the history of two closely related lives from beginning to end.' (Griest p. 109)

Secondly, the role of the libraries as mediators in purveying fiction to the middle-class public inevitably had its effect on content. Although Victorian prudery is legendary the restricted range of the British novel in matters of sex (as compared with the French) was not a simple matter of demand and supply. Libraries, writers, authors and public all became complicit in excluding certain matters from fiction altogether and treating others as covertly as possible. The three-decker acquired a reputation for evasiveness if not escapism, summed up in some verse Rudyard Kipling wrote at the moment of its disappearance:

We asked no social questions, – we pumped no hidden shame –
We never talked obstetrics when the Little Stranger came.
                                                    (quoted in Griest p. 7)

The censorship of fiction could take many forms. A library could refuse to accept a novel from a publisher at all – as Smith banned George Moore's *Esther Waters* with the comment: 'We are a circulating library and our subscribers are not used to detailed descriptions of a lying-in hospital'; it could disapprove of a title – as Mudie is said to have objected to Wilkie Collins' *The New Magdalen*; or it could effect actual editorial changes in the text – altering 'fat stomach' to 'deep chest' for example. Mudie and Smith were both Nonconformists and conservative in their social and religious views. Mudie in particular used the title of his 'Select Library' to justify a positive role of intervention, telling Carlyle in 1850: 'In my business I profess to judge books only from a commercial standpoint, though it is ever my object to circulate good books and not bad ones.' (Griest p. 35)

For Mudie 'bad books' would certainly have included those, whatever their literary quality, which offended or were thought to offend the standard of Victorian taste, 'the Young Person'. Of course Mudie often correctly reflected the genuine prejudice of his middle-class and largely female readership. His justification for not stocking George Moore's *A Modern Lover* was that: 'Two ladies from the country wrote to me objecting to that scene where the girl sat to the artist as a model for Venus. After that I naturally refused to circulate your book.' (Griest p. 83) It is equally true, however, that publishers and authors pre-empted censorship or suppression by omitting anything that libraries might regard as questionable. 'Publishing at Mudie' became a policy which must have affected more than just the library editions and also more than just matters of sex. Two possible examples of the libraries' indirect influence are Dickens's alteration of the ending to *Great Expectations* to make it more 'agreeable' and Alexander Macmillan's rejection of Hardy's first novel, *The Poor Man and the Lady*, with these words: 'Your pictures of character among Londoners and especially the upper classes, are sharp, clear, incisive and in many respects true, but they are wholly dark – not a ray of light visible to relieve the darkness, and therefore exaggerated and untrue in their result'. (Griest p. 136) He meant of course that the typical borrower would have found it 'untrue'!

The circulating libraries through their distribution of the three-decker built up an audience for fiction which no other system could have done. But it was an audience accustomed to what was on the whole a bland, uniform, unadventurous product, a taste which was not invented by Mudie and Smith but which they cultivated in preference to forms of fiction for which they had an ideological hostility. However, the inadequacy of the diet they offered is suggested by the fact that when eventually 'daring' or 'modern' novelists such as George Moore and Emile Zola were published in one-volume editions which by-passed the libraries they found a ready public.

'Oliver Twist': Serial Form

Dickens's first novel published in serial format makes an ideal illustration of the influence of this mode of publication on writer and readers and through them on the text itself. *Pickwick Papers* had been published in 1836 in the revolutionary (for fiction) format of the monthly part-issue. For his second novel Dickens exploited his position as editor of the two-shilling monthly magazine *Bentley's Miscellany* (named after its publisher) and produced *Oliver Twist* in the more traditional guise of magazine instalments, shorter than the part-issues but spread over a longer period: *Oliver* ran from February 1837 to April 1839 inclusive, with three short breaks. Both serial methods relied on the same basic principle: readers were attracted because the immediate financial outlay was less than for a three-volume

edition but only remained attracted, and made a profit for the
publisher, if the instalments were sufficiently gripping to encourage them to buy the next part or the next issue of the
periodical. (For periodicals this was less crucial since there
were several other ingredients intended to 'hook' the reader and
this may have been one reason why this form of serialisation
eventually ousted the part-issue.) These requirements would
probably have affected Dickens's approach to novel-writing
even if his temperament had been different; however, his hand-
to-mouth method of composition made them even more significant.

Serial publication demands a series of narrative sequences
that engage the readers' interest, curiosity and emotional involvement, often through the use of suspense. Each instalment
needs to be relatively self-contained but the writer must keep
the design of the whole novel in view, especially if the successful
story is to be reprinted in three-volume form. In his comments
on the nature of reading Wolfgang Iser has said that if such a
balance is achieved:

> [readers] often found a novel read in instalments to be better
> than the very same novel in book form. . . . The difference
> arises out of the cutting technique used in the serial story. It
> generally breaks off just at the point of suspense where one
> would like to know the outcome of a meeting, a situation etc.
> The interruption and consequent prolongation of tension is
> the basic function of the cut. The result is that we try to
> imagine how the story will unfold, and in this way we
> heighten our own participation in the course of events.
> Dickens was a master of this technique; his readers became
> his 'co-authors'. (*The Act of Reading*, p. 191)

With modern television serials the imaginative participation of
the audience can be stimulated almost to hysterical proportions.
(For example the identity of the attacker of 'JR' in *Dallas*
became an international obsession after a carefully planned
break in the transmission of this serial in the 1970s.) There is no
shortage of anecdotes to show that nineteenth-century readers
responded in a similar way to serial fiction. During the publication of Marryat's *Japhet in Search of his Father* (1834–36) one

ship passing another in mid-ocean sent a message using the naval signal flags: 'Has Japhet found his father yet?' Kathleen Tillotson quotes contemporary readers who claimed that each serial episode 'is anticipated with more anxiety than the Indian Mail, and is a great deal more talked about when it does come'. (*Novels of the 1840s*, p. 34) Such popular involvement crossed oceans and frontiers as is proved by stories of crowds lining the quays of New York to wait for the latest Dickens instalments to arrive from England.

An example of the use of the 'cut' to create suspense in *Oliver Twist* occurs at the end of the original sixth instalment (now Chapter 13), when Fagin sends the Artful Dodger to retrieve Oliver from Mr Brownlow with the sinister concluding threat: 'If he means to blab us among his new friends, we may stop his windpipe yet.' The following instalment ended in equally bloodcurdling fashion with the description of the brutal kidnap of Oliver:

> In another moment he was dragged into a labyrinth of dark narrow courts and was forced along them at a pace which rendered the few cries he dared give utterance to, unintelligible. It was of little moment, indeed, whether they were intelligible or no; for there was nobody to care for them, had they been ever so plain. (Penguin edn, p. 158)

The reader is left between episodes with the haunting image of Brownlow and Grimwig keeping their useless vigil: 'still the two gentlemen sat perseveringly, in the dark parlour, with the watch between them'.

Archibald Coolidge in his book *Dickens as a Serial Novelist* (1967) and Lance Schactele in '*Oliver Twist* and its Serial Predecessors' (1980) have suggested that Dickens solved the problem of the 'double perspective' (self-contained units in an overall design) more successfully than the writers of previous magazine serials. This is astonishing in view of his method of working. It was rare for Dickens to have more than the first few instalments of a work available when publication began and he was frequently only one instalment ahead of his readers. Even this 'instalment in hand' might be completed only a few days before the publication deadline. We know from the 'Letters' about a moment of panic

which came in a stationer's shop when he overheard a woman
enquiring for the latest number of *David Copperfield* which was
due to appear at the end of the month. Dickens, who had not yet
written a word of it commented: 'Once, and but once only in my
life, I was – frightened!'

John Butt and Kathleen Tillotson in their account of Dickens's
working routine (*Dickens at Work*, Methuen 1958) have shown
how he injected the necessary discipline into this hand-to-
mouth existence by the use of standardised formats. His single
sheets of manuscript, or 'slips', contained slightly more than
enough to fill one page of print. (In fact thirty slips equalled the
thirty-two pages of print in each monthly instalment, the
surplus words being removed at the proof stage.) Dickens knew
that on average he could complete two to three of these slips in a
day, working from nine in the morning until two in the afternoon; this meant that he could postpone the start of the next
part-issue or monthly serial instalment as late as the third or
fourth day after the previous one had appeared on sale. Allowing
for time for the actual printing this usually left him a bare
fortnight for writing the episode and drawing up instructions
for the illustrator. In the case of the shorter weekly instalments
the pace was much the same – he had a month's work or four
instalments in hand at any one time.

Clearly such a tight schedule was vulnerable to mishap. On
three occasions instalments of *Oliver* did not appear in the
Miscellany. In June 1837 Dickens stopped writing, probably
because of the death of Mary Hogarth, his sister-in-law. A gap
in October 1837 may have arisen from uncertainty or disagree-
ment over the form and length of the serial and subsequent
renegotiations with the publisher. In September 1838 the
reason may have been to delay completion of the serial so that
the three-volume edition (which was about to be published)
would maintain its sales.

Hand-to-mouth methods naturally made revision difficult,
since Dickens's stock of material was mostly in print at any one
time. However, they also allowed him to exploit to the full the
great advantage for the novelist of serial publication, the close
relationship between writer and readers and the ability of the
former to respond to the reception from the latter: what – in
terms of the communication model – has been called 'feedback'.

There were two significant indicators of reader response: the weekly or monthly sales figures for the instalment or periodical and the nineteenth-century equivalent of 'fan-mail' or the reverse. We know that Dickens responded to the latter by for instance altering a character in *David Copperfield* because the woman on whom she was based had written a letter of complaint. The most drastic response he made to poor sales figures was probably in the case of the part-issued *Martin Chuzzlewit* where the hero's departure for America and the enlargement of the character of Mrs Gamp were both successful devices for reviving interest. Serial publication had the potential to achieve what Thackeray described as 'communion between the writer and the public . . . something continual, confidential, something like personal affection'. (Tillotson p. 33) It partly overcame the weakness of the written word as against oral storytelling, the lack of immediate contact between narrator and listener. Dickens's own method of composition, in which each instalment was written only when required, allowed maximum intervention by the readers whom he could defer to or ignore as he wished. (Many of his public vainly begged him to reprieve Little Nell from her celebrated death.)

In his analysis of Dickens's serial methods (*Dickens as a Serial Novelist* Iowa State Press, 1967) Archibald Coolidge relates them to a need for *progression*, coupled with a desire to present a broad canvas, packed with detail and incident, but composed in a relatively short time, with little chance for prior planning. The need for progression is met by the use of a plot with multiple strands or 'lines'; the need for multiplicity of character and incident required of the bulky Victorian novel is met by the deployment of stock characters and situations.

If we analyse *Oliver Twist* in the form in which its first readers received it, divided into twenty-four episodes of two chapters each (three chapters in the case of those instalments which followed the breaks mentioned above) we can see how often the plot proceeded on two different levels. In instalment 11, for example, Chapters 23 and 24 take us back to Oliver's birthplace and reintroduce Mr Bumble while Chapter 25 continues with the account of Fagin's behaviour after the burglary. The instalment leaves the reader in a state of shocked curiosity on both counts – the significance of the gold locket stolen by Old

Sally in one case, the revelation that Oliver has been left behind after the burglary in the other. The next instalment opens with a chapter (Chapter 26) which follows Fagin after this news, and then reverts to the Bumble strand of the story with his hilarious wooing of Mrs Corney. The two 'curtains' in this instalment are the appearance of the ghostly shadow of the woman on the wall and the author's promise to return to the situation of Oliver – but not until the *next* instalment. Although not all episodes were multistranded in this way, there were enough to ensure that the reader became intrigued by or anxious about the characters on at least two different fronts.

Dickens was self-conscious about the use of this technique, as is shown by a famous passage of authorial comment at the beginning of Chapter 17. Although the passage is concerned with justifying an alternation of *mood*, from tragedy to comedy, this alternation also involved narrative – the switch from Fagin's den and Oliver's plight there to Oliver's birthplace and the hen-pecked Bumble:

> It is the custom on the stage, in all good murderous melo-dramas to present the tragic and the comic scenes, in as regular alternation as the layers of red and white in a side of streaky bacon. . . . As sudden shiftings of the scene and rapid changes of time and place, are not only sanctioned in books by long usage, but by many are considered as the great art of authorship: an author's skill in his craft being, by such critics, chiefly estimated with relation to the dilemmas in which he leaves his characters at the end of every chapter: this brief introduction to the present one may perhaps be deemed unnecessary. (Penguin edn, p. 168)

Dickens's justification for the sudden switch is that 'real life' is also prone to transitions 'from well-spread boards to death beds, and from mourning weeds to holiday garments'.

The use of climactic or cliff-hanging finales to chapters and of alternating plot-strands are two methods by which Dickens met the demands of serial publication for progression. In *Oliver* there are three main clusters of characters: Oliver himself, later joined by Mr Brownlow and later still by the Maylies; Fagin and his gang, including Sikes, Nancy and Monks; and Bumble and his wife and the inhabitants of the workhouse. Dickens switches the focus of the plot constantly between the three, which usually involves a change of locale as well. In order to help deal with the plethora of characters and situations which arise in his novels Dickens resorted to a third technique – identified by Archibald Coolidge – the employment of stock situations and stock characters. (Coolidge pp. 53–55)

It is not necessary to accept the whole of Coolidge's argument classifying all of Dickens's characters into a relatively small number of categories, to agree that there are family resemblances in the casts of many of the novels. Brownlow and Grimwig (benevolent plutocrats) are paralleled by Mr Pickwick, the Cheeryble brothers in *Nicholas Nickleby* and more distantly by John Jarndyce in *Bleak House*. The neglected orphan features in many novels – most tellingly of course as Dickens's autobiographical stand-in, David Copperfield – and so does the 'oppressed and brutally treated woman' for whom Nancy is an early model. Nevertheless Coolidge is at pains to point out that the systematic inventory he is able to draw up does not reduce Dickens to a mere manipulator of stereotypes; what makes the characters come alive for the reader, despite the fact that their *functions* are often similar, are the individual quirks which Dickens gives them, such as the gruff contrariness which seems to contradict Grimwig's nature as a benefactor.

Sometimes the demands of the serial format and Dickens's improvisatory approach to it left flaws and contradictions in the writing. Critics have attacked *Oliver Twist* for its implausible plot and the mechanical way in which it is resolved in the final chapters. Even if we ignore the extent to which Oliver himself simply disappears as a focus of interest in the latter half of the novel, there remains a lack of preparation for the conspiracy between Monks and Fagin to criminalise Oliver and the revelations about the significance of the gold locket and Oliver's true parentage. One critic has suggested[5] that these weaknesses reflect a basic change of course while the novel was actually being serialised. Originally it may have been planned as a short serial of half-a-dozen episodes, describing how the brutal treatment of Oliver in early life led him to crime and eventually to the gallows. (The novel's subtitle *The Parish Boy's Progress* seems to support this.) However, Dickens had a written agreement to supply his publisher, Bentley, with a complete new novel, specified as 'three volumes post octavo'; possibly accumulating pressure of work may have forced him to persuade Bentley to accept the expanded *Oliver* as a replacement. (He was already deep into *Barnaby Rudge*, described in the same agreement as 'three volumes of 320 pages each and 25 lines in each page'!)

Perhaps the need to expand *Oliver* to three-volume length, though not at first three-volume format, explains inconsistencies and deficiencies in what had started out as a much shorter production. There was obviously no chance of altering what had already been printed but when the three-volume version eventually appeared in 1838 Dickens took the opportunity to make revisions, some of which may have been intended to smooth out 'knots in the grain'.

These revisions also took into account the different readership expected for the three-volume novel which the libraries would stock for family readership as opposed to the more male-oriented *Miscellany*. It has already been shown how much power the libraries wielded in this area; the pressure on authors even when not writing specifically for three-volume publication is clear from Dickens's defensive preface to the third (1841) edition of *Oliver*, where he states explicitly that Nancy is a prostitute as contrasted with the text itself which only hinted at this even in the original serial version. In the same preface Dickens defends in the interests of factual accuracy the sordid aspects of his own novel in contrast to the romantic portrayal of crime which the 'Newgate novel' had popularised:

Here are no canterings on moonlit heaths, no merry-makings in the snuggest of all possible caverns, none of the attractions of dress, no embroidery, no lace, no jack-boots, no crimson coats and ruffles, none of the dash and freedom with which 'the road' has been time out of mind invested. The cold, wet, shelterless midnight streets of London; the foul and frowsty dens, where vice is closely packed and lacks the room to turn; the haunts of hunger and disease; the shabby rags that scarcely hold together; where are the attractions of these things? (Penguin edn, p. 34)

Yet even for Dickens such realism had limits when it came to the *speech* of the low-life characters. The revisions made for the three-volume version include the deletion of a large number of oaths, also from the speech of middle-class characters like Dr Losberne, and the removal of other language considered unsuitable for a family audience: for example the word 'mouth' was substituted for 'windpipe' in Fagin's threat quoted above. Despite all this the novel was regarded as still inappropriate for use in schools at the end of the century.

Oliver Twist: the Absent Hero

We might consider that the process of bowdlerisation and the constraints that underlay it affected only superficial details in Dickens's text. However, the deference to a particular readership had more wide-ranging repercussions. The novel is celebrated for the representation of cant, or criminal slang, and we know that in his revisions Dickens took pains to make this aspect more realistic and consistent as long as he did not think it would cause offence. Yet there is one glaring inconsistency. Although Oliver himself has been brought up in the workhouse since birth and spends a considerable time in the company of Fagin's gang, his language is always what Victorian readers would have regarded as acceptable – as bland and characterless as that of the Maylies and the other middle-class figures.

Oliver's invulnerability to the influence of his life companions robs the book of credibility for modern readers who have been educated to the significance of 'environment' as against 'heredity' in determining human characteristics. It is scientifically impossible that Oliver should have inherited middle-class speech patterns from his parents. Only slightly less implausible and more important to the theme is his moral behaviour – his ready reliance on prayer for example, his spontaneous charity towards Dick, his fellow orphan, his total imperviousness to the corruption of Fagin's den and even his risking his own safety in his priggish condemnation of Dodger and Charlie Bates.

Oliver's incorruptibility contrasts with the experience of the hero of another 'Newgate novel', Edward Bulwer's *Paul Clifford* who explicitly condemns social inequality for warping the lives of orphans like himself. The fact that Dickens failed to develop such a theme may be a sign of the conflict which he underwent in making Oliver both acceptable to his respectable middle-class readers and at the same time a convincing symbol of the ill-treatment of paupers which he tried to publicise in the early chapters.

Many critics have observed that a passive central character appears in most of Dickens's early novels and this character is generally a child. Like Little Nell, Paul Dombey and later on Little Dorrit and Jo the crossing-sweeper, Oliver Twist largely functions as the passive victim of malign social forces. In terms of plot, the technique of stimulating anxiety about a vulnerable character is one that Dickens may have picked up from the Gothic novelists, as Coolidge suggests. (p. 104 ff.) (It conforms with the Gothic imagery which is abundant in *Oliver* – for example the term 'merry old gentleman', a euphemism for the devil, which is used to refer to Fagin.)

However, Dickens's practice may have had deeper roots in his own life. Brought up in a lower-middle-class family, the son of a naval pay clerk, he suffered the most powerful experience of his early years – probably of his whole life – when his father was imprisoned for debt and he was sent off to work in the blacking factory. The trauma appears in his account to John Forster: 'My whole nature was so penetrated with the grief and humili-ation of such considerations, that even now, famous and caressed and happy, I often forget in my dreams that I have a dear wife and children, even that I am a man; and wander desolately back to that time of my life. (See Edgar Johnson *Charles Dickens: His Tragedy and Triumph* Penguin 1977 p. 33) For Dickens, who never in fact mentioned the episode to his wife and children, the nightmare lay not in the actual conditions of work, which were not harsh, but in the shame and degradation for him, a boy of middle-class though poverty-stricken parent-age in being forced to consort with the pauper boys who were the regular employees in the blacking factory. This aspect of social collision appears in his semi-fictional account of the experience in *David Copperfield*: 'Though perfectly familiar with them, my conduct and manners were different enough from theirs to place a space between us. They, and the men, always spoke of me as "the young gentleman".' It is not too fanciful perhaps to see a resemblance between the relationship among the boy-workers at the factory and Dickens (whose shame only lasted a few weeks) and that between the boys in Fagin's gang and young Oliver – even if we leave aside the ambiguous significance of the name of a boy who befriended the young Charles, one Bob Fagin. (See Stephen Marcus *Dickens from Pickwick to Dombey*, Chatto and Windus 1965, for one interpretation of this parallel.)

Concerning the long-term effects of the blacking factory episode, Edgar Johnson, one of Dickens's biographers, has said: 'Somewhere deep down inside, he made the decision that never again was he going to be so victimised'. (p. 41) It is not surprising that victimisation plays such a prominent part in Dickens's work or that he consciously regarded it as a tactic, writing to Wilkie Collins that something unjust could only be conveyed to the Victorian public by depicting a young girl victimised as a result. What should be clear now that we have a perspective on the nineteenth-century novel as a middle-class art form is how difficult it was for the portrayal of victimisation to be fully converted into social criticism. According to Terry Eagleton, Dickens belongs to that group of 'petty bourgeois' writers whose ambiguous intermediate position between the classes gave them unique insights into their society. In Dickens's case, his class location between the blacking factory and his childhood middle-class home with its books and their 'glorious host' of fictional characters gave him access to a rich range of experience. However, the pressure of his middle-class allegiances and those of his readers was to force an ambivalent presentation of Oliver's plight. In Eagleton's words: 'The novel argues at once that Oliver is and is not the product of bourgeois oppression, just as the "real world" of bourgeois social relations into which he is magically rescued is endorsed against the "unreal" under-world of poverty and crime, while simultaneously being shown up by that underworld as illusory.' (*Criticism and Ideology*, p. 128)

Oliver's 'magical rescue' is carried out by the middle-class philanthropists such as Brownlow and the Maylies, but the weakness in Dickens's case is that he fails to relate them explicitly to the equally middle-class 'philosophers' whose design and implementation of the Poor Law has made this rescue necessary. This evasion of the structural origins of social problems and the contradictions which it creates in the text was first noted by George Orwell, who pointed out that often the outcome of a Dickens novel turns on the benevolence of a 'good rich man', despite the fact that 'anyone who was so anxious to give his money away would never have acquired it in the first place'. ('Charles Dickens' in *Decline of the English Murder and other Essays* Penguin, 1965, p. 85) In the case of *Oliver Twist* the presence of this contradiction tends to shift our interest from Oliver, whose 'uncorrupted' character obviously cannot with credibility be presented to us too closely, and the Maylies, in whose pallid rural utopia we only half believe, to the active and vivid 'underworld' figures of Sikes, Nancy and Fagin; even the most conventional Victorian reader must have felt less absorbed in the convolutions of the plot surrounding the Leeford will than in the hounding and death of Sikes.

The reader feels for the murderer as he does later for the condemned Fagin that 'attraction of repulsion' which Dickens himself admitted he felt for their real life equivalents. John Lucas has pointed out (*The Melancholy Man*, Methuen 1970) that this sympathy is increased by our sense of the full weight of the vengeance of middle-class justice being visited on the Dodger and Fagin – in Fagin's case for crimes which did not attract the death penalty even in Dickens's day. This paradoxical emotion, which is easily powerful enough to overwhelm any residual interest we might have in the fate of Oliver, the nominal hero, may well have had its roots in the ambivalence of the young Dickens towards his protector, Bob Fagin, in the blacking factory. Steven Marcus has suggested that in the novel this protectiveness is transformed into the initial friendliness of the fictional Fagin, designed to inveigle Oliver into the criminal world in order to corrupt him. Just as young Charles felt his innate status as a 'young gentleman' threatened by the familiarity of the other boys, so Oliver's more material claim to the status (the inheritance) is directly threatened by his involvement in the gregarious life of Fagin's den.

Dickens's 'withdrawal of sympathy' from the victims of class conflict can be surmised from the structure of his work; that of Elizabeth Gaskell can also be traced in the publishing history of hers.

The Transformation of 'John Barton'

Elizabeth Gaskell's first novel, *Mary Barton*, provides a particularly striking example of the way in which the concerns of a nineteenth-century publisher, based in turn on an assessment of the expectations of readers in the late 1840s, were able to affect at a deep level the ability of an author to communicate through fiction. The summary which is included here can be fleshed out from Mrs Gaskell's own letters,[6] and Edgar Wright's book *Mrs Gaskell: The Basis for Re-assessment* (1965), which prints the first draft of the novel originally entitled 'John Barton'. (The draft is reprinted in the Penguin edition of *Mary Barton* as an appendix.)

In 1848, Elizabeth Gaskell, the wife of a Manchester Unitarian minister, was just beginning to involve herself in the literary world and her lack of experience must have made her vulnerable to pressure from publishers and editors. Her first full-length novel, which we now know as *Mary Barton*, is said to have been undertaken partly as a therapeutic exercise after the death in childhood of her only son, in 1848. She sent it (like the three stories she had previously published under the name of Cotton Mather Mills) to William Howitt, who passed it on to Edward Chapman of Chapman and Hall, Dickens's publishers at this time. The price of the copyright was agreed at £100 which Howitt advised her was highly acceptable for an 'unknown' writer. It was a fee, however, which she later considered forgoing in view of the influence which Chapman acquired over the final form of the text.

One concern of Chapman, who kept the manuscript for fourteen months before taking further action, was that the novel should be long enough to fill two volumes at least and not be forced into the despised one-volume format associated with cheap reprints. In response to the demand for more text Mrs Gaskell added what is now Chapter 37, which centres on the long debate between Carson, the mill-owner whose son was murdered by John Barton, and Job Legh, the old, self-educated working-man. The effect of this passage is to tone down the despondent mood of confrontation between mill-hands and their employers which is 'worked up' in the early part of the book and is given violent form by the murder of Harry Carson.

Job Legh is offered as a mediating figure who not only explains to Carson the roots of John Barton's hatred (without excusing it) but also proposes a quasi-religious act of reconciliation:

> If we saw the masters try for our sakes to find a remedy – even if they were long about it, – even if they could find no help, and at the end of all could only say, 'Poor fellows, our hearts are sore for ye; we've done all we could, and can't find a cure' – we'd bear up like men through bad times. No-one knows till they've tried, what power of bearing lies in them, if once they believe that men are caring for their sorrows and will help if they can. If fellow creatures can give nought but tears and brave words, we take our trials straight from God, and we know enough of his love to put ourselves blind into His Hands. (Penguin edn, p. 458)

The result is that Carson is slowly moved towards a change of heart. Although still considered, we are told, hard and unfeeling by those who do not know him, he is converted to the desire 'that a perfect understanding', and complete confidence and love, might exist between masters and men; that the truth might be recognised that the interests of one were the interests of all' (ibid. p. 460). So great is the weight of the author's endorsement for the position of Carson and Job Legh in this apparently supplementary chapter that the reader is left in no doubt that he or she should accept, like them, 'the Spirit of Christ as the regulating law between both parties'. (p. 460) The idea of Christian reconciliation at this stage in the novel complements Mrs Gaskell's condemnation in earlier chapters of the violent and sinister behaviour of John Barton and his radical trade-union friends.

The most important change between the manuscript and published versions of the novel was the shift of focus implied by the change of title (specifically asked for by the publisher) from *John Barton* to *Mary Barton*. At one level this merely reflects the current convention of using a woman's rather than a man's name in the title. But also, as the existing first draft shows, it is the result of a change of emphasis, the motive for which is not entirely certain, but which affected the ideological slant of the novel as well as the plot. It was not done without resistance, since we know Mrs Gaskell contemplated surrendering part of her copyright fee rather than make the changes. Edgar Wright, whose book *Mrs Gaskell: The Basis for Re-assessment*, OUP 1965, was the first to print the original draft for *Mary Barton*, comments: 'Between this rough sketch and the completed novel Mrs Gaskell laid the foundation for her command of technique.' (p. 268) But it could equally well be argued that in making the alterations she deferred to what she or her publisher regarded as acceptable to contemporary middle-class readers.

The draft implies that she was originally thinking in terms of a three-volume novel since it is divided explicitly in this way, though it seems to incorporate *less* material than eventually went into the *two*-volume edition. Since, as we have seen, three-volume novels were felt to carry most prestige, the omission of certain items from the original plan seems to point to ideological rather than commercial factors at work. As the change of title suggests, the original concentrated much more on the character of the murderer – here called 'Wilson' not 'Barton'. In addition there are these major differences:

(1) The mill-owner not his son is the victim of the murder.
(2) In the draft Job Legh is instrumental in introducing 'Wilson' (i.e. Barton) to a Chartist club (whereas in the final version Job keeps aloof from politics, so retaining his value as a mediating figure).
(3) The episode of the chase to Liverpool, the character of William Wilson, and the whole 'cliffhanging' atmosphere of the second half of the published version are only hinted at in the draft, in the one line: 'How she proved an alibi with Margaret Clegg's help.'

All three changes drastically affect our reception of the novel. The first one, by leaving the mill-owner alive, allows him to repent, as a representative of the employers, the behaviour towards his workers that led indirectly to his son's death; the result is the dominance of the theme of reconciliation at the end. The second change, by inserting into the story a 'neutral', non-revolutionary working-class character, whose energy is diverted into natural history rather than Chartism, makes that reconciliation easier to stage-manage. The third change, the expansion of the purely sensational element of the plot, is the obverse of the other two. The published version shifts attention from John Barton (who virtually disappears from the narrative between Chapters 17 and 35) despite the fact that the author had once claimed: 'Round the character of John Barton all the others formed themselves; he was my hero, *the* person with whom all my sympathies went.' (*Letters* ed. Chapple and Pollard, Letter 42, p. 74) As a result the element of adventure and suspense needed to be pumped up in the later chapters to distract from and replace the insoluble conflict between mill-owners and workers dramatised by the murder of 'Chadwick' (as he is called in the draft).

Some critics have seen in these changes the operation of a self-censorship rather than explicit recommendations from the publisher – though either would clearly derive from some concept of what readers would tolerate. One aspect of the novel that may throw light on this is the treatment of dialect. We have seen that in *Oliver* Dickens was unprepared to use dialect for the main sympathetic characters, notably Oliver himself; Mrs Gaskell on the other hand has been praised for the confidence with which dialect is handled in *Mary Barton* almost from the first page. She regarded this, however, as a practice needing justification as is shown by her inclusion of two lectures on dialect in the 1854 edition, and by the footnotes in the text which not only *explain* the words used but relate them to Anglo-Saxon originals, that is legitimate them by reference to the history of the standard language. Moreover, although dialect speech is put into the mouths of the Wilsons and Bartons generally, it is, in the words of Edgar Wright, 'symbolic' rather than true dialect since 'the complex sentence construction, carefully-placed adjectives and general balance are those of written and practised prose'; he points out that where dialect words and phrases appear, it is in an unsystematic fashion, for example 'could not' and 'could na' appear in the same speech. Mary Barton herself, as befits the conventional romantic heroine, shows almost as few traces of dialect in her speech as Oliver. Her words in the trial scene, for example, contain no non-standard syntax and only one or two non-standard expressions, such as 'I'd a deal to bear'. Wright comments: 'The heroine at an emotional climax needs dignity of expression as well as dignity of emotion. So does the repentant and dying Barton.'

It is important to remember that the correlation between dignity and 'educated' speech would have been uppermost in the expectations of Mrs Gaskell's original readership. This readership would undoubtedly have been disturbed by any other ending to the novel more radical than the one which incorporates an ideology of reconciliation through 'the Spirit of Christ' and the convenient resolution of the Bartons' problems through their emigration to Canada. It was an ideology which was characteristic of the faith of Unitarians, for whom Wright says 'religion is regarded as a conciliating and stabilising force, teaching acquiescence and patient endurance, as well as a sense of human rights.' (p. 28) In the light of this there may be some validity in David Musselwhite's idea that the very names 'Carson' and 'Barton', which are more similar phonetically than the 'Wilson' and 'Chadwick' of the draft version, symbolise the emphasis on a common interest between masters and men, implied by the published text. It is probably unnecessary to support Musselwhite's rather far-fetched idea that in omitting the 'I' from the name of Job Legh (Job Leigh in the original draft) 'Mrs Gaskell has shut herself out of her work';[7] there is no need to consider evidence on unconscious suppression, when it is clear that the interaction of author, publisher and readers, in which Mrs Gaskell had a relatively inexperienced role, provided little room for manoeuvre in the revolutionary atmosphere of 1848.

6. The Novelist on the Margins: Hardy and Lawrence

The last years of Queen Victoria's reign saw the end of the three-decker novel which had served British fiction as a standard since Scott and with it the collapse of the dominance of the circulating library system. By the 1890s pressures which had been steadily gathering strength through the century combined to effect a literary and publishing upheaval which has had consequences lasting up to the present day. Before looking in detail at the work of Hardy and Lawrence for evidence of these changes this chapter gives an overview of the factors which brought them about: social context, readership, literary or institutional context and authors.

Social Context

Under the unifying symbol of the 'old Queen' late-nineteenth-century Britain had settled into some sort of stability in class terms. This does not mean that there were no political, social or industrial conflicts but that the thrust with which the middle classes had sought to displace the old aristocracy of land from the main centres of power – economic, administrative, legislative and cultural – had ended in almost total victory. On the other hand the threat of unrest from below which had seemed to these same middle clases so real in the Chartist agitations of Mrs Gaskell's time was now dissipated. In Hobsbawm's words, the Reform Act of 1867, which brought about a drastic extension of the franchise, was accepted by the middle class 'because they no longer regarded the British working class as revolutionary

. . . they now saw it as divided into a politically moderate aristocracy of labour, ready to accept capitalism and a politically ineffective, because unorganised and leaderless, proletarian plebs, which presented no major danger.' (*Industry and Empire*, Penguin 1969 p. 126) One aspect of the 'acceptance' of capitalism was a process of subordination to middle-class 'hegemony' as represented by cultural norms. The urban working class was offered the benefit of cultural assimilation – if only as a means of securing a docile workforce. (Introducing his 1870 Education Bill in Parliament, William Forster commented: 'On the speedy provision of elementary education depends our industrial prosperity . . . if we leave our work folk any longer unskilled . . . they will become overmatched in the competition of the world.') Two factors in this process are especially relevant here; the development of universal elementary education and the growth of the popular – or more accurately, mass – press. Although the second of these may not be as clearly a result of the first as was once thought, they can be seen as joint influences in assimilating the majority of the population to the dominant 'print culture'.

Richard Altick has commented that the 1871 Education Act did not lead to a revolutionary jump in education or even literacy but merely consolidated a movement which had been gathering force for most of the century. The percentage gain in literacy ten years after the Act was 7.9 per cent as opposed to 10.5 per cent for the ten preceding years. (Altick, pp. 171–172). Nevertheless after 1871 nothing would ever be quite the same again as every child was pushed through the reading and writing mill, though with varying success. Despite the sterility of much of the education provided and the methods employed, which were satirised in novels from *Hard Times* onwards, the development of ability to handle the written word among the population proceeded apace. One by-product of this was the increasing use of English literature (first poetry, but later prose) as matter for practice and assessment in the schools. Newspaper circulations also rose rapidly after 1871 and particularly in the 1890s: the invention of steam printing (later electrically-powered printing) greatly increased the capacity of the newspaper presses, while the abolition of the newspaper Advertisement Tax in 1855 and of the Paper Tax in 1861 helped to bring down the cover price of each issue, so that by the end of the century the penny newspaper (the *Daily Telegraph*, first published in 1856 at this price) and then the halfpenny daily (the *Daily Mail*, launched by Lord Northcliffe in 1896) became a possibility. The success of the *Mail* doubled the size of the newspaper-buying public between 1896 and 1906; between the beginning and end of the nineteenth century the total daily sales of all newspapers rose from about 5,000 a day to over a million.

Raymond Williams lists the three 'transforming factors' which created this mass press out of an older popular tradition as: the vast improvement in productive and distributive methods caused by industrialisation; the social chaos and the widening franchise, caused by industrialisation and the struggle for democracy; and the institution, as a basis for financing newspapers, of a kind of advertising made necessary by a new kind of economic organisation, and a differently organised public. (See *The Long Revolution* Penguin 1965, p. 200) Although he omits rising literacy (pointing out that as early as 1850 there were enough readers available to support a large-circulation newspaper) both Alfred, Lord Northcliffe and George Newnes (the founder of the magazine *Tit-Bits*) referred to their intention of reaching the new 'market' educated in the post-1870 Board schools. Newnes's cynicism, particularly about the attention span of his potential readers, is well captured in the words of the character Whelpdale who represents him in George Gissing's novel *New Grub Street* (1891):

> I would have the paper address itself to the quarter-educated; that is to say, the great new generation that is being turned out by the Board schools, the young men and women who can just read, but are incapable of sustained attention. People of this kind want something to occupy them in trains, and on 'buses and trams. . . . Everything must be very short, two inches at the utmost; their attention can't sustain itself beyond two inches. Even chat is too solid for them; they want chit-chat. (Penguin edn, p. 496)

We could therefore perhaps regard the 1870 Act as symbolic in that it suggested to publishers, editors and writers a large change in the market and increased their efforts to reach this new readership. Indeed Leavis and his followers see this sort of cynical appeal to 'the lowest common denominator' as the start of a process of simplification, stereotyping and standardisation of responses which they claim characterises reading matter (and contaminates fiction) in the twentieth century. The importance of fiction as an ingredient in the new reading matter is shown by the success of *Tit-Bits* in offering a prize of £1,000 for an original short story in 1881 and receiving 20,000 entries.

Williams, however, argues against blaming literary debasement on the mass media, regarding the new popular press as doing no more than satisfying appetites that were once met by other means: 'A number of tastes which would formerly have been gratified in pre-literate and therefore largely unrecorded ways are now catered for and even fostered in print.' (*Culture and Society*, Penguin 1961, p. 298) The least disputable statement about the process seems to be that as literacy and education rose, reading matter expanded to meet a demand, but in some cases this only involved the supplanting of older forms (such as very cheap fiction reprints) by new, such as cheaper newspapers and penny magazines. There can be no denying, however, that the mass press had a part to play in spreading the habit of reading fiction; like many contemporary novels *Tess of the d'Urbervilles* was first published in a newspaper as was D. H. Lawrence's first short story – earlier in the century magazines would have filled the same role – and the practice of syndicating fiction became common by the 1890s.

Readers

The rise in the literacy rate during the century, from 67.3 per cent in 1841 for males to 97.2 per cent in 1900; from 51.1 per cent in 1841 for females to 96.8 per cent in 1900) would obviously have made potential readers of the social groups who previously had no access to literature. However, it did not automatically provide these working-class readers with the income to spend on books or even library subscriptions. It is therefore worth asking two questions about this theoretical expansion of the reading public: to what extent was it interested in fiction, as opposed to the more utilitarian functions of reading, and how were the needs of these readers for fiction likely to be met within their available income?

Louis James in *Fiction for the Working Man* (1963) argues that efforts to cater specifically for the working classes go back to the beginning of the nineteenth century, if not before. In 1820 John Linbird's *The Mirror of Literature, Amusement and Instruction* was published at twopence (2d.). The readership to whom it appealed can be gauged from its price and the fact that it had to be sold by such agents as a shoemaker in Manchester or a tinman in Cornwall because bookshops refused to stock it – though it sold 150,000 copies in the first edition. As cheaper paper and mechanical printing methods brought down production costs and the advance of literacy enlarged the market publishers increasingly turned to providing fiction for the poorer social groups. This tendency became especially pronounced after the great outburst of working-class radicalism in the 1840s had subsided. James is careful to stress that the failure of the latter is not to be blamed on the former. However, it is possible that the opposite may be true: the disappointment of working-class political aspirations and the waning influence of the 'radical' press may have meant that an appetite for reading news and political opinion was diverted into one for cheap fiction. (The historian Gareth Stedman Jones has argued that the success of the music hall can be explained in this way.[1])

The need for low prices meant that publishers were hard pressed to provide *original* material for this market. At first they reprinted eighteenth-century novels, but the move to magazine publications gave them a chance to commission original work: as serials or short stories. By carefully targeting a working-class readership the publisher was able to maximise his audience and make a profit even at a very low price, just as a tabloid newspaper publisher does today. James quotes surveys from the 1840s which show that of the eighty cheap periodicals circulating in London, twenty-two contained nothing but romances and stories and in the next ten years no less than fifty publishers were involved in serving this market, in many cases through penny-publications alone. (*Fiction for the Working Man*, p. 31) By the 1890s Agnes Repplier was suggesting that the readership for 'penny-fiction' was over seven million (mostly women, it is now thought, though James does not address this question despite the title of his book!). At these prices it is not difficult to explain the poor quality of most of this fiction; writers were often paid by the page and included plenty of space-filling dialogue to expand their earnings. (See Victor Neuburg: *Popular Literature, A History and Guide*, Penguin 1977, p. 224.)

The barrier of price could also be overcome by part-publication, in the form of the penny-number, the 'downmarket' equivalent of the shilling-number in which Dickens first made his mark. This was the format in which G. M. Reynold's notorious and sensational *Mysteries of London* caused such an impact in 1845; alternatively it could be bought in monthly rather than weekly parts, at sixpence. Reynolds, a supporter of the Chartists, clearly thought of his readership as working class; he addressed a weekly article in his magazine *Reynolds' Miscellany* to 'the industrial classes' and included explicit social comment in his fiction. However, low prices were not the only distinguishing feature of working-class reading matter. Although Dickens was never as universally popular as was once thought his fame did encourage publishers to try to extend his appeal to a wider market. Often this took the form of quite cynical plagiarisms; *Pickwick Papers* appeared in various bastardised forms: plays, illustrated sheets, sequels and penny-editions in which the common element was not the narrative but regurgitations of the main characters who were seen as almost being 'common property'.

The most interesting aspect of these plagiarisms, which sold enormous numbers at very low prices – *The Penny Pickwick* boasted a circulation of 50,000 a week – was the way in which they were adapted to a working-class readership unfamiliar with the authentic version. For example the plagiarist 'Bos' turned Pickwick from an innocent into a pompous eccentric and made his valet Sam Weller into the true hero; in his adaptation of *Oliver Twist* Fagin is given an eloquent plea for social justice: 'If the wealthy of the land choose to lay claim to those things that are intended as much for the use of the poor man as for the rich one, we cannot be much surprised that men are to be found who will resist the laws that have been made for the purpose of depriving them of their share of the gifts of heaven.' (*Fiction for the Working Man*, p. 70)

The market testing for this sort of material could be quite specific. One publisher of Dickens imitations commented: 'Our publications circulate among a class so different in education and social position from the readers of the three-volume novels that we sometimes distrust our own judgement and place the manuscript in the hands of an illiterate person – a servant, or machine boy, for instance. If they pronounce favourably on it, we think it will do.' (Neuburg p. 172) It is interesting to note the purely *relative* use of 'illiterate' in this context.

Most of the volume-length fiction which the working class could afford was reprinted versions of works from which the libraries no longer expected a profit. The reprinting of Dickens (as opposed to the plagiarisation of his novels) became almost a minor industry in itself. As well as pirated reprints, there were legal ones made possible when the original publisher sold the copyright of a novel, which he had originally bought from the author. There was also some new fiction available in volumes at low prices, such as William Milner's New Novelists' Library, and the so-called 'railway novels'. By the end of the century paper-covered 'penny novels' had begun to appear; they sold largely to women readers, consisted of simple plots and well-defined characters and emphasised the ultimate triumph of virtue over vice. Of these nineteenth-century equivalents of Mills and Boon, Victor Neuburg, a historian of popular literature, has remarked: 'the dividing line between a paper-covered book and a periodical becomes blurred.' (See *Popular Literature: A History and Guide*, p. 230) The end of the three-volume novel and its replacement by 6s. (30p) single volume novels may have brought new serious fiction of a good standard within the price range available to a few working-class readers. Darko Suvin rejects Altick's notion that by the end of the century 'most readers could afford a freshly-published novel' but nevertheless mentions H. G. Wells's *The Time Machine* (1895) as one work that might have appealed to the more literate working-class reader and even been within his financial reach. (Suvin p. 22) How this happened can now be examined.

The Downfall of the Three-decker

In 1894 publishers brought out 184 novels in three-volume

format at the standard price of 31s. 6d., in 1897 only 4. This dramatic decline is a fascinating illustration of how a cultural form changes as a result of a number of interacting factors – in this case economic pressure from publishers exerted on a resistant library system, coinciding with a new artistic impulse which found an eloquent champion.

In 1852 Gladstone had attacked the high price of fiction in Parliament. In his evidence to the Royal Commission on Copyright Matthew Arnold accused the lending libraries of conspiring to keep good books dear: 'The three-shilling book is our great want.' (Altick p. 309) The premium which the system put on length was recognised as discouraging rather than promoting quality. Reardon, the novelist hero of Gissing's *New Grub Street*, a mine of information about literary practices of the 1880s and 1890s, is shown resorting to the usual solution:

> Description of locality, deliberate analysis of character or motive demanded far too great an effort for his present condition. He kept as much as possible to dialogue; the space is filled so much more quickly, and at a pinch one can make people talk about the paltriest incidents of life. (Penguin edn, p. 154)

As Reardon saw it the crucial issue was that in the absence of a system of royalties the author had to sell his copyright outright to the publisher in order to survive:

> An author of moderate repute may live on a yearly three-volume novel – I mean the man who is obliged to sell his book out and out, and who gets from one to two hundred pounds for it. But he would have to produce four one-volume novels to obtain the same income; and I doubt whether he could get so many published within the twelve months.' (p. 236)

The 1860 Royal Commission on Copyright did nothing to affect this practice, however. Three-deckers remained attractive to authors and lending libraries; meanwhile the publishers (who owned the copyrights) still had the option of bringing out cheap reprints of novels which had been successful and for which they often did not have to pay the writer a penny. Despite publishers' lipservice to the library system these reprints multiplied as the century advanced and the interval between the three-volume edition and the single-volume 6s. reprint grew shorter and shorter. The lending libraries began to be threatened economically by this practice at the same time as the spread of free public libraries reduced their potential custom.

By the 1880s dissatisfaction with the selectiveness and prudery of the libraries had found a spokesman. The Irish-born novelist George Moore made Mudie his target in his championship of the French novelist Zola: 'At the head . . . of English literature sits a tradesman who considers himself qualified to decide the most delicate artistic questions that may be raised, and who crushes out of sight any artistic aspiration he may deem pernicious.' (Griest p. 149) Henry Vizetelly, who was to be imprisoned in 1888 for publishing Zola's allegedly obscene *La Terre*, issued Moore's novel *A Mummer's Wife* as a single-volume novel in 1885 and this format became a way of evading the censorship of the libraries (who were interested only in three-deckers). Meanwhile a series of *Times* leaders attacked the libraries for encouraging a superficial attitude towards reading and one- and two-volume first editions started to appear in increasing numbers. In the light of Mudie's complaint that 'not one in twelve of the three-volume novels pays its way' it is not surprising that libraries started to resist buying novels at a high nominal cost per volume when no one else was expected to.

In 1894 the libraries banded together to try to get publishers to agree to two conditions: that they would not be asked to pay more than 4s. a volume for fiction and that no reprints would be issued until at least twelve months after the publication of the three-volume 'library' edition. Some publishers had already decided, however, that they could manage without libraries; in July 1894 William Heinemann announced the publication of a single-volume novel, *The Manxman*, by the very popular novelist Hall Caine, with the warning that there would be no three-volume edition of this work. As *The Manxman* sold at 6s. the libraries would have had to pay 2s. more than their new top price per volume to get it and would only be able to circulate one volume at a time instead of three. In retaliation for this blatant breach of the understanding between publishers and libraries, Mudie refused to purchase at the full price copies of *Sons of Fire*, the latest novel of another popular author, Mrs Braddon.

Sons of Fire, Mrs Braddon's forty-eighth novel, was her last in three-decker form. Over the next few years there was a sudden collapse in the number of such novels offered to libraries; by 1898 the 'triple-headed monster' which had tyrannised Victorian fiction was as dead as the dinosaur (which it resembled in size and sometimes in intellect). Although the libraries were freed of their obligation to buy their stock at inflated prices the death of the three-decker knocked the props from under a system which depended on institutions lending high-priced books rather than individuals buying them. The decline of the libraries can be dated from this point although the 'snob' value of subscribing to a commercial library rather than the new free public libraries allowed them to cling on until well into the next century.

For the reader the benefit was that 'the whole price structure was revised downward' (Altick, p. 313) so that after 1894 first editions sold at 5s. or 6s. while reprints were available at 2s. 6d. or 3s. 6d. and works out of copyright for as little as 3d. Prices might have fallen further still but for the Net Book Agreement of 1899 under which bookshops and other retailers agreed not to give a discount on any book priced at 6s. or more. (By this time competition had reached the point where copies of Dickens were given away with packets of tea.) As a result for fifty years the price of new fiction stabilised around the figure of 6s.–7s. 6d. and during the twentieth century has consistently stood at about 10 per cent of the average weekly wage. Is it therefore true to say that the end of the three-decker led to a massive expansion in the fiction market?

Certainly the number of *titles* increased massively from 381 in 1880 to 1,825 in 1899. Some of these new single-volume novels also had very large sales; for example Marie Corelli's *The Master Christian* (1900) had a pre-publication printing of 75,000 copies.[2] If this looks huge compared with the sales of the average three-decker (about 600 copies bought by the libraries) it should be remembered that in 1894 the Authors' Society estimated that the libraries had 60,000 subscribers – many of course being households. Nevertheless it is very likely that the new low price structure combined with the impact of greater literacy meant there were many more readers even for the better quality original fiction.

What seems indisputable is that the end of the three-decker encouraged the writing and publishing of a new type of novel, more flexible in length and subject matter. Whereas the average length of the three-deckers (Henry James's 'loose and baggy monsters') was 150,000 to 200,000 words, a more 'modern' length was 70,000 to 80,000. Whereas the puritanism of Mudie and Smith had given priority to protecting 'the young person', publishers were now free to bring out more adventurous work. One aspect of the new shorter length requirement was the abridgment of existing three-deckers, such as Rider Haggard's *She* which sold 500,000 copies in the shorter version.

In 1913 Holbrook Jackson tartly commented on the end of the three-decker: 'Actually it was the capitulation of a type of novel: the old sentimental lending-library type novel of polite romantic atmosphere which was guaranteed to tax no brain by thought and to vex no code of morals by revolutionary sugges- tions' (quoted in Malcolm Bradbury *The Social Context of Modern English Literature*, Basil Blackwell 1971, p. 208).

New Modes of Consumption

Even without the 'three-decker crisis' of 1894 Mudie and his fellow proprietors would have found the climate more wintry in the face of competition from the new free public libraries. These institutions, open to all and open outside working hours, were made possible by an Act of 1850 which empowered local authorities to raise a rate of one (old) halfpenny to purchase or erect premises for them. (The argument that carried the day in Parliament was that libraries offered a road to working-class self-improvement which was an insurance against the attrac- tions of movements like Chartism.) However, few special rates were actually levied in the earlier years and even by 1896 forty- six authorities, including some big ones like Glasgow, were without public libraries. In many places the gaps were filled by the philanthropy of the American millionaire, Andrew Carnegie.

Given the emphasis on edification with which the 1850 Act

was promoted, it is not surprising that there were reservations
about the libraries' justification in stocking fiction. Nevertheless
in industrial centres, especially, 'fiction on the rates' was in
such demand that in Sheffield in 1856–67 it comprised half the
total of books circulated. Librarians split between those who
wanted to give the public what they demanded and those who
wanted to provide what was felt to be good for them. It was
pointed out that even 'penny dreadfuls' could inculcate a taste
for reading and by the 1890s libraries had yielded so much to
demand that between 65 and 90 per cent of their borrowings
were fiction. Although a certain prejudice against novels remained – until the 1950s many libraries issued one 'fiction' and
one 'non-fiction' ticket – there was clearly here a new force in
distribution, less censorious than Mudie, although public libraries also had their Mrs Grundys, and less prone to vacillations
in popular taste. By the 1970s three-quarters of book loans were
fiction and libraries would typically buy 1,200 of a printing of
1,500 for a new novel.[3]

Who were these new borrowers? The middle classes were still
liable to regard the libraries as charitable institutions, beneath
their dignity, and figures from Bristol in 1891 show 'artisans' as
the largest single group who read books on the premises and
'assistants' (from shops?) the largest group who took them
away to read at home. (Altick, p. 236) Even if these proportions
do not reflect the actual numbers from these groups in the
community (and Altick suggests only 3 to 8 per cent of the
population of a given town were active borrowers), it is surely
an indication that among the lower middle classes – the huge
army of clerks and shop-keepers of Victorian England – and the
better educated working classes there was now an avenue to
fiction other than the penny novelette.

A second incentive to reading fiction was its inclusion on
school syllabi. This was less important for the working class,
since at the level of elementary education which was the only
one attained by most poor children, the methods of teaching
reading were so mechanical they probably discouraged any
spontaneous interest in literature. In his school inspector's
report of 1860 Matthew Arnold commented that the 'literary
selections' used for reading practice in these schools consisted
of 'the writing of second or third rate authors, feeble, incorrect

and colourless.' (Altick, p. 159) However, in 1883 a new stipulation empowered inspectors to hear children read from 'such works as *Robinson Crusoe*, Voyages and Travels or Biographies of eminent men' and publishers started to bring out school editions, though at first these were largely selections of poetry. By 1871 English Literature was given a separate place in the syllabus, though examination of it mostly consisted of testing the power of pupils to memorise sheaves of verse.

In the secondary and grammar schools the largely middle-class pupils were increasingly given a diet of English 'classics' instead of the Latin and Greek authors who had been the staple of education up to this time. A commentator in 1867 remarked that: 'In schools where pupils are not destined to proceed from there to University, or to a life of studious leisure and opportunity, English should, I think, be made the prominent linguistic and literary study.' Some impetus came from the inclusion of 'English Literature' in examinations such as that for the Indian Civil Service, where it was instituted as early as 1855. By 1875 boys leaving secondary school could choose between seventeen different exams, most featuring an English Literature component, though this was often a test of factual knowledge rather than literary critical skill. Imaginative writing in English therefore became accepted as subject matter by the 1880s and 1890s, though it was some time before it was taught as a humane subject rather than a compendium of facts or as a vehicle for absorbing grammar. (A witness to the Taunton Commission on secondary education of 1868 had recommended: 'The classical English writers should be read in class, sentences analysed, synonyms distinguished . . . and compositions written in imitation of particular writers.')

At the higher education level the principal factors which ensured the study of English Literature a permanent place were the needs of vocations such as elementary school teaching – English was included in the examinations for teachers in 1862, although for them as for their pupils the emphasis was on rote learning – the spread of the education movement for adults – Henry Morley of the Working Men's College was probably the first full-time academic in English Literature – and finally the needs or presumed needs of women students. Not only did women dominate the new profession of elementary school teaching, but it was felt in many quarters that English Literature enshrined values which women were expected as mothers to pass on to their children. In his inaugural lecture as Professor of English at Queen's College, London Charles Kingsley told his audience that reading English literature would produce an understanding of the 'English spirit' which would counter the tendency to national degeneration ('the minds of young women are becoming un-English'). Even when English Honours degree courses were established, not without a struggle at the traditional universities, the appeal was at first largely to female students: for example at Oxford from 1873 onwards. In Eagleton's words, degree-level English Literature was regarded as 'an untaxing sort of affair, concerned with finer feelings rather than with the *bona fide* academic "disciplines", it seemed a convenient sort of non-subject to palm off on the ladies.' (*Literary Theory: An Introduction*, Blackwell 1983, p. 28) The 'social mission' of English, as Chris Baldick has called it, only came into full flower after the First World War, when I. A. Richards and F. R. Leavis transformed university English from a dilettante subject to a discipline which claimed to embody the deepest moral values through a personal response to prose, poetry and drama.[4]

Authors

Eagleton has suggested that the leading novelists of the early and mid nineteenth century came from the 'petit bourgeoisie', the lower middle and professional class, which gave them a 'privileged' position from which to examine the society dominated by the upper middle class. He instances George Eliot (daughter of a land agent), Dickens (son of a naval pay clerk) and the Brontë sisters (daughters of a country clergyman). (*Criticism and Ideology*, p. 125) This pattern was still strong at the end of the century: Gissing's father was a chemist, Bennett's a solicitor and H. G. Wells's a small shopkeeper. Most of these writers were reasonably comfortably off but few of them came from the upper gentry – compare the poets Shelley and Byron – or from the class of the captains of industry. In general it seems to have been the pattern of Richardson rather than Fielding which prevailed. Can this subjective assessment be supported by any statistical evidence and did it change in the course of the century or afterwards?

It is staggeringly difficult to generalise about the social origins or status of writers. Diana Laurenson has pointed out that this is reflected in the classification of the Registrar-General which in 1961 demoted writers from Social Class I – where they were placed alongside the other professions – to Social Class II along with actors and musicians. Should we categorise novelists by their parents' employment, or by their own, since many had other full-time jobs? In the case of women writers, is their husband's profession relevant? It certainly was to the publishers Chapman and Hall who dealt with Mrs Gaskell through her husband. The first systematic attempt to classify writers by social origin was made by Raymond Williams; in *The Long Revolution* (1961) (pp. 254–269) he examines the origins of 350 writers, including poets and dramatists, as well as novelists, born between 1480 and 1930. The question of selection is clearly crucial. Sticking to the 'great names' can be subjective and unrepresentative, but there is no possibility of including everyone who set pen to paper. Williams compromised by drawing names from the *Oxford Introduction to English Literature* and using the *Dictionary of National Biography* as evidence of their background. He groups the names into periods by taking the year in which the writer was aged ten ('a crucial age in one of the decisive factors – education'). In the earlier periods this produces some very low numbers and even in the nineteenth century there is a danger they may be too small to be meaningful.

To summarise Williams's conclusions by period.

1730–1830: the largest group of writers come from professional families (25 out of 57); 13 are from the families of tradesmen and craftsmen, 8 from the gentry and one from the nobility.
1830–80: 'the dominant impression is of a more highly organised upper-middle class making the major contribution'. Out of 53 writers, 44 come from the merchant class, professional class or gentry ('now commonly closely related') and only 9 from the tradesman and craftsman class. Williams comments: 'this is a notably less varied social origin, to the

disadvantage of poorer groups, than in the earlier part of the nineteenth century.'

1880–1930: 'the pattern is basically similar to that of the previous period'; i.e. only one writer from the nobility, 39 out of 53 from the gentry, merchant and professional class and 13 from tradesmen and craftsmen, farmers and labourers.

There are clearly arbitrary factors at work in Williams's classifications, for example in the placing of 'professionals', which later research has shown to be the most important group. The most interesting of Williams's observations is that in the late nineteenth and early twentieth centuries English literature sought revitalisation from 'outsiders' such as, among novelists, the Pole, Joseph Conrad, the American, Henry James, and the Irishman, James Joyce. He claims:

> already in the nineteenth century there were signs of a break, with individuals deviating from the majority patterns, and, by the end of the century, a distinct and organised minority deviation. The social situation of literature in the twentieth century has been largely the interaction of continuing minority patterns, with an increasingly standard route into them, and this marked dissenting minority, which has tended to support and value writers from outside the majority pattern, and to provide an alternative outlet and affiliation for dissenting members of the minority groups. (p. 266)

In his list of writers from the 'dissenting minority' Williams includes both Hardy and Lawrence, though whether because of their class or their regional affiliation is not made clear.

Williams's pioneering study was followed by Richard Altick, who in 1962 attempted a more comprehensive survey,[5] which looked at the origins of 1,100 British authors ('all but the lowest stratum of hacks') active in the period between 1800 and 1935. Altick's most significant conclusion is that the highest proportion of writers (who again are not divided into novelists, poets and playwrights) originate from what he calls 'the professional and artistic grades of the middle class' – with the children of clergymen outnumbering those of every other single profession. He comments: 'Literary ambitions, it appears, were more likely to be nurtured in a social group traditionally favourable to literature than one – such as the commercial class – whose members had only recently begun to have books about them.' ('The Sociology of Authorship' *Bulletin of the New York Public Library* LXVI vi June 1962, p. 395)

In terms of change over the period Altick's evidence seems to support Williams's that during the century the small percentage of working-class writers declined but recovered in the first half of this century. Unfortunately these figures are too small to be significant in showing change and are further confused by the fact that Altick (perhaps working on American assumptions) includes the children of artisans (i.e. craftsmen) among the 'middle class'. If we reassign this group, then the percentage of working-class writers over the four subperiods are: 6.8, 4.7, 4.8 and 6.6 per cent. This shows a perceptible but not very significant dip in the middle period (1835–1900).

Diana Laurenson's short article 'A sociological study of authorship' (*British Journal of Sociology* 20, 1969) is confined to the period 1860–1910 but has the merit from our point of view of including only prose writers. Out of the 128 male writers, 56 were novelists, and out of 44 women, 33 were fiction writers. Like Altick she finds in her sample an overwhelming predominance of middle-class authors; within this group there is a majority of children from professional and artistic households, and the biggest percentage by far of these are the children of clergymen. She concludes: 'the predominance of homes where intellectual training necessitated books, and some sophistication in the discussion of ideas, where immediate money-making was not the prime consideration, is not surprising.' (p. 515) The percentage of writers from the upper classes over this period is by contrast 5.6 per cent of men and 13.6 per cent of women; for the working classes it is 6.3 and 4.5 per cent respectively. Even the lower-middle classes (the shopkeepers and small traders) contributed only 6.3 per cent of male writers and 9.1 per cent of female. By comparison the percentage from professional households is a massive 63.7 per cent for men and 19.2½ per cent for women. (The discrepancy with respect to sex perhaps deserves more study.)

On this evidence there seems to be a lot of truth in the stereotype of the writer suggested by Malcolm Bradbury: 'His parents would come from various levels of the professional middle classes; his father is likely to be a surgeon or doctor, a lawyer or solicitor, a clergyman or a dissenting minister, a merchant or a businessman, a schoolmaster in a private or a state school, a civil servant or an army officer.' (*The Social Context of Modern English Literature*, p. 139) It is possible such a pattern can be reconciled to Eagleton's ideas of the 'petit bourgeois' origins of the leading Victorian novelists, though there are obvious exceptions to both. It is another question how far the pattern was changing even by the 1890s, especially in the case of the outstanding rather than the conventional novelists; as Williams points out, Conrad, Hardy and Lawrence are evidence only of a 'minority entry' into the solid ranks of middle-class novelists. (*Long Revolution*, p. 265)

If there was even a modest increase in the number of novelists from working-class origins by the twentieth century, it could be attributed to two nineteenth-century developments having their full effect. One was the increase in educational opportunity, the other the tendency of writing itself to become a profession at which a living might be made.

Professionalisation and Alienation

It has been suggested that in the later nineteenth century authorship was professionalised, so that writing fiction could be seen as a full-time and remunerative occupation. On the other hand Swingewood and Laurenson and Bradbury argue that the writer becomes increasingly 'marginalised' in the same period and in the early twentieth century; under a developed capitalism writers lose their function in society and a secure position in their social class. The effect is an alienation which is reflected in the subject and treatment of fiction itself, which shows an increasing tendency towards the 'neurotically self-conscious'. This can be interpreted in straightforward Marxist terms, as a symptom of the decadence of Western society, or as a positive attempt to rescue the best aspects of that society. Malcolm Bradbury suggests: 'When the writer thinks of himself as an 'outsider', this is not by any means necessarily because he finds himself in hostile detestation of liberal culture.

Rather he often sees himself as the continuation of it into unpropitious circumstances.' (*The Social Context of Modern English Literature*, p. 123) What evidence is there for either thesis and can they be reconciled?

The end of the pre-nineteenth-century patronage system (under which literature had been financially supported by the cultivated rich) meant that writers without private means were likely to need to support themselves by a second job: Altick lists government (i.e. politics or the civil service), the arts, and the church as the chief professions subsidising literature in this way. However, by 1881 census figures show that there were 6,111 full-time authors, editors and journalists, a figure which rose to 11,060 by 1901. Although most of these may have been journalists, this itself may indicate the existence for authors of another source of income compatible with their work and not too uncongenial.

Financial horizons for authors may have been widened by changes in the method by which they were paid. Before the 1880s most novelists sold the copyright of their work outright to a publisher. A very successful writer such as Scott or a financially astute one such as Dickens might do well under this system but middle-rank authors made only £300 to £500, at a time when £300 a year was regarded as the lower income limit for the middle class. Even an established author like George Gissing was still selling a copyright for as little as £150 in 1901. The 'half-profits' system was equally unsatisfactory to authors; publishers were accused of inflating their costs in the accounts, so as to increase the 'half' owed to them. Only with the institution of the royalty system did writers gain the chance of a regular income and new authors lose the fear of being deprived of most of the profit from a successful novel. The basis for the spread of the royalty system was the Net Book Agreement of 1895 which by forbidding retailers to discount books costing 6s. or more (the new standard price for fiction) ensured a stable price structure on which royalties could be calculated.

Pressure for these changes, and for improvements in the copyright laws to prevent piracy at home or abroad, came from the Society of Authors which was set up in 1883 under the secretaryship of the energetic and successful novelist Walter Besant. This body also pressed the professional status of authors by campaigning for improvements in the way in which agreements with publishers were drawn up; for a time it even acted as a 'literary co-operative' to place work with publishers. Another support for the profession was the Royal Literary Fund, a charity established as long ago as 1790, which gave money to D. H. Lawrence among others. The profession of literary agent, an intermediary between writers and publishers, which itself denoted an expansion of both professions, became regularised in the 1890s; one agent, J. B. Pinker, was influential in the careers of Conrad and Arnold Bennett among others.

Despite these developments it remained true that at any given period only a small minority of novelists would have supported themselves solely by writing. In Laurenson's sample only four were in this position, though 32½ per cent of the men and 20 per cent of the women supported themselves with the aid of journalism. Nevertheless for women writers in particular the rewards could make the difference between penury and relative comfort; this is shown by the comment of the prolific Mrs Oliphant whose autobiography laments the need to be chained to her pen: 'as I am growing old I have more and more desire for a regular quarter day, a regular occupation and so much more money coming in. . . . This is where men have such a huge advantage over us, that they generally have something besides their writing to fall back upon for their bread and butter.' (Quoted in R. C. Terry *Victorian Popular Fiction* Macmillan 1983, p. 33)

Diana Laurenson remarks that the changes in the market situation of writers during the nineteenth century can be seen as producing conflicting images of the writer – as salesman and as artist. The typology she develops from this conclusion may help to reconcile the tendencies to 'professionalisation' and 'alienation' already referred to. Laurenson postulates two stereotypes, emphasising that many writers fall between the two and some change from one to the other. On one hand there is the 'institutionalised' writer, marked by a commitment to the market; he or she produces prolifically to a regular schedule and writes for a specific audience, responding (as Dickens did) to the demands of readers, publishers and others. Psychologically this type has a well-integrated energetic personality, an extrovert interest in the contemporary world and a self-image of himself or herself as a 'professional'. By contrast the 'individualised' writer is sporadic and perfectionist in his or her working practice, discounts the popular audience and ignores the role of publishers. Characteristically this type lives a life of sensitive reaction to physical and/or mental stress, is immersed in the private world of his or her creativity and has the self-image of an artist, often a withdrawn or rebellious one. This contrast may underlie the distinction between Dickens and Mrs Gaskell in the first half of the century and Hardy and Lawrence in the latter decades and the early twentieth century.

Hardy and Lawrence: Dissident Voices

Thomas Hardy's *Tess of the D'Urbervilles* was published in 1891, at the very end of the dominant period of the three-decker when the conventions that had sustained it were being publicly challenged. D. H. Lawrence's *The Rainbow* was published, then suppressed, in 1915 when the three-volume novel ('the old sentimental lending library novel') was definitely dead; its publishing history – even more chequered than that of *Tess* – spans the shift to a new, more adventurous style and content.

There is some reason to follow Williams in enrolling Hardy in that 'minority' group of writers who revitalised British fiction, along with the Americans and the Irish. (*Long Revolution* p. 265) Although Hardy's father had worked his way up from a simple stonemason to a small builder, employing other workmen, his humble origins and relatives were a source of embarrassment to the novelist for his whole career. Robert Gittings in *The Young Thomas Hardy* (1978) shows how in his autobiography Hardy tried to expunge all trace of connections which seem to have been as shameful as the blacking-factory episode was to Dickens. Hardy's first novel, *The Poor Man and the Lady*, which was not accepted by a publisher, deals with marriage across class barriers and the subject of social mobility clearly concerned him up to the writing of his last novel, *Jude the Obscure* (1895).

Hardy's contribution as a consciously regional novelist is even more relevant. Although Scott had founded his reputation on Scots dialect speech and customs, Scotland was traditionally seen as another country rather than a mere region, its dialect used in the eighteenth century even by heavily intellectual figures such as Hume and Adam Smith. Hardy's original success in novels like *Under the Greenwood Tree* (1872) lay in his recreation of the landscape, customs and language of the region he christened Wessex. At first this resulted in an enthusiasm among the conventional public for a fiction which seemed to regenerate the old pastoral convention. However, as the later novels begin to insert darker and darker themes and to fore-ground characters who were less socially respectable (the sunken Durbeyfields and the rootless Jude) and social and sexual relationships were emphasised, Hardy's reviewers smelt treachery. In 1896 Edmund Gosse wrote:

> Is it too late to urge Mr Hardy to struggle against the jarring note of rebellion which seems growing upon him? . . . His early romances were full of calm and lovely pantheism; he seemed in them to feel the deep-hued country landscapes full of rural gods, all homely and benign. We wish he would go back to Egdon Heath and listen to the singing in the heather. (See J. Holmstrom and L. Lerner (eds) *Thomas Hardy and his Readers* Bodley Head 1968, p. 121)

Hardy did not completely betray his middle-class readers, however. Although he explicitly tells us that Tess Durbeyfield is bilingual ('the dialect at home more or less; ordinary English abroad and to persons of quality') the language she speaks is nearer to standard than that of the minor characters, even before we are told that Angel Clare has been coaching her. A dialogue with Marian goes:

> 'Tess – Mrs Clare – the dear wife of dear he! And is it really so bad as this, my child? Why is your cwomely face tied up in such a way? Any body been beating 'ee? Not *he*?'
> 'No, no, no! I merely did it not to be clipsed or colled, Marian.' (Penguin edn, p. 357)

In this passage Tess uses dialect *vocabulary* ('clipsed or colled') but Marian alone is given non-standard pronunciation ('cwomely') and grammar ('ee' for 'you'). This is despite the fact that Hardy in a letter of 1878 had claimed that it was his practice when representing dialect to show 'in the ordinary way most of those local expressions which are but a modified articulation of words in use elsewhere'. (*Life and Art* p.113) The effect in *Tess* is to differentiate the heroine from the subsidiary rural characters though her speech also contrasts with Oliver Twist's flawless Standard English.

Dialect is also assigned to the hero in Lawrence's *Sons and Lovers* where Paul Morel uses it in intimate conversation. This usage seems to reflect Lawrence's status as a 'minority' voice in the authorship of fiction. His place as the first major British novelist of working-class origin has not been convincingly challenged by those who have tried to argue that his father Arthur Lawrence held a supervisory job in the local colliery; it has been demonstrated by Colin Holmes that the 'butty' was not an independent contractor but a foreman, in charge of a group of men but not socially distinct from them.[6] On the other hand Mrs Lawrence's status and aspirations – though not her lifestyle – were middle-class, as befitted a former teacher. The fraught relationship between the two parents (the Morels of *Sons and Lovers*) may have contributed to the writer's tormented history; certainly his early identification with his mother nourished his artistic bent and may have encouraged his interest in theories of the relationship between the sexes. Part of the tension between the class origins of the Lawrences/ Morels was symbolised by the issue of language.

In the following passage from *Sons and Lovers* Lawrence uses the idea of class 'bilingualism' ironically in the account of Paul's refusal to pick up his father's wages from the colliery; Paul is as contaminated by dialect as the men he claims to despise:

'I'm *not* going to the office anymore,' he said. . . .
'They're hateful and common, and hateful, they are, and I'm not going any more. Mr Braithwaite drops his "h's" an' Mr Winterbottom says "You was".'
'And is that why you won't go any more?' smiled Mrs Morel. The boy was silent for some time. His face was pale, his eyes dark and furious. His mother moved about at her work, taking no notice of him.

'They always stan' in front of me, so's I can't get out,' he said. (Penguin edn, p. 93)

On the very next page to this one, dialect even enters the narrative – though possibly this could be regarded as 'free indirect speech' (see the discussion of Flaubert's 'discovery' of this in Chapter 2, p. 56):

> Mrs Morel usually quarrelled with her lace woman, sympathised with her fruit man – who was a gabey, but his wife was a bad 'un.

This passage seems to bear out Raymond Williams's comment in relation to Lawrence that 'what is new here, really new, is that the language of the writer is at one with the language of his characters'. (*The English Novel from Dickens to Lawrence* Paladin 1974, p. 140)

Both Lawrence and Hardy show signs of strain by contrast in their handling of the 'standard' language, the conventional non-dialectal language of narrative. Hardy's occasional resort to a ponderous and inflated style perhaps reflects his deliberate attempts to model his early writing on the leaders of *The Times* and other contemporary patterns of 'fine writing'. For example, this account of Mr and Mrs Durbeyfield at the village pub:

> Troubles and other realities took on themselves a metaphysical impalpability, sinking to mere mental phenomena for serene contemplation, and no longer stood as pressing concretions which chafed body and soul. The youngsters, not immediately within sight, seemed rather bright and desirable appurtenances than otherwise; the incidents of daily life were not without humorousness and jollity in their aspect there. (Penguin edn, p. 60)

Here the laborious strings of abstract nouns ('impalpability', 'phenomena', 'concretions') combined with homely language ('chafed', 'youngsters') and elaborate syntax ('not without humorousness and jollity in their aspect there') result in an incongruous account of the mental processes of the illiterate Durbeyfields. The passage appears stilted in comparison to Hardy's deft use of Mrs Durbeyfield's own language to highlight the ironic side of her husband's delusions of ancestral grandeur: ' 'Twas on this account that your father rode home in the vlee; not because he'd been drinking as some people supposed.'

In relation to Lawrence W. W. Robson has referred to a lack of polish which betrays him as an 'uneducated' writer:

> When Lawrence lapses from his highest level, he is apt to move towards Marie Corelli or Rider Haggard, not towards Galsworthy. In his good as in his inferior works he has something in common with the great 'lowbrow' bestsellers: the vitality which they have and the 'middlebrow' novelists have not, though the best sellers are coarse where Lawrence is sensitive and spiritual. ('D. H. Lawrence and *Women in Love*' in Boris Ford (ed.) *The Pelican Guide to English Literature* vol. 7 Penguin 1964, p. 284)

Even in the highly regarded *The Rainbow* there are traces of stylistic clumsiness, especially in the later chapters about the relationship between Ursula and Skrebensky. (It is not always excused by Walter Allen's comment that Lawrence is 'fumbling for words, words with which to describe the strictly indescribable'.) For example:

> When she had roused him to a pitch of madness, when she saw his eyes all dark and mad with suffering, then a great suffering overcame her soul, a great inconquerable suffering. And she loved him. For oh, she wanted to love him. Stronger than life or death was her craving to be able to love him. (Penguin edn, p. 463)

Clearly there is a deliberate attempt to transcend traditional prose in this passage. However, this is hampered rather than helped by the repetition of 'suffering' (which merges Skrebensky's and Ursula's different *kinds* of suffering); by the impression of archness left by the short sentence beginning with 'And'; by the unfortunate colloquial intonation of 'all dark and mad'; by the rather artificial spontaneity introduced by the 'oh'; and finally by the last sentence with its pseudo-Biblical inversion ('Stronger than life or death was') and vocabulary ('craving').

The Textual Adventures of 'Tess'[7]

In the 1880s and early 1890s Hardy became one of a 'stable' of writers retained by W. F. Tillotson and Son of Bolton. This firm, which published a number of Lancashire newspapers, had introduced fiction into their publications to boost sales; eventually this developed into a Newspaper Fiction Bureau, specialising in what is now called 'syndication'. Tillotsons would negotiate with authors for the right to serialise their work and would then resell the copyright to other non-competing provincial newspapers. Tillotsons, whose impressive list included Wilkie Collins, Charles Reade and at a later date Kipling and Conan Doyle, first approached Hardy in 1881, who must have been impressed by their evident capacity for attracting and supplying a vast new group of readers. Unfortunately in his eagerness to extend his public Hardy seems to have overlooked the fact that W. F. Tillotson, the original proprietor, was a strong Congregationalist, who held decided views about the content of the fiction which his firm accepted, and these also influenced his successor after his death in early 1888.

We know that Hardy like some other established writers of the 1880s was becoming increasingly dissatisfied with the literary system. His essay 'Candour in English Fiction' (1890) tried to dispel the idea that the lack of 'sincerity' (as he put it) found in later nineteenth-century novels was due to some faltering of imagination or insight on the part of the writers. In Hardy's view, the contemporary spirit demanded a 'tragic vision' in which the individual was shown pitted against 'merely social' laws and the 'commonplace majority' was triumphant over the exceptional few. Only conscientious truth to life – however unpalatable – would do, and this implied a genuine account of relations between the sexes and a determination to avoid artificial endings typified by the phrase 'they married and were happy ever after'.

The main obstacles to a move towards 'sincerity' were the serialising magazines and circulating libraries, particularly in so far as they sought to satisfy the demand for 'household' or family reading. As long as the adults in the Victorian family tried to protect the younger members from the impact of this 'sincerity' the result would be artificial and bland novels which not only failed to meet the requirements of 'sincere fiction' themselves but 'directly tend to exterminate it by monopolising all literary space'. If any author did try for sincerity, Hardy claimed the pressure was on him not to allow his characters and their careers to develop in a logical and plausible way but to 'belie his literary conscience, do despite to his best imaginative instincts by arranging a *dénouement* which he knows to be indescribably unreal and meretricious, but dear to the Grundyist and subscriber.' As a remedy Hardy advocated the return of book-buying in place of book-lending (as Arnold had done thirty years previously), so that books would 'naturally resolve themselves into classes instead of being, as now, made to wear a common livery in style and subject, enforced by their supposed necessities in addressing indiscriminately a general audience.' As for that other cornerstone of the system, serial publication in magazines, it was too deep-rooted to be supplanted; Hardy's answer here was to restrict 'sincere fiction' to a *feuilleton*, or pull-out supplement intended for adults, as was done in France. (See 'Candour in English Fiction' in *Life and Art*, Greenberg 1925)

Hardy's fervent belief in the value of fiction as something more than mere entertainment ('mental enlargement' he calls it in another essay 'The Profitable Reading of Fiction') predates Leavis and the twentieth-century academics. When he wrote 'Candour in English Fiction' he had already clashed with Tillotsons over the content of some short stories and clearly the issues raised by this clash impressed him deeply. Since through most of his career Hardy had used the system of serial publication followed by three-volume editions it is not surprising, given his views on the inertia of the system in general, that he did not feel justified in forsaking it. As a writer without a private income, he could scarcely afford to turn down serialisation fees. What is strange is that he ignored what he knew about the squeamishness of Tillotsons and some of their newspaper clients when he offered them his next novel: *Tess of the d'Urbervilles*. Its manuscript form contained a seduction and the birth and death of an illegitimate child as well as a more frankly sensual account of the relationship between the sexes than the Victorian public were thought able to tolerate.

Tess was turned down by Tillotson and two magazines

before it was accepted in November 1889 by the editor of the *Sunday Graphic*, a newspaper which mixed sensational but inoffensive and generally undemanding fiction with a news content largely based on the snob appeal of the nobility and royal family. The price which Hardy had to pay (though it is not clear whether he himself or Locker, the editor, wielded the blue pencil) was the elimination of the seduction of Tess by Alec d'Urberville in Cranborne Chase, the birth and death of little Sorrow (Chapters XI and XIV) and the substitution of a false marriage ceremony, initiated by Alec, which we first hear of when Tess reveals it to her mother on her return from Trantridge. There are also lesser differences between this serialised version and the Wessex Novels edition of 1912, which forms the basis of what the modern reader knows of *Tess*. They are mostly bowdlerisations, the most hilarious of which is that Angel Clare is made to transport Tess and the other milkmaids across the puddles in a wheelbarrow instead of in his own arms (Chapter XIII).

Hardy describes himself as making these changes (which are set out in full in the Appendix to the Penguin edition) with 'cynical amusement'; the cynicism was born no doubt of financial necessity, but the overall effect was to make the impact on the first readers a substantially different one. The story of the false marriage contract makes Tess's predicament much closer to that of the put-upon heroine of the conventional three-decker – though it is possible to assume with the Penguin editor David Skilton that the 'aware reader' would actually assume it implied repeated sexual relations – thereby demonstrating the ambiguity of censorship. (Penguin edn. p. 499) Readers who came upon the story in this form would have found no irony in Hardy's subtitle 'A Pure Woman' and Tess must have had a closer resemblance to Sue Bridehead of *Jude the Obscure*, with her neurotic insistence on the absolute validity of the marriage contract.

Hardy attempted to rescue some of the censored material by publishing it separately even before serialisation of the rest began. The seduction scene appeared as a story, 'A Saturday Night in Arcady' in May 1891, in the *Fortnightly Review*, a notoriously radical publication edited by the campaigner against Victorian prudery, Frank Harris. The episode of little Sorrow was similarly published in free-standing form in the Edinburgh *National Observer* in November 1891, when the *Graphic* serialisation was almost complete. It has been suggested that Hardy's intention was to alert the more sophisticated reader of the *Graphic* version to the 'true' story of *Tess*: whether this is so or not, it is interesting to note that the material could be published provided it was dissociated from the conventional novel heroine and targeted at a suitable readership.

When Hardy soon afterwards attempted to 'piece the trunk and limbs of the novel' together by restoring the censored episodes, the resulting three-volume edition did not receive the cold reception which the wariness of Tillotson and Locker had implied. Perhaps publishers were less solicitous of conventional readers and more concerned to gain liberal-minded ones, given that in 1892 the conflict with libraries was at its peak. In sales terms the 1892 three-volume edition was highly successful, partly because changes in American copyright law enabled the publishers to keep control of it in the United States; nor was the reviewing Establishment particularly horrified by the daring nature of the theme (although Andrew Lang objected to the inclusion of such 'vulgar objects' as the carving knife with which Tess murders Alec).

The transition to book form was a creative one in that it enabled Hardy to make other changes, apart from restoring the cuts. For example whereas in the serial Tess made her visit to the tombs of her d'Urberville ancestors on her way to work in the Vale of the Great Dairies, in the later version the episode occurs more poignantly at the point of her family's lowest fortunes when they arrive in Kingsbere without shelter for the night. Dialect and colloquialism also increased, and did so again in later editions, up to the standard Wessex Edition of 1912. (Interestingly Tess's use of dialect *decreases*, perhaps because Hardy wanted to provide more basis for the suggestion that Angel Clare deliberately attempted to 'improve' Tess's speech.)

Although Hardy was enough encouraged by the reception of Tess to state in an interview in 1892 that he believed Victorian sensibilities were changing ('I do feel strongly that the position of men and women in nature, things which everyone is thinking and saying, may be taken up and treated frankly' (see *Thomas Hardy and his Readers*, p. 90)) many reviewers (and presumably readers) were appalled by the painful realism of the novel and its pessimism. Gosse's reaction (quoted above) and several similar ones bear out Eagleton's claim that Hardy was felt to have violated the old tradition of literary 'pastoral' in which the countryside was presented as a soothing and morally uncorrupted alternative to town life and sophisticated society. In *Thomas Hardy and Rural England* (1972) Merryn Williams supports this view by showing how both *Tess* and *Jude the Obscure*, which appeared two years later, and which both feature main characters drawn from the less privileged classes, undermine the tradition of country writing in which 'the poor were usually noticed as objects of charity or not at all'. In both novels the behaviour of the hero and heroine to some extent symbolises the plight of the majority of rural inhabitants in the period after 1880.

As his 1883 essay 'The Dorsetshire Labourer' shows, Hardy was alert to the fact that country life, far from being changeless, was vulnerable to outside economic pressures. Importation of wheat from North America had a specially severe effect on cereal-growing counties in the South such as Dorset, where wages were already low because of lack of competition from employment in industry. There were two notable agricultural depressions in 1875–84 and 1891–9 during which the effect of this pressure combined with poor harvests was to force many labourers and their families into the towns or into overseas emigration. Although in his 1883 article Hardy is surprisingly optimistic about the fate of these workers, in *Tess* he depicts the decline of another class dependent on a thriving rural economy. The Durbeyfields are precipitated into catastrophe as a result of the accident to the horse from which they earn their living as carters, but in any case they belong to a precarious minority:

> The village had formerly contained, side by side with the agricultural labourers, an interesting and better informed class, ranking distinctly above the former – the class to which Tess's father and mother had belonged – and including the carpenter, the smith, the shoemaker, the huckster, together with nondescript workers other than farm-labourers; a set of people who owed a certain stability of aim and conduct to the

fact of their being lifeholders like Tess's father, or copyholders, or, occasionally, small freeholders. (p. 435)

This intermediate class, whose members in *Tess* are being threatened by the expiry of their tenancies and leases as well as by the contraction of the rural economy, is the one to which Jude Fawley also belongs (as ward of the local baker and later an itinerant stonemason) and Hardy himself, whose father was a small builder, had direct experience of it. Arnold Kettle's assertion therefore that *Tess* is chiefly about 'the destruction of the peasantry' is not precise enough; it is doubtful whether 'the peasantry', meaning a class of subsistence landholders, had existed in England for many years before 1891 – they had been replaced by labourers working for a daily wage. However, Kettle was right to stress the previously undervalued social context of the novel, which may have made it unpalatable for some Victorian critics. The two crises in which the economic plight of the Durbeyfield's is most extreme – the accident to Prince and the eviction on Lady Day – lead to Tess's two disastrous involvements with Alec: her initial seduction and the liaison in Sandbourne which she undertakes for the sake of her homeless family.

The theme of seduction was a traditional one in novels about the countryside, as Merryn Williams shows, and therefore acceptable to conservative readers; they must have been less happy, however, with the depiction of the heroine's degradation, at Flintcombe Ash, as the most exploited kind of agricultural worker and later under the inhuman work-regime imposed by the threshing-machine in which 'her arms worked independently of her consciousness'. ('The Dorsetshire Labourer' had described a real-life incident of a woman made so dizzy by a similar machine that she was unable to find her way home until the early hours of the morning.) However, it was *Jude the Obscure*, set in the unromantic county of Berkshire and dealing with the wanderings of uprooted rural workers on the fringes of the expanding towns that really seemed to signal the end of Hardy's reputation as a 'country writer' of the traditional sort.

Although *Jude*, like *Tess*, was originally published in a bowdlerised serial form, the book version was an example of the new single-volume novels, published in 1894 at the 'democratic' price of 6s., as one of a series which included reprints of Hardy's earlier works. In this case, however, the taste of the publisher was ahead of that of the reviewers who referred to 'grime', 'nightmare', 'hoggishness and hysteria' and most memorably 'Jude the Obscene'. Although the novel's treatment of sexual themes is foreshadowed in *Tess* (for example Tess observes of Alec on p. 442: 'It was not her husband, she had said. Yet a consciousness that in a physical sense this man alone was her husband seemed to weigh on her even more') perhaps the stronger reaction arose because the Sue Bridehead of *Jude* was an educated young woman rather than a working-class girl. At any rate a new anxiety was voiced by the Bishop of Wakefield who, having thrown his copy of the novel into the fire, complained: 'It is a disgrace to our great public libraries to admit such garbage, clever though it may be, to their shelves.'

The bishop's concern for the protection of others, in this case the lower-middle and working-class users of public libraries, is a variant of the protective attitude to young women underlying Victorian attitudes to fiction. That this protectiveness had lost its old power is shown by the comment of a French observer, Wyzewa, a year after *Jude* was published: 'The New English novel differs above all from the old in that it is sexually-oriented [sexualiste]. What the English call sexually-oriented literature corresponds exactly to what we recently used to call naturalism. . . . French mothers can no longer purchase novels in England for their daughters with confidence.' The old happy relationship between the English novel and chastity, first described by Mme de Staël, was decisively broken.

'The Rainbow' Comes and Goes

The composition and reception of *The Rainbow* can be seen as a significant stage not only in Lawrence's own career but also in the transition of the novel from Victorian to modern form. As prelude to *The Rainbow*, however, we need to look at the nature and impact of Lawrence's earlier work, especially *Sons and Lovers*. Graham Holderness in *D. H. Lawrence: History, Ideology and Fiction* (1982) has examined in detail Lawrence's early life and environment. Holderness argues that Lawrence's relations with his parents and his social position in his home town, the mining community of Eastwood, exposed him to conflicting pressures – towards individuality and isolation on the one hand and 'communal' consciousness and integration on the other. In artistic terms this became a conflict between an 'aesthetic' style, concentrating on the sensuous perception of beauty, and a 'realistic' style, portraying individuals in a recognisable community. The first mode can be found in earlier novels like *The White Peacock* and *The Trespasser* which centre on super-sensitive, artistic characters, reminiscent of the 'decadent' 1890s. However, with *Sons and Lovers* Lawrence shifts to a style corresponding to Lukács' definition of 'realism', that is the recognition of the interdependence of 'inner' and 'outer' being, the presentation of the individual as a 'social animal'; the portrayal of 'social types' – the synthesis of particular and general found in the classical realism of Balzac and Tolstoy; and an attempt to convey a social 'totality', but with the 'inward' aim of realism rather than the superficial exterior plausibility of 'naturalism'. (see Holderness, p. 7)

According to Holderness Lawrence's ambiguous relation-ship to the community of his birth and upbringing derives from the contradictions in that community itself. Leavis, in his early championship of Lawrence, had tended to stress the 'organic' and integrated nature of the East Midland coalfield com-munities. By contrast Holderness picks out the social stresses and divisions to which, like many similar industrial com-munities, Eastwood was subjected. He mentions the series of strikes and industrial conflicts through which the miners strove to improve their pay and conditions and the social segregation and exclusiveness of the Congregational church to which Mrs Lawrence belonged. On this view the harmonious idealised community, balancing the virtues of industry and the country-side, which sometimes appears in *Sons and Lovers*, was a mere temporary phenomenon, achieved by a stand-off between employers and miners in the years of Lawrence's childhood and youth (1890–1910). Underlying it were powerful tendencies towards conflict and disintegration which resurfaced in the 1920s with the General Strike, and which caused Lawrence gradually to substitute for 'the country of the heart' of East-wood/Bestwood a debased and nightmarish alternative, the

Wyggeston of *The Rainbow* and the Tevershall of *Lady Chatter-ley's Lover*.

Lawrence's perception of this divided community was sharply focused by the dual class loyalties thrown up by his birth to a barely literate miner and a schoolteacher, the daughter of an engineer. Eagleton, who attributes Lawrence's fascination for 'dualistic philosophies' to this fact, comments:

> Lawrence's dualistic metaphysics is ridden with internal contradictions, for a sufficient significant biographical reason; his mother, symbol of primordial sensual unity, was in fact petty-bourgeois, and so also represented individuation, aspiring consciousness and active idealism in contrast to the mute sensuous passivity of his working-class father. This partial inversion of the parents' sexual roles, as defined by Lawrence, contorts and intensifies the contradictions which his metaphysic tries to resolve. (*Criticism and Ideology* p. 159)

Like the fictional Gertrude Morel, Lydia Lawrence (*née* Beardsall) represented a drive towards individuality and an escape from the communal living and interdependence which was particularly associated with the male miners because of their working conditions underground. (In his essay *Nottingham and the Mining Countryside* Lawrence explores the different outlook of the two sexes in such communities.) However Mrs Lawrence could not, any more than the culturally provincial Eastwood setting could, provide her son with a 'role model' for the life of the artist he wished to lead. Her aesthetic taste was determinedly middlebrow and her aspirations for her children limited to that 'respectability' which would divide them off from the life centred on the pit. (In the same way Mrs Morel puts her son Paul into a 'desk job' against her father's wishes.) As a result it seems that the only encouragement for young Lawrence's artistic development came from Jessie Chambers (the Miriam of *Sons and Lovers*). Holderness quotes her account of the contrast between the aesthetically-dominated world they shared and the workaday environment of Eastwood:

> I dreaded to hear a footstep approaching to break the magical quality of our association. When we were alone

together we were in a world apart, where feeling and thought were intense, and we seemed to touch a reality that was beyond the ordinary workaday world. But if his mother or sister returned, bringing with them the atmosphere of the market place, our separate world was temporarily shattered, and only recaptured with difficulty. (see Holderness p. 74)

Lawrence's isolation within his family was reproduced in his isolation among what there was of the Eastwood intelligentsia, since that had a slant towards socialism rather than aestheticism and sexual freedom. Isolation and detachment characterise the heroes of the earliest novels who are dedicated to a sensuous exploration of life, unshackled by the presence of any surrounding society in which they participate. Such a society, with its strange but not disharmonious interpenetration of collieries and countryside, takes precedence for the first time in *Sons and Lovers*, published in 1913. It is surely significant that by this date Lawrence had decisively distanced himself from it in time – the death of his mother which closes the novel occurred in 1910 – in space – by the move first to Nottingham and then to Croydon – and finally, socially and psychologically. His elopement with the German aristocrat Frieda Richthofen put him outside the pale not only of Eastwood non-conformist middle-class but of all 'respectable' society. In the words of Harry T. Moore, Lawrence's biographer: '*Sons and Lovers* was a partial reconquest of the past, because in it Lawrence faced that past and battled with it.' (*The Priest of Love*, Penguin 1974, p. 217)

Holderness therefore regards *Sons and Lovers* as the triumph of Lawrence's realist style. It certainly breaks new ground in a number of ways. Richard Hoggart has compared the direct, vivid and concrete style of the opening paragraphs with the obliquity and irony which a middle-class highly educated novelist such as E. M. Forster employed. (*Speaking to Each Other* vol. 2 Chatto and Windus 1970, p. 197) There is the extension of the use of dialect (the 'unfashionable' dialect of Nottinghamshire rather than the rustic speech in Hardy's novels) and the enlargement of the novel's range to a milieu scarcely touched since Mrs Gaskell's period. Although slum neighbourhoods in London had been brought to life in the

1880s and 1890s by writers such as Gissing and Arthur Morrison, using Zola-esque 'naturalistic' methods, a new note is sounded by Lawrence's detailed, non-sensationalising but socially sensitive account of Eastwood's back streets. Anyone reading the following passage could not doubt that this writer knew what he was talking about:

> The dwelling-room, the kitchen, was at the back of the house, facing inward between the blocks, looking at a scrubby back garden and then at the ash-pits. And between the rows, between long lines of ash-pits, went the alley, where the children played and the women gossiped and the men smoked. So the actual conditions of living in the Bottoms, that were so well-built and that looked so nice, were quite unsavoury because people must live in the kitchen and the kitchens opened on to that nasty alley of ash-pits. (Penguin edn, p. 8)

This tone of patient explanation of living habits is extended in the next paragraph into an obviously authentic account of the minute social differences which fed Mrs Morel's aspirations towards 'respectability' and textured the apparently unified community of Bestwood:

> Mrs Morel was not anxious to move into the Bottoms, which was already twelve years old and on the downward path, when she descended to it from Bestwood. But it was the best she could do. Moreover, she had an end house in one of the top blocks, and thus had only one neighbour; on the other an extra strip of garden. And, having an end house, she enjoyed a kind of aristocracy among the other women of the 'between' houses, because her rent was five shillings and sixpence instead of five shillings a week. But this superiority in station was not much consolation to Mrs Morel. (ibid., p. 8)

Of course this detailed social background is important as context for the 'tragedy', to use Lawrence's own term, at the heart of the novel. This tragedy arises from social conflict, stoked up by the ideology of social mobility. Paul Morel, the hero of this 'third person autobiography' is isolated and loses his inner harmony because of the aspirations of his mother to rise above the culture of the mining community. The conflict is at its most naked in scenes like the row between Gertrude and Walter over the cutting of young William's hair and the argument over whether Paul should go into a clerical appointment. Holderness illustrates the destructive character of this conflict by borrowing a term from Macherey and identifying the one 'significant absence' of the novel – the middle class itself. As there is no substantial representative of the bourgeoisie in *Sons and Lovers*, so Mrs Morel's aspirations are seen as leading literally nowhere and end for Paul in his turning away from his natal community towards the alluring but unknown attractions of the city. (Just as his real-life equivalent Lawrence at about this time launched himself into a cosmopolitan, rootless life of exile.)

On Holderness's interpretation Paul's rejection of Miriam parallels Lawrence's rejection of his former 'aesthetic' ideology, represented by the pastoral world which Miriam inhabits. However, Lawrence did not remain committed to the mode of realism, initiated by this novel. In his very next work he makes the transition to a mode of myth and symbol, which transcends reality just as surely as the aestheticism of the 1890s. Yet in the effort towards this transition there opened up a breach between Lawrence and the majority of his middle-class reading public.

From the beginning Lawrence's editors had insisted on changes in the text of his novels. The original of *The White Peacock* contained the passage:

God! – we were a passionate couple – and she would have me in her bedroom while she drew Greek statues of me – her Croton, her Hercules! . . . Then gradually she got tired – it took her three years to have a real bellyful of me. (see Moore, p. 166)

In the published version this was altered to:

Lord! – we were an infatuated couple – and she chose to view me in aesthetic light. I was Greek statues for her, bless you: Croton, Hercules, I don't know what! . . Then gradually she got tired – it took her three years to be really glutted with me.

These changes encapsulate what it was felt would offend the 'respectable' reader of the time – blasphemy, sexual explicitness, and direct colloquial language. In the light of this prevailing attitude it is not surprising that Heinemann turned down *Sons and Lovers*, according to Lawrence because they regarded it as an 'unclean' book, or that before Duckworth would publish it their editor, Edward Garnett, carried out extensive bowdlerisations. However, Lawrence's next novel was one in which the 'unclean' was so much a thematic strand in the story that there was no possibility of tinkering with it, and it led to the book's suppression. This fact alone justifies (although there are other reasons) regarding its publication as marking a boundary between the Victorian and the modern novel.

The innovatory nature of *The Rainbow* has been referred to both by Lawrence himself, who spoke of his aim to transcend 'the old stable ego of character', and by Marvin Mudrick in his essay, 'The Originality of *The Rainbow*'. Mudrick finds Lawrence in this novel abandoning the traditional concerns of British, as opposed to European or American fiction:

> If the novelist creates his characters as more or less aggressive bundles of recognisable traits, as egos stabilised by manners and morals, and his novel as a sequence of collusions between such bundles he will produce the kind of novel that Lawrence is now giving up, the novel preoccupied – whether in affirmation or protest – with manners and morals, the class novel, the standard English novel. If, however, the novelist creates his characters in a life-size medium, fictional and communal, which nurtures, provokes, and makes room for the strength of impulse, he will produce a novel like *The Rainbow*. . . . Characters in novels like these are not caricatures or even conventional heroes, mere victims or arbiters of manners and morals, they are passions and first principles; and they are all the more human and individual for being so.
> ('The Originality of *The Rainbow*' in *D. H. Lawrence: Twentieth Century Views* Prentice Hall 1963, p. 39)

Mudrick goes on to suggest that Lawrence has excluded from his novel that pursuit of material success which previous British novelists had prescribed for their heroes and heroines.

In conventional novels that pursuit had taken place in a dense, complex social setting, marked by those traditional reference points which the American Henry James complained were lacking in *his* national heritage:

> No sovereign, no court, no personal loyalty, no aristocracy, no church, no clergy, no army, no diplomatic service, no country gentlemen, no palaces, no castles nor manors, no old country houses, no parsonages nor thatched cottages, nor ivied ruins; no cathedrals, nor abbeys, nor little Norman churches; no great universities nor public schools. (*Life of Hawthorn* (ed. Tanner) Macmillan 1967, p. 55)

Within this traditional and highly stratified society the fictional character had found his or her niche – often via marriage. The British hero or heroine was not typically an outsider who 'made good' despite his opposition to the values of society, but an insider whose place in society was temporarily compromised by accident compounded by malice (Oliver Twist) or by an insufficiently socialised temperament (Emma). By contrast in Lawrence the 'societal impulse' is shown as thwarted finally by the pressure of industrial society. In its place Lawrence substitutes the 'sexual impulse', suppressed hitherto in English novels, which had conformed to the 'bourgeois imperative'.

Despite Mudrick's theory there are moments of social density in *The Rainbow*, for example in this reference to the relations between the Brangwen children and their village neighbours on the one hand and the local middle classes on the other:

> However the Brangwen-Pillins coalition readily broke down, owing to the unfair superiority of the Brangwens. The Brangwens were rich. They had free access to Marsh Farm. The school teachers were almost respectful to the girls, the vicar spoke to them on equal terms. The Brangwen girls presumed, they tossed their heads. (Penguin edn, p. 263)

Like Gertrude Morel and the real-life Lydia Lawrence, Anna Brangwen (Ursula's mother) encourages distinctiveness for her children: 'When Ursula was twelve, and the common school and the companionship of the village children, niggardly and begrudging, was beginning to affect her, Anna sent her with Gudrun to the Grammar School in Nottingham.' (ibid. p. 263) However, these 'societal' elements are not followed up; it is the *sexual* relationship between Skrebensky and Ursula which dominates the second half of the novel and it was this intimate exploration of sexual frustration which led to the novel being withdrawn soon after publication.

Although Mudrick finds that in *The Rainbow* the 'societal impulse' is eclipsed or obscured, he concedes that in the novel Lawrence has created a convincing community, based on Marsh Farm: 'In his historic moment, Lawrence has before him the life of the last English community . . . a life rich in productive labour and in continuity with the passing seasons.' ('The Originality of *The Rainbow*' p. 34) For Leavis likewise, who invokes Lawrence's community in an idealised way – the 'organic community', *The Rainbow* is the story of a transition over three generations from semi-rural community to the alienated isolation of Ursula at the end. (See *D.H. Lawrence: Novelist* Chatto and Windus 1972) Graham Holderness, however, denies that this positive portrayal of a community is present. He proposes that the novel should be read 'backwards' from the account of Wiggiston, the mining town where Ursula's Uncle Tom manages the colliery, and which is another artistic transposition of Eastwood. Wiggiston lacks any sense of identity or community: 'The rigidity of the blank streets, the homogeneous amorphous sterility of the whole suggested death rather than life. There was no meeting place, no centre, no artery, no organic formation' (p. 345). Its ugliness and monotony – 'Everything was amorphous, yet repeated itself endlessly' – makes it symbolic of the system, which Ursula learns to call 'the machine', which excludes all relationships except the one between employer and employee: the cash nexus of Carlyle and Marx. According to Tom Brangwen:

> Marriage and home is a little sideshow. The women know it right enough, and take it for what it's worth. One man or another, it doesn't matter all the world. The pit matters. Round the pit there will always be the side shows, plenty of 'em. (p. 349)

The vehemence of this attack on the industrialised community contrasts with the relative integration of town and countryside in *Sons and Lovers* and even with the treatment of Walter Morel and his relationship with his family. Most critics, recognising this, have suggested that Marsh Farm is used as a positive contrast, an antidote to the industrialised social chaos of Wiggiston. For example Raymond Williams reads the novel as an account of the breakdown of community:

> The given reality of men and women is the experience and the method of the early chapters, and then under pressure – the pressures of altering ways of life, economic and social and physical changes – such a reality radical and irreducible has to be made or found; it is not given. It is then made and found – attempted to be made and found – in certain kinds of relationship: physical certainly but physical mainly as a discovery of being, of spirit. (*The English Novel from Dickens to Lawrence*, p. 144)

In contrast Holderness maintains that the 'community' represented by Marsh Farm is an illusion and not a real alternative to Wiggiston. In this respect, *The Rainbow* offers us an example of how fiction, because it is a reworking of ideology, to use Eagleton's terms, can allow us to perceive the operation of that ideology more clearly. Holderness claims that 'Marsh Farm' is a pure ideological construct, which enables Lawrence to contrast Wiggiston with an idealised 'organic' community from which all pressures and contradictions have been removed: 'There is actually no rural community at all in this earlier part of the novel: there is only a family . . . this family exists as an autonomous unit, with as little connection with a contingent or contextual community as a country house in Jane Austen – and without even other similar families to connect with' (*D. H. Lawrence: History, Ideology and Fiction*, p. 183).

For Holderness the ideological quality of 'Marsh Farm' is brought out by the deliberately heightened, poetic language in which it is described, in the well-known passage at the beginning of Chapter I ('The young corn waved and was silken, and the lustre slid along the limbs of the men who saw it'). In *The Rainbow* Lawrence abandoned the realism of *Sons and Lovers* for the juxtaposition of two myths: 'The myth of Marsh Farm *grows through* the solid nightmare of Wiggiston, in the presence of Ursula, as grass (to use one of Lawrence's favourite metaphors) grows through a concrete pavement and effectively negates it.' (Holderness, p. 187) Consequently the ending of *The Rainbow*, with its vision of a transformed society, results from an evasion: 'The novel's ideological images of social completeness, harmony and fulfilment – arch and rainbow – were offered as symbols of the old organic society, and were permitted, by the mythological mode, to stand unmolested by real history.' (ibid., p. 187)

By 'real history' Holderness presumably means the Marxist conception of history as 'class struggle'; for him *The Rainbow* is a failure, an indication of Lawrence's inability to overcome the 'ideological crisis' brought about by the First World War and a resort to myth and symbol as a substitute for the Lukácsian realism of *Sons and Lovers*. It has already been suggested that in the depiction of the early life of Ursula there is more 'social density' than Holderness seems to find – though admittedly it is introduced incidentally. Ironically what contemporary critics found in the novel was an excess of 'realism', of an explicitly sexual nature. Shortly after its publication in September 1915 (when the respected reviewer Robert Lynd referred to it as 'windy, tedious and nauseating') it was the subject of an action brought by the Purity League, under the Obscene Publications Act of 1857. The League's solicitor, Muskett, had in mind such passages as the Anna Victrix chapter, the account of Winifred Inger, and the whole Ursula-Skrebensky relationship when he described the novel as 'a mass of obscenity of thought, idea and action throughout, wrapped up in a language which . . . would be regarded in some quarters as an artistic and intellectual effort.' (see *D. H. Lawrence: The Critical Heritage* ed. Draper, RKP 1970, p. 102) The publishers, Methuen, who made no defence at the magistrate's court hearing, were fined ten guineas and compelled to destroy all unsold copies.

In my view *The Rainbow* is a novel which critically describes the social changes associated with industrialisation, though it is not directly about the network of social relationships in an industrialised society. Ursula's experiences bring her more and more into conflict with the machine-like nature of this new society and lead her to reject one by one its most cherished totems: education at school and university, industry (in the shape of Wiggiston), the armed forces (represented by Skrebensky) and respectable married life. It is not surprising therefore that in a period of wartime hysteria and anxiety the novel was seen as a threat to political as well as sexual conformity – a threat which seemed to be substantiated by Lawrence's own public opposition to the war and its most jingoistic supporters, his refusal to volunteer, despite the lack of religious qualifications which would have allowed him to become a conscientious objector, and his marriage to a German.

The suppression of *The Rainbow* shows how difficult it was still for society to tolerate criticism from its most influential literary genre. However, the effect of the war itself on social conventions was far-reaching and in 1920 the novel could be published again without hindrance. By this date the threat to patriotism had lost much of its relevance – Ursula's criticism of the soldier Skrebensky could no longer be held to be damaging to the war effort – and a general relaxation of morality had taken place. Robert Graves and Alan Hodge record in *The Long Weekend*: 'The shameless abandon with which the new free woman danced, allowing her partner a near-sexual embrace, her immodest dress and coiffure and her profane looseness of language were by no means the only charges against her. A letter in *The Spectator* in 1919 complained that young women were learning to frequent public houses.' (*The Long Weekend* Faber and Faber 1941, p. 42)

Another reason why the novel appeared less damaging in 1920 may have been Lawrence's increasingly marginalised position on the British literary scene. By that date he had adopted his role of 'exile', had started on his long series of journeys across Europe and the world, and had become estranged from the London literary circles who had given him support and encouragement. In Holderness's words: 'He had been displaced as a miner's son to become a respectable professional, displaced from that to become a writer, and then displaced by the war from the role of writer itself. He was now a writer without a public, without access to publication.' (p. 200)

The last remark hints at Lawrence's suggestion in his letters that *Women in Love*, his next novel, would be circulated among

a small group of acquaintances or published by subscription –
both methods that by-pass the market system and return to the
pre-capitalist origins of literature. It illustrates the extent to
which the hearty two-way relationship between author and
reader found in the heyday of Dickens had broken down. It was
replaced by isolation (incipient in Hardy and total in Lawrence)
or by the attraction of a complete commitment to the expanding
market, which is the subject of the next chapter.

7. The Challenge of the Popular

This final chapter deals with the so-called 'popular' work of fiction and its relationship both to the literary market and to the society in which it was written. It also considers the problem of how popular fiction should be studied, given the inappropriateness of conventional forms of literary criticism. The text on which the chapter is based is the Ian Fleming thriller *Thunderball*. Many other texts might have been used, going back to the early nineteenth century or beyond – however there are advantages, given the plan of this book, on carrying the discussion of the socio-cultural context of fiction into the mid twentieth century.

Popularity and the Reading Public

In 1932 appeared one of the earliest academic attempts to grapple with the popular novel, Q. D. Leavis's *Fiction and the Reading Public*. As might be expected from a book written by the wife and collaborator of F. R. Leavis, it is based on an essentially gloomy prediction: standards of fiction writing will inevitably decline, in correspondence with the general debasement of standards attributable to industrialisation. Mrs Leavis argues that the evolution of the nineteenth-century novel was marked by a series of pressures on what she regards as 'good taste': circulating libraries, the serial mode of publication (which she blames for encouraging sensational effects), the proliferation of cheap reprints and finally the 6s. novel. For a long time the extension of the reading public – which in itself Mrs Leavis seems to regard as a dubious benefit – was held in check by the high price of new fiction and what she describes as 'the slow rate of absorption' of the working class into the readership for novels. By the 1860s, however, this readership had split into two – a 'serious' one prepared to put in the work to understand Eliot, Thackeray and Trollope and a more frivolous one, satisfied by Dickens (regarded by the Leavises at this time as lightweight), Charles Reade and Wilkie Collins. This distintegration of the reading public was then hastened by the impact of the alien and morally suspect French novelists of the later nineteenth century on whom the 'highbrow' writers such as James and Conrad to some extent modelled themselves.

Fortified with this historical account and with a firm belief in the malign influence of advertising and the press, Mrs Leavis divided the novels of her own day into four types: 'highbrow'; 'middlebrow' read as 'literature'; 'middlebrow' not read as 'literature' but not writing for the lowbrow market; absolute bestsellers. She then describes the result of a questionnaire which she sent to sixty novelists and from whom she received twenty-five replies. The contemporary popular novelist is portrayed by his answers as a cynical technician, working to a hackneyed formula to produce a saleable work, intended at best to 'pass the time'. The result contrasts glaringly with the 'good novel' which she defines as being able to administer a 'series of shocks to the readers' preconceptions, usually unconscious of how people behave and why, what is admirable and what reprehensible; it provides a configuration of special instances which serve as a test for our mental habits and show us the necessity for revising them.' (*Fiction and the Reading Public* Chatto and Windus 1932, p. 256)

The scenario which is constructed from this fairly superficial research is a bleak one: bad novels drive out the good. The high cost of advertising makes it uneconomic to market novels other than those with a mass appeal and 'mass appeal' in Leavisite theory necessarily implies a poor aesthetic standard. The effect of this economic pressure combined with the cheap and vulgar clichés encouraged by the popular press will soon reduce most literature to the level of the cinema (a favourite Leavisite model for mass vulgarity).

It is not difficult to find flaws in Mrs Leavis's factual account and in the arguments she draws from it – where these are arguments and not mere assertions. In factual terms the work of Louis James and others has since shown how there has always been an undertow of second-rate literature, some of it at a level of crudity Mrs Leavis does not even contemplate. If this literature was popular, in the sense of appealing to the poorer people who constituted the mass of the community, it was partly because they had a lower standard of education and were unable to afford even in lending library form the works of Thackeray, Eliot and Trollope. An effective rejoinder to the scenario of a twentieth-century collapse in standards can be found in this comment by Robert Mayo, a historian of eighteenth-century magazine fiction (dating from a period long before the rot was supposed to have set in): 'Almost any volume of the *Monthly* or *Critical* from their earliest years will show that vulgar romances, scandalous histories and trashy pseudo-biographies outnumbered the acceptable novels by two or three to one – and later the ratio became even more unfavourable. The literature was different in many respects, naturally, from modern bestsellers, but not superior in literary quality. In some respects it was worse.' (*The English Novel in the Magazines 1740–1815* Oxford University Press 1962, p. 357)

To this criticism Q. D. Leavis would doubtless reply in a phrase she quotes in her book: 'Formerly, no doubt, the mob had a lower class of books than at present but they did not then set them up for the best.' The suggestion that standards imposed from outside are to be preferred to honestly-expressed personal preferences only shows up her own elitism, however: *who* is to decide whether a novel deals a 'shock to the sensations'? what are the criteria for the fourfold categorisation of novels? Moreover events since 1932 have not borne out the truth of her predictions – worthwhile novels are still being written alongside bestsellers.

Nevertheless despite Mrs Leavis's prejudices and the meagreness of her data, there is something in her methodology that deserves further attention. She herself defined her approach as 'anthropological' (sometimes 'sociological'), aware that she was pioneering beyond the boundaries of conventional literary criticism. To the extent that labelling a novel as 'popular' in itself conventionally implies a low regard for its aesthetic value there is some justification for adopting such an approach. Unfortunately the innovative elements in her work (the use of the questionnaire – slight as it is – and the search for formulae to identify popular fiction) are overshadowed by her moralistic assumptions. Since 1932 it has been commonplace to apply the socio-cultural approach to popular fiction; to question its validity as has recently been done by such writers as Tony Bennett involves discussion of such questions as: how is 'popular' fiction distinguished from 'serious' fiction? can *only* sociological or socio-cultural methods be used to study it? and so on. Some of these questions will crop up again later in this chapter.

Mrs Leavis's scenario has been reassessed by John Sutherland in his book *Fiction and the Fiction Industry* published in 1978. Sutherland finds little evidence to bear out the prophecies of literary degeneration to be found in the writings of the Leavises or later writers such as Richard Hoggart. In the mid 1970s there was no sign of the market for books reaching saturation point: the number of new titles – fiction and non-fiction – published in 1974 was three times what had made one publisher afraid of a 'glut' when writing in 1934. Many publishers had been swallowed up by large conglomerates with interests in other media but this tendency had not led to the extinction of the small, independent 'literary' publisher, prepared to take a risk on new fiction. Neither was there any evidence that the 'mediocre best-seller' dreaded by Mrs Leavis had driven out the 'serious' novel. On the contrary, Sutherland shows how the profits from the sale of popular successes can frequently be used to subsidise serious works by publishers who for reasons of prestige or loyalty to aesthetic standards sought to publish 'good authors'. (Ian Fleming's novels were used to subsidise Jonathan Cape's other ventures in this way.)

Nevertheless Sutherland sees a threat to the expansion of the market for 'good' fiction which is related to a crisis within the publishing industry. In the mid 1970s rises in publishing costs had pushed up publication prices to levels at which resistance was met from customers. By far the most important customers for new fiction were the public libraries whose problems were increased by cuts in their own funding. Since public libraries had become almost monopolistic purchasers of new fiction, on the same lines as Mudie and his colleagues had been a hundred years earlier, the impact of their loss of resources was critical for the novel. Sutherland quotes an estimate that of 1,200 copies of a new novel published, all but

300 would be bought by the public libraries; as funds started to dry up the libraries tended to concentrate them on purchases which seemed to provide more 'value for money' and to buy 'the new Alastair Maclean or Catherine Cookson because it will be read by from 60 to 100 people before it falls apart, rather than spending the same amount of money on a marvellous first novel . . . which will probably be borrowed only six or seven times.' (Sutherland p. 13)

In Sutherland's view the effect of these tendencies, together with the economic pressure on bookshops and serious magazines, which publicised new fiction by reviewing it, was almost as momentous as the disappearance of the three-decker in the 1890s. When the price of novels fell to 6s. this transferred purchasing power from the subscription libraries to the private consumer and the fiction-carrying magazine. It inaugurated an era of stability lasting fifty years in which the price of new novels was maintained at the level of 6s.–7s. 6d. (30p–37½p). This equilibrium which allowed British novels to survive on much lower sales than their American counterparts was supported by the Net Book Agreement which was designed to prevent undercutting of the new standard price and thus ensure that less popular novels sold at the same price as bestsellers. Above all, however, it was sustained by the public libraries which had the advantage over Mudie's in being less subject to commercial values (Sutherland points out that: 'no-one, for example, takes a public library to task for there being only one date-stamp in a three-year-old novel' (p. xxvi)); they also exercised an educational role in encouraging the public to read far more novels than they could possibly afford to buy, an average of three a week per adult according to Sutherland.

The breakdown of this new equilibrium was becoming obvious in the economic climate of the 1970s. One factor in it, however, had its origins before the Second World War. Paperback publishing now deserves separate consideration.

Paperback Writers

Q. D. Leavis might have added a bemused footnote to *Fiction and the Reading Public* if it had been published in 1935 rather than 1932. She would have had to take account of the first Penguins in their (by contemporary standards) garish orange and white covers which, despite the fact that they were reprints of highly respected works of fiction and non-fiction, were sold over the counter at Woolworths because Allen Lane had not persuaded the traditional bookshops to stock them.

In retrospect it is difficult now to imagine why this new publishing form seemed so revolutionary. Sutherland in fact asks why new fiction needs to be published in hardback at any stage, when it is normally only read once. However, the actual physical composition of the paperback is only one ingredient in its success. It is probably the least important ingredient although such technological developments as the use of the rotary magazine press and the application of synthetic glue rather than sewn bindings have brought about greater cost savings than simply substituting paper for boards.

In fact the paperback is simply the most recent of a series of ways recorded in this book in which publishers have sought to counteract the high cost of new fiction by reprinting established successes. Sutherland expresses the relationship between the new novel and the reprint in a succinct way:

> Since 1832 [date of the publication of Colburn and Bentley's Standard Novel reprints] English publishing of the novel has been marked by a reciprocation in which new novels are produced in a first form which is expensive and conservative in make-up, but capable of being experimental and adventurous in content. Meanwhile reprints (or 'nearly new novels') are, as regards titles, safe-choice, unadventurous works which appear in a form that is strikingly innovative in marketing and technology – like the paperback. (*Fiction and the Fiction Industry*, p. 172)

The paperback therefore, like the single-volume reprint in the nineteenth century, soon occupied a niche in the literary context where its intrinsic advantages of low production costs and cheap materials were supported by guarantees of large sales at a low price. This guarantee resulted from the fact that almost all paperbacks were reprinted versions of titles that had proved their worth.

Penguins themselves were soon seen to be attempting to rise above the cheap reprint image. They lost their chain-store connection and were marketed like hardbacks, being sold in bookshops on separate stands arranged in alphabetical order, rather than being shovelled in and out as each new batch of titles arrived. However, as the advantages of the reprint system became clear other brands of paperback proliferated; by the mid 1960s most traditional publishers either overtly or covertly owned a paperback imprint. As competition increased some of these imprints survived by doing what Penguin had largely abandoned – exploiting outlets other than conventional bookshops, such as newsagents, supermarkets and general stores. This tendency imitated a much more pronounced one in America where lack of an equivalent to the Net Book Agreement meant that bookshops were scarcely viable in any but the biggest cities. It would in any case have probably been the norm for one distinct category of paperbacks – 'genre' paperbacks which were normally original works without literary pretensions, such as the Mills and Boon novels.

The growing paperback market (30 per cent of the total book market by the 1970s) made it possible to fulfil the long-standing dreams of publishers, as quoted by Janice Radway in her study of the romantic novel: 'it was possible to make book sales predictable and more profitable if one could establish a permanent conduit between a publishing source and a consuming audience and keep that conduit constantly filled with material that would continue to satisfy individual readers.' (*Reading the Romance* University of North Carolina Press 1984) One way of establishing predictability was to build on existing success. Therefore the majority of paperbacks remained as reprints, though the pressure for novelty and from competition gradually shortened the gap between the first publication of a novel in hardback and the paperback edition (just as in the last century the interval between three-decker and single-volume edition became very short). Whereas seven years elapsed between the hardback and paperback versions of *Lucky Jim* (1954), in the case of *The French Lieutenant's Woman* (1969) this delay was only twelve months. The logical outcome was a more respectable image for the paperback accompanied by a rise in price and quality and even the occasional first appearance of a serious novel in paperback.

Hard selling and heavy advertising have supported this 'reprint pattern', in which the emphasis is on a new wave of titles making an impact each month. A second approach is one which emphasises not the novelty but the uniformity of the product; its dependability provides the appeal to readers who seek security rather than challenge in their reading habits. This approach is associated with publications like the romantic novels put out by Mills and Boon which are 'original' rather than reprints but are written to an obvious formula. Even critics of Q. D. Leavis would concede that these novels are difficult to discuss in the same breath and using the same techniques as the subjects of traditional literary criticism, though they are not necessarily liable to lead to the debasement of the latter or seduce its readership away.

Ian Fleming's Bond novels share the characteristics of both types of paperback. The Pan editions were reprints of hardback novels in the first instance. However, their success in paperback can largely be put down to their exploitation of a strong formula element, characteristic of such publications and of much 'popular' fiction before:

In 1965 the Bond books sold 6m of Pan's 21m. They were in a real sense a breakthrough comparable in some ways to Lane's, thirty years earlier [i.e. the first Penguins]. Hitherto the million-sellers in paperback had been largely haphazard, lucky shots, sex soap operas or long servers. (The first five were *Lady Chatterley*, *Peyton Place*, *Saturday Night and Sunday Morning*, *Dam Busters Odyssey*. . . .) The importance of the Bond books was that they revealed a new reliable market for a certain kind of book that was not trash and could be marketed as a 'brand name' (i.e. 'the latest Bond'). (Sutherland, p. 176)

This suggestion of Sutherland's indicates that the Bond novels offer particularly fruitful examples of social and cultural factors at work. Studying them involves a consideration of the related issues of 'genre' and 'formula'.

Genre

Genre has been used elsewhere in this book in its traditional literary-critical sense – for example to describe the specific fictional category of 'the historical novel' as pioneered by Scott. However, the term acquires particular socio-cultural overtones when it is used not just in a retrospective way by literary critics but by publishers of current works which are targeted on a specific readership. In this narrower sense it might apply to the output of the Minerva Press in the early nineteenth century, which specialised in Gothic sensationalism, just as much as to Mills and Boon romances today. The American term 'genre fiction' is perhaps more appropriate for this commercially-oriented conception of genre. (It has also been called 'category fiction' or 'semi-programmed' fiction.)

Genre fiction emerges when readers seek the security of themes and treatment with which they are familiar and publishers respond by meeting those needs, which provide for them the advantage of a stable and reliable market. In extreme forms this can lead to a de-individualising process, in which the identity of the individual novel or author can take second place to the publisher's imprint (seen by the market as a guarantee of the form); authors may be anonymous or pseudonymous or shift identity, as is shown by Janice Radway's study of the American Harlequin romances.[1]

Extreme forms of genre fiction are characterised by writers with a prolific output and highly organised (sometimes crippling) work schedules. Sutherland mentions the 560 books written over forty years by the detective-story author John Creasey, while Janice Radway points to the apparently insatiable demand indicated by the fact that American publishers were issuing thirty-five titles *a month* in the 'gothic romance' category alone between 1969 and 1972, each with a typical first printing of 800,000. She quotes one of the latter publishers as saying: 'Readers of books of this kind ask not 'Have I heard of this book?' but, 'Did I enjoy the last dozen Silhouettes I read?' His publishing house retains a 'test group' of readers who try out each new romance for 'acceptability' just as if it were a new detergent.

Genre fiction is one in which in Sutherland's words: 'Plot

automatism is common and becomes more so as one goes down into the pulpier depths'. (ibid. p. 193) As such it seems to bear out Q. D. Leavis's fears about a debased fiction which simply panders to what she refers to as a desire for 'substitute living' – mindless escapism. Yet it can be argued that this demand has always been met, for example in the penny novelettes of the Victorian period, and there is no evidence that what is aesthetically distinctive in fiction is being extinguished by the stereotype. Some genre writers have transcended the apparent limitations of the conventions and subject matter – for example, Isaac Asimov and Ray Bradbury in science fiction or John Le Carré in spy fiction – while 'serious' writers have raided genre for plots, settings and themes. Although genre is said to be distinguished by a 'high ratio of familiar to strange elements' this only corresponds in extreme cases to the ratio of 'inartistic' to 'artistic'. The pressure of readers (their 'horizon of expectation') for 'more of the same' can be withstood, though at the cost of financial and artistic isolation. The dilemma is illustrated by a young science-fiction writer whom Sutherland quotes: 'If ever I was going to achieve an outlet as a writer of fiction I saw I would have to go to the commercial markets, the mass or genre markets, that is to say, and while partially converting myself to the strictures of category fiction *sneak in* my literary intentions.' (Sutherland, p. 195)

The case of the so-called 'spy novel' illustrates the idea that there is not necessarily a rigid distinction between 'genre' and other fiction. Although most authors of such novels have been 'popular' in the sense of aiming at and attracting large readerships and having few literary pretensions, on the whole publishers have not packaged and marketed the genre in quite such a uniform way as they have tended to do for 'romances' or 'mysteries'. Nevertheless the authors have been aided by the existence of certain conventions that have enabled at least the less inventive of them to regard their output as a market product rather than a work of art.

The tradition on which the spy genre draws goes back to Kipling's *Kim* (1901) and Erskine Childers' *Riddle of the Sands* (written in 1903 and relating to the invasion hysteria which preceded the First World War). The original spy heroes, at least in British as opposed to American novels, were 'gentlemen' who regarded espionage as an elaborate game; the term 'The Great Game', describing manoeuvring between Russia and Britain on the boundaries of their respective 'spheres of influence' in Asia, is symptomatic. The writers of these earlier stories had themselves often worked in the Secret Service (authenticity remains an important requirement of this genre up to the present day); they modelled their heroes on their colleagues – public school, Oxbridge, often xeno-phobic and racist and glorying in physical not mental culture.

Later spy heroes became 'professionals' paid a regular salary – whereas their predecessors often became involved in espionage by accident – and were familiar with the more sordid techniques of the trade. The heroes of Len Deighton and Le Carré (conceived in the 1950s and 1960s) often have lower-middle or working-class origins, lack sympathy with the values of their superiors, and are very much concerned with routine matters of 'pay and conditions'. Joan Rockwell, who has charted this development, points out that it coincides with and reflects the taking-over by 'gentlemen' civil servants of the control and management of the 'real life' secret service; the relationship between Le Carré's plebeian Leamas and his upper-class superiors reverses that of Somerset Maugham's gentleman-spy Ashenden and his boss, whom he regards as socially inferior.

Within the genre there is therefore a range of possible ways in which the portrayal of espionage may relate to social realities – or to the reflection of them in contemporary values and ideology. Nevertheless there is an acceptance by readers and writers of this kind of novel as constituting a 'genre'. They are essentially contracts between a writer and his readers, in which promises are made to fulfil certain expectations. The longer the history of the genre the firmer those expectations become, but on the other hand the greater the firmness of the conventions the greater the aesthetic effect to be achieved by bending or breaking them. In the Bond novels the variations to the basic formula are only of the most superficial kind, sufficient to sustain novelty and interest, but Le Carré's work, particularly in its analysis of characters and values, is individual enough to make us question the application of the term 'genre fiction' to his novels at all, while the fiction of Graham Greene, though it deals in novels like *The Human Factor* with the same subject matter clearly belongs to a different dimension altogether.

Thrillers, Spies and Secret Agents

Critics disagree as to the boundaries of the spy genre. Jerry Palmer in his book *Thrillers* (1978) takes the broadest view which locates 'spy fiction' as a subcategory in the 'thriller' genre, other subcategories being the 'classic' detective story of Arthur Conan Doyle and Agatha Christie (based essentially on a puzzle) and the more violent American private-eye novel of Raymond Chandler, Micky Spillane and James Hadley Chase. The common characteristic of these narrative-types is the element of suspense.

The Danish writer Lars Ole Sauerberg on the other hand while accepting the category of suspense fiction, finds distinctive elements in what he calls 'secret agent fiction'. (This term unlike Joan Rockwell's 'spy fiction' takes account of the hero who is engaged purely in counter-espionage or *agent provocateur* activities – as Bond largely is.) Like Palmer, Sauerberg identifies a common structure in the novels he examines but also like another critic, Umberto Eco, he finds a formula peculiar to Fleming's novels alone, though related to the common elements.

One useful model for the analysis of genre in terms of formula and structure is the analysis of oral literature (for example ballads and folk-tales) with which it shares some characteristics, for example the relative subordination of the individual author. Propp's work on Russian folk-tales is often taken as a starting point for this method of analysis which consists of isolating the individual elements and then examining how they are structured and sequenced over a number of instances. In his study *Secret Agents in Fiction* (Macmillan 1984) Sauerberg, using this approach, finds resemblances between the three authors, Le Carré, Fleming and Deighton, and traditional romances with their basis in the *quest* and *conflict* between hero and adversary. This explains the universal appeal underlying secret agent fiction but it is the *particular* characteristics which seem to explain its peaks of momentary popularity (for example in the

period from the 1950s to the 1980s). The five particular characteristics are:

(1) A 'dichotomous' structure, based on a contrast between
    the hero's activities at 'home' in England and 'abroad',
    in an alien environment.
(2) A concern with *ethical* issues (particularly as raised by a
    clash between the demands of national security and
    personal morality).
(3) A *plot* which takes the standard form of: assignment –
    departure and return – preliminary ordeal – conclusive
    ordeal – clarification.
(4) *Standard roles* for hero, adversary and 'hero's helpers'.
(5) A *theme* concerning British decline in power in inter-
    national affairs.

In his discussion of the 'thriller' Palmer identifies fewer
characteristic elements, as one would expect given the wider
category. The two essential ingredients he identifies are a hero
who acts as a *professional* and the *defeat of a malign conspiracy.*
The hero's professionalism contrasts on the one hand with the
'bureaucratic inflexibility' of his adversary (the members of the
conspiracy) and even of his own allies; on the other hand it
shows up the 'amateurism' or 'incompetence' of other involved
parties, for example his female helpers. This professionalism
usually exploits a flexibility which derives from the ability to
learn from experience; possession of it gives the hero a position
of glamorous isolation before and after the assignment.

Because of the hero's success and self-reliance Palmer describes him as *competitive* (he competes against allies as well as
enemies). The conspiracy on the other hand is essentially
mysterious in that its motivation seems irrational in the ordered
world which the hero is assigned to defend: 'What the thriller
asserts at root, is that the world does not contain any inherent
sources of conflict: trouble comes from people who are rotten,
but whose rottenness is in no way connected with the nature of
the world they infect.' (p. 87)

Both Palmer and Sauerberg prove to their own satisfaction
that the Bond novels exhibit the characteristics they identify.
Before examining the truth of this, however, there is another

and more specific analysis to consider – that of the Italian structuralist Umberto Eco who has attempted to isolate the formula which characterises the Bond novels and which is peculiar to them (though of course it relates to the overall structures to be found in the genre). In *The Role of the Reader* (Hutchinson 1981) Eco sees each Bond novel as structured around fourteen sets of *oppositions*. Four of these relate to the main characters:

(1) Bond–M
(2) Bond–Villain
(3) Villain–Woman
(4) Woman–Bond

Two are based on political and cultural opposites:

(5) Free World–Soviet Union
(6) Great Britain–Non-Anglo-Saxon Countries

Eight are based on values:

(7)   Duty–Sacrifice
(8)   Cupidity–Ideals
(9)   Love–Death
(10) Chance–Planning
(11) Luxury–Discomfort
(12) Excess–Moderation
(13) Perversion–Innocence
(14) Loyalty–Disloyalty

Not only do these opposing values characterise Bond and his adversary, but they are reflected in other characters (the Woman is torn internally between Purity and Perversion) or character oppositions (the Villain–Woman opposition can be characterised as a Love–Death opposition).

The fourteen oppositions form the structural building blocks of each Bond novel. The *sequence* of the novels, however, follows this pattern of eight moves – in Eco's analogy of a chess game 'move' refers to one character taking the initiative in relation to others:

(A) M. moves and gives a task to Bond.
(B) Villain moves and appears to Bond (perhaps in vicarious forms).
(C) Bond moves and gives first check to Villain or Villain gives first check to Bond.
(D) Woman moves and shows herself to Bond.
(E) Bond takes Woman (possesses her or begins her seduction).
(F) Villain captures Bond (with or without Woman or at different moments).
(G) Villain tortures Bond (with or without Woman).
(H) Bond beats Villain (kills him or kills his representative or helps at their killing).
(I) Bond, convalescing, enjoys Woman whom he then loses.

This sequence, which Eco punningly refers to as 'Bond moves and mates in eight [sic!] moves', is the equivalent of what Palmer, following Propp, refers to as the 'dominating' procedure of the Bond novels. Fleming's work can be described as highly formulaic, if Eco is right, since all these elements appear in each novel, though there can be minor alterations in sequence and repetition is allowed to cater for the occasional duplication of Woman or Villain. After the reader has read one or two of the novels he is familiar with the 'pieces' and 'moves' and thenceforth the appeal lies in appreciating the author's skill in varying and applying the formula:

> It would be more accurate to compare a novel by Fleming to a game of basketball played by the Harlem Globetrotters against a local team. We know with absolute confidence that the Globetrotters will win: the pleasure lies in watching the trained virtuosity with which they defer the final moment, with what ingenious deviations they reconfirm the foregone conclusion, with what trickeries they make rings round their opponents. (*The Role of the Reader*, p. 160)

It should be clear from this summary that the formulae identified by Palmer, Sauerberg and Eco respectively are not contradictory; each can be seen as a more detailed variant (or 'inflection') of the previous one, reflecting Palmer's treatment of 'secret agent' fiction as a subcategory of the thriller. It is when we come to the question of *ideology* that we notice significant differences between Palmer and Sauerberg arising from the concern of the latter with a more specific, narrower group of texts. Before considering this, however, we need to see how the formulae are employed in a specific Bond novel.

'Thunderball': Formula in Action

Thunderball was the eighth Bond novel, written in 1960 and published in 1961, an important turning point in Fleming's career, the year of the filming of *Dr No*, the first Bond film. As a result of the associated publicity, the novels which had previously had a large but not phenomenal readership now took off; in 1961 alone sales rose from 370,000 to 670,000. *Thunderball* was itself partly based on a filmscript which Fleming had developed with the aid of a film producer called Kevin McClory and a scriptwriter, Jack Whittingham; this fact led to some expensive litigation over the copyright which has resulted in all subsequent editions bearing the names of these two men. *Thunderball* also marks a change in the theme of the Bond novels, since the conspiracy which confronts Bond is no longer the Russian spy organisation SMERSH, but the criminal syndicate SPECTRE.

The structure of the novel shows some interesting variations on that outlined by Eco (and even on Sauerberg's looser pattern). The story begins conventionally enough with a summons from Bond's superior, M, but instead of providing the hero with an assignment M reprimands Bond for his physical state, especially his addiction to alcohol and tobacco, and orders him to a health farm. In this unlikely environment the 'preliminary ordeal', to use Sauerberg's term, takes place, but it is set up not by the Villain (whom we have yet to meet) but by his representative, one Count Lippe.

After Bond successfully turns the tables on Lippe, the focus switches to the headquarters of SPECTRE in Paris; the following chapter which introduces us to its leader, Blofeld, Bond's adversary in this and succeeding books, bears out Palmer's suggestion that Fleming's method involves increasing suspense by presenting some passages in each novel from the Villain's point of view. (See Palmer's contribution to *Popular Literature and Social Change* ed. C. Pawling, 1984) Blofeld shares many features with Fleming's other villains: physical abnormality – he is twenty stone in weight, sexless and has a mouth like a 'badly-healed wound' but 'long silken black eyelashes that should have belonged to a woman'; indeterminate ethnic origins – his mother was Greek, his father Polish and he himself owes allegiance to no particular nation; and an extremely powerful personality. The latter aspect is emphasised in the scene in which Blofeld ruthlessly destroys a disobedient member of his organisation. When he goes on to outline the conspiracy which is to form the basis of the plot – the theft of two atomic devices and the extortion of money from Britain and America in exchange for their return – we learn that Count Lippe is Blofeld's agent. He too is ethnically-mixed, partly Portuguese but with a 'dash of the Chinaman' as befits Blofeld's vicarious self.

The first six chapters form a sort of rehearsal for the main plot: the assignment is the health farm; the preliminary ordeal – Bond's experience on 'the rack'; the major ordeal is the Turkish bath; the girl, whom we never hear of again, Patricia Fearing. Chapter 7 which recounts the first episode proper, the setting of the main assignment (recovery of the bombs), finds not only Bond but the whole world in a state of uncharacteristic relaxation: 'With the Cold War easing off, it was not like the old days.' (Triad Panther edn., p. 67) However, the assignment involves Bond in departure for the challenge of alien territory (although nominally British the Bahamas are overshadowed by American influence); his departure means a return to his old eating and drinking habits as he prepares himself physically for the struggle against the ruthlessness and omnipresence of SPECTRE which is further emphasised by the murder of the disposable agents, Count Lippe and the Italian pilot of the bomb-carrying aeroplane.

In the Bahamas we meet another of the Villain's representatives, Emilio Largo, who resembles Blofeld in his physical distinctiveness – his hands are almost twice the normal size – and mental superiority. ('Always he had seen the essential step ahead that would have been hidden from lesser men'. (p. 96))

As usual he has power over the Woman, in this case Domino Vitale, who runs true to Fleming type in her beauty, her mixed origins (Austrian-Italian) and physical impairment (a limp). Bond for his part receives the assistance of a 'helper', Felix Leiter of the CIA, who is clearly cast in a 'supporting role' although the action takes place in America's own backyard.

According to the Eco structure Bond must seduce the Woman, so as to release her from the Villain's control and any implication of guilt (Eco's Move E). In the course of this he discovers that Largo is masterminding operations in the Caribbean and arranges with her to signal to him if she finds any trace of the bombs on Largo's hydrofoil. The last phase of the story sees Bond and Leiter pursuing the hydrofoil aboard an American nuclear submarine (having characteristically disobeyed their instructions). Domino is discovered while searching for the bombs and tortured in line with Eco's move G; however in *Thunderball* Bond himself is not captured. Instead he launches himself into the *major ordeal* (the preliminary one having already taken the form of an underwater fight against Largo's frogman). The climax of the novel is a hand-to-hand fight between Bond and Largo, in which Bond is rescued by Domino who shoots Largo as the hero is on the point of death. The novel closes with hero and Woman united but we know on the experience of previous Fleming novels (and thanks to Eco's analysis) that the very next Bond book will open with their separation.

Bond: the Ideology

Thunderball illustrates well enough how the Bond novels follow the structural requirements of a genre. However, if socio-cultural theories of fiction can be applied to popular novels we should also expect an explanation of the dominance of the genre itself in the mid twentieth century, in terms of the ideological needs it serves.

Palmer's account of the 'thriller' attempts this through the two factors which for him characterise the genre: the *competitive hero* and the *mysterious conspiracy*. Palmer points out that although Edgar Allan Poe had invented the detective story in the

1840s it was not until Conan Doyle that the form (the earliest sort of thriller) became established and popular, in the 1880s. This can be attributed to two developments: by the end of the century the ideology of competitiveness derived from bourgeois individualism had infected even the better paid working class, and in the same period growing middle-class fear of crime had merged with a suspicion of working-class political agitation, to create a generalised anxiety over the threat to 'respectable society'. In literary terms the threat was transmuted into the mysterious and irrational conspiracy against the prevailing order.

In the inflection of the thriller we call the spy novel this 'pathological irruption' has taken the traditional, almost fossilised, form of a threat to the security of the Western world. In the pre-Second World War spy stories (for example by John Buchan) the threat was to Britain and her Empire; however, the onset of the Cold War simplified the complicated international politics of the 1930s into a straight polarity of East versus West. From the pre-war spy fiction, however, there was derived a crude racial doctrine of sophisticated Europeans opposed by scarcely human non-Europeans. Therefore in early Bond novels (up to *Thunderball*) the threat to Western security (now conceived of as British plus American interests) is represented by the Soviet conspiratorial organisation SMERSH; however an additional *frisson* is provided by the presence of Oriental and other non-European ingredients, particularly in the Villain, which relates these stories to such writers as Buchan, Sapper and Saxe Rohmer. The theme of racial contamination may even account for the fact that Bond always loses the Woman, since she is usually not Anglo-Saxon and often not European.

Eco believes that Fleming's racialism (as seen for example in the Haitian origins of Mr Big in *Live and Let Die*, the Jewish Goldfinger and the Chinese-German Dr No) is merely opportunistic; the alien-ness of the non-European races helps to provide maximum contrast between heroes and villains. It can be argued, however, that the play upon xenophobia is significant and becomes more important in the later books because it partly substitutes for the declining power of the Soviet menace. *Thunderball* which replaces SMERSH by SPECTRE (which is significantly a non-Anglo-Saxon organisation) is the first and starkest illustration of this change, which can be partly attributed to the general relaxation of international tension which followed the defusing of the Berlin crisis and other events of the early 1960s such as the signing of the nuclear test-ban treaty and the relatively liberal leadership of Kennedy in America and Khrushchev in Russia.

It is misleading to say, however, that *Thunderball* is a straightforward thriller based on international crime. The plot itself, in which NATO's own nuclear weapons are used for blackmail, threatening first a rocket base and then a Western city, depends on the Cold War legacy which produced the weapons in the first place. As Tony Bennett says: 'If the early novels play on the tensions of the Cold War period, the latter ones play on the fragility of the newly forged structures of detente.' (*Politics, Ideology and Popular Culture* Open University U203, Unit 21, 1982, p. 10) Fleming knows even as he plays down the cruder East–West hostility that he can rely on his readers' perception that it has not disappeared but merely entered a new phase of secrecy and suspicion. In doing so, however, he deliberately tampers with historical reality in one extraordinary way; it is Britain not America which is made to act as the senior partner in the Western alliance, through the primacy given to James Bond as the British representative.

Lars Ole Sauerberg sees concern with Britain's loss of a role in the world as a feature of the work of Fleming, Le Carré and Len Deighton, each of whom resolves it in a different way. Fleming's solution is simple anachronism; he puts the clock back by assigning Bond and the British Secret Service an authority and influence they could not possibly have had even in the late 1950s. The aftermath of Suez (in which Britain was revealed to be both unethical and ineffective in her foreign policy) and the collapse of Britain's efforts to maintain a truly independent 'nuclear deterrent' were just two of many ways in which Britain's declining status became evident in this period; the response of the conservative media and the Establishment was to insist on a 'special relationship' with America, giving rights of consultation over the economically more powerful nations of Europe and Japan. According to Tony Bennett: 'As Britain's imperialist status visibly and rapidly waned . . . the novels were successful, at least in part, because they offered an imaginary outlet to a historically blocked jingoism.' (ibid. p. 9) This jingoism was identical with that of the *Daily Express* at the time, the newspaper in which the Bond stories were usually serialised after publication; pandering to it meant that Fleming had to reverse the status of America and Britain in the persons of Bond and the CIA man Leiter, who features in the novels as Bond's brave but slightly less perceptive subordinate. The relationship is reflected even in the *structure* of the plots since Bond takes the initiative in each case, leaving Leiter to offer American financial or technical support. It also appears in details such as Bond's implausible comments on the superiority of British atomic submarines, at a time when historically the British government was begging America for a share in the Polaris programme. Ideologically, the Bond novels conceptualise America as a powerful but musclebound giant, whose resistance to hostile attack needs to be directed by British skill and strength of purpose.

Even so there are suggestions in *Thunderball* that American rivalry may be dangerously close to becoming superiority. The Bahamas setting illustrates perfectly that this can take a cultural form. Bond stays at a hotel 'to which had recently been applied a thin veneer of American efficiency and tourist gimmicks – iced water in his room, a Cellophane-wrapped basket of dingy fruit "with the compliments of the management" and a strip of "sanitised" paper across the lavatory seat.' (p. 117) The threat of cultural Americanisation, in all its cheap pretentiousness, challenges British supremacy just as radically though less overtly than the gangsters of SPECTRE. In *Thunderball* these two threats are complemented by a third – that of subversion from within, brought about by the collapse of traditional standards and values.

This theme receives its bluntest expression at the beginning of Chapter 2 where Bond is conveyed to the health farm by a young taxi-driver whose 'cheap self-assertiveness' the hero identifies with high wages, adolescent rebelliousness and the dawn of what later came to be called 'pop culture'. ('This youth, thought Bond, makes about twenty pounds a week, despises his parents, and would like to be Tommy Steele.' (p. 16)) Although Bond's rather incongruous 'retired colonel' mood soon breaks down, his crustiness betrays his sense of threat; the meritocratic assertiveness that grew out of post-war affluence and full employment is introduced here as one of a number of challenges to the hero's integrity.

All Fleming's readers notice and are charmed or repelled by the atmosphere of high living evoked by the novels. Even Hugh Gaitskell, theoretically an enemy of upper-class luxury, wrote to Bond's creator: 'The combination of sex, violence, alcohol and at intervals good food and nice clothes is, to one who lives such a circumscribed life as I do, irresistible.' (J. Pearson *The Life of Ian Fleming*, Cape 1966) Certainly the environments which Bond frequents with ease – expensive clubs, a Park Lane apartment, rich men's sports – identify him with the upper-class heroes of the inter-war spy stories of Buchan and 'Sapper'. It is scarcely surprising therefore that he recoils from a changing English society that allows young working-class people unprecedented economic and social power.

'Food' is one area in which the battle over standards emerges. As Eco has pointed out meals are always prominent in the novels and described in loving and knowledgeable detail. In *Thunderball* this aspect of Bond's life-style is threatened in two ways. The onset of Americanised commercialism and a new classless ostentatious affluence is represented by a pretentious menu that Bond and Leiter are offered at the Royal Bahamian Hotel where the advertised 'Tender Farm Chicken, Broiled to a Rich Brown, Basted with Creamery Butter and Disjointed for Your Convenience' turns out to be 'five shilling's worth of badly cooked rubbish'. (p. 124) Secondly, a threat to traditional values in eating and drinking is posed by the health farm, Shrublands, to which M exiles Bond.

At Shrublands the threat of 'crankiness' or 'progressivism' is symbolised by the alien Central European names of the dietary authorities: 'Kneip, Preissnitz, Rikli, Schroth, Grossman, Bilz.' In the anachronistic imperialist world of Bond it seems unlikely that they would have anything to teach the hero and so it proves: although Bond's stay at Shrublands superficially energises him, it also makes him vulnerable to Count Lippe's machinations. When the actual

Thunderball assignment begins Bond immediately abandons the Shrublands regime for the traditional diet of a red-blooded hero:

> I can't do my work on carrot juice. I've got to be off in an hour and I need some proper food. Be an angel and make me your kind of scrambled eggs – four eggs. Four rashers of that American hickory-smoked bacon if we've got any left, hot buttered toast – your kind not wholemeal – and a big pot of coffee, double strength. And bring in the drink tray. (p. 82)

The ideology of masculine heartiness expressed here can be related to a primitive belief in the need of the hero to maintain his strength by eating the proper food. (The protein-rich breakfast also connects with the imperialist ideology by being symbolically 'British'.) Goat's milk yoghurt and low-tar cigarettes may revitalise the body in times of idleness but the tension of action must be fed with traditional fare – meat, alcohol and stimulants. In this passage the class-based and masculine authority of Bond is (for the unsophisticated reader) comfortingly reasserted over the progressive, namby-pamby influences which are represented as too strong in post-war Britain.

Reference to 'masculinity' prompts a mention of one final facet of the Bond ideology – the rampant sexism in which the books abound. This is so obvious and has been so extensively documented that it is probably unnecessary to describe in detail how women are subordinated by Bond's 'love 'em and leave 'em' style and by the structural device of introducing a fresh heroine in each novel. The long comments on p. 109 of the Pan edition of *Thunderball* show how blatant and unashamed Fleming's sexism can be; and how the reader is expected to go along with it. As with the political ideology a traditional role for women is asserted, though this does not prevent Domino, for example, acting with bravery and initiative. Possibly the ambiguity of the Woman, who is less than completely passive, suggests, as with Bond's anxieties about social change, that in the novels Fleming was unprepared to bolt down tightly the ideological lid; however, the film versions were able to exploit this gap in the general sexist ideology, as the next section shows.

'Incrustations' of Bond

It may seem perverse to have proceeded so far without mention-
ing the Bond films from which many people receive their most
vivid mental impression of the hero. One factor in popular
fiction which should not be ignored is the ease with which its
characters can take on a 'life of their own'. This tendency is not
confined to modern examples: Watt has shown how Crusoe
became the semi-mythical figure of folklore and pantomime in
a very short space of time, and Pickwick and Sherlock Holmes
provide nineteenth-century examples. In the modern cultural
context, however, there may be two distinct stages; the first is
the deliberate transfer under copyright of concepts and characters to other media and the second is the appropriation of them
by the public consciousness in a semi-mythical role. The first
stage may of course affect the shape which the myth eventually
acquires and Tony Bennett claims that in relation to the Bond
'myth' the novels have no special privileged position: 'Even our
reading of the "originating" texts can never be naïve; it is
influenced by such later "texts of Bond" as the films, visual
representations like the comic strip version which ran in the
Daily Express, and "continuations" of the Bond series by authors
like Kingsley Amis, Christopher Wood, and John Gardner.
('Text and Social Process: the Case of James Bond' *Screen
Education* Winter/Spring 1982, p. 11) Also significant are the
contexts in which Bond was serialised: first the *Express* and
later *Playboy*, publications with connotations of imperialist
nostalgia and male hedonism respectively.

Although it is stimulating to examine, as Bennett does, the
different forms in which Bond has been 'appropriated', the aim
of this chapter is not to detail the various 'incrustations' of
Bond (to use Bennett's term) but to throw light on the role of
popular fiction as the centre of a web of commercial and
cultural pressures and expectations. Bennett recognises this
centrality of the novels when he writes: 'The novels are undoubtedly privileged in the sense that historically they came
first. They function as a textual source for the film, and as
legitimators – both culturally (an authentic Bond film must,
however loosely, be based on a Fleming source) and legally
(Eon productions owns the film rights to all the Bond titles

except *Casino Royale*).' (ibid. p. 12) On the other hand if we take into account the effect on book sales of the first Bond film in 1961 (they rose from 300,000 in 1960 to 670,000 in 1961, one and a half million in 1962 and seven million in 1965) the films are clearly of first significance: 'The figure of Bond established by Sean Connery's portrayal for example, is likely to have cancelled out and over-ridden other-mind's eye images of the hero that might earlier have been constructed in relation to the novels.' (ibid. p. 12) This is supported by a comment of Fleming himself (who is said originally to have wanted the more traditional officer-and-gentleman actor David Niven to play the star part): '[Connery is] not quite the idea I had of Bond . . . but it would be if I wrote the books over again.'

Bennett identifies two important ways in which the films modify the theme of the novels: The Cold War element disappears (SMERSH is replaced by SPECTRE even in adaptations of the earlier novels and the conspiracy, as befits a period of detente, threatens both America and Russia *and* the West) and the Bond/Woman relationship is given greater prominence and spiced with an element of rivalry. In *The Spy Who Loved Me* for instance interest is focused less on Bond's conflict with the Villain than his competition with Anya, the KGB agent assigned to work alongside him. (This may have been encouraged by the fact that in this case the Fleming estate had stipulated that none of the original plot was to be used for the adaptation.) Bennett comments that the change in the sexual theme may have accounted for the popularity of the films even in a period when the women's movement was gathering strength: 'In trivialising the aspirations of that movement and, at the same [sic], projecting women as ultimately dependent on men, the films served to bolster threatened sexual identities, and this may have been reassuring for many women as well as for men.' (Open University Unit, p. 29)

Following Bennett's argument encourages seeing the Bond novels as merely one of a string of 'signifying practices', at the centre of which is the Bond figure. This figure is also constructed by the 'incrustations' in the original conception – films, commercial and marketing applications, biographies of Fleming and interviews with the stars of the films, both male and female. As a consequence the myth becomes the bearer of what Bennett calls a 'series of related ideological tensions' that enable Bond to exert a 'broad, cross-class, cross-gender and international popular appeal'. (ibid. p. 32)

The significance of this approach for the study of popular fiction is that the same process can be seen at work on other novels – and not on popular ones alone. It is in a sense the raising to the nth degree of the marketing pressure that Q. D. Leavis envisaged as the downfall of the serious work of fiction. At a time when the novel is under financial threat (as Sutherland has shown) a 'fiction industry' able to transform itself into many shapes – films, television adaptations, children's comics, even computer games – provides the promise of economic viability. The application of this even to fiction not primarily conceived as entertainment is documented in John Sutherland's account of the marketing of Ed Doctorow's novel *Ragtime* in *Fiction and the Fiction Industry*, pp. 63–83. In that case the publishers attempted to tap the vein of nostalgia running through America's bi-centennial year in the interests of a novel set in the early twentieth century. As well as exploiting the traditional film tie-in (novels are now publicised in book trade journals with the boast 'Film Rights Sold') there was pressure to enhance the prestige of the book and enlarge its captive readership by getting it accepted as a school set text. The aim (which was not achieved) was to sell a *fictional concept* rather than a novel, supported by the period associations behind the Scott Joplin revival and the ragtime score to the contemporary film, *The Sting*.

One result of this kind of trend may be a tendency for fiction to go in one of three directions. There will be formula or genre fiction which is available at very low prices because of its huge volume of sales and meeting ideological needs for well-defined readerships. There will also be 'high fiction', heavily subsidised by library purchases, and stimulated by literary prizes and other modern forms of patronage. This category is likely to be increasingly difficult for new writers to break into as sources of public and corporate funding dry up. Sutherland notes interestingly that when William Golding switched to writing full-time (underwritten by the steady sales of his previous books) his work became 'complex', 'artful' and 'difficult'.

Thirdly there is a direction in which the distinctiveness of the novel as a genre becomes blurred, in the wake of film adaptations and television serialisations (the 'novelisation' of original TV productions contributes to this), and some writers such as Fay Weldon or Frederick Raphael move between written fiction and other media. In this direction the 'text' becomes a concept, at the mercy of public reinterpretation and 'incrustation' only limited by the copyright laws, for as long as they apply. Study of this process would form a fascinating strand in any discipline of 'signifying practices' or 'cultural studies'. Its texts might include *Jaws* (sold by Peter Benchley to the film-makers on the basis of a four-page outline of a book not yet written) and the interconnecting versions of *Cabaret* (the film of the musical of the play of the novel).

The Challenge of the Popular

This last section considers how the study of popular fiction can raise a challenge to conventional literary criticism, some aspects of which the reader will probably have noticed surfacing in the preceding pages. Some examination of the term 'popular' is necessary first of all.

Although 'popular' originally implied 'of the people' the term is often used colloquially to mean 'appealing to large numbers'. Since historically the largest numbers have been those of the uneducated, 'popular' has also come to mean appealing to this group, facilitated by low price, in contrast to a more sophisticated elite. (It may still have an attraction for the latter in their 'off-duty' moments, as is shown by the 'don and the detective-story syndrome'.) In this sense 'popular' has also acquired the connotations of 'simple' and 'unsophisticated', 'untaxing'.

'Popular' has connections with 'folk' but is generally held to differ from it in the sense of not being created by 'the people' themselves, but provided for them, often (though not uniquely) in a cynical and manipulative fashion. Popular fiction resembles traditional folk art in such respects as the de-individualisation of the author, reliance on formula and stereotype and the tendency of character and situation to take on a mythical status, cut free from their original context or like James Bond 'incrusted' with later deposits.

Finally, from the perspective of traditional literary-criticism 'popular' is often defined implicitly and negatively as that which is outside the accepted canon. It is used in this sense by R. C. Terry in the title of his *Victorian Popular Fiction* (1983), where it refers to neglected but heavy-selling Victorian texts, three of which Terry rescues from obscurity by identifying in them some aesthetic qualities which at least give them a second-rank status. Such 'raids on the popular' are sometimes undertaken as a means of reassessing or revitalising the canon, but do not breach the fundamental principle of a barrier between 'popular' on the one hand and 'literary' on the other.

Breach of the principle is precisely the rallying-cry of radical critics such as Eagleton, who have come to reject the notion of a canon in itself and seek to replace a study of distinctively 'literary' texts by one of 'signifying practices'. These critics point out that criteria for including works in the canon are subjective, vague and ultimately amount to little more than 'custom and practice'. The problem is aggravated by the difficulty of evaluating very recent literature (when is it sufficiently in perspective to allow an assessment?), the intermediate status of certain texts (Trollope, Stevenson, Iris Murdoch and Tolkien might all be damned as 'middlebrow'), and shifting valuations within the canon itself (Scott, once unassailable, is now a borderline case, Raymond Chandler is almost 'respectable').

Secondly, it has been observed that in an age of varied and overlapping media to make a distinctive category of what is printed, the other sense of 'literary', is artificial and anachronistic. Yet if we open out criticism to include film and television, as has been advocated by critics, the aesthetic approach, which is associated with the study of the literary, itself comes under fire. If we can study the socio-cultural implications of *Coronation Street* without needing to bother about assessing its 'worth', why not do the same for Frederick Forsyth, Adrian Mole, or for that matter Dickens and Graham Greene?

This book is obviously based on a sympathetic response to the last question, since it has shown how socio-cultural factors can be used to illuminate the 'privileged texts' of the canon and how they can be even more easily applied to such as James Bond. Indeed conventional critics would scarcely deny the truth of the latter; they would simply disclaim it as none of their business. Having failed to find much of aesthetic or ethical interest in Bond they would leave the novels to the investigations of 'pure' sociologists before moving on to the ninety-first interpretation of flower symbolism in D. H. Lawrence.

The current situation can be summarised in a diagrammatic form (see Figure 2). This four-fold classification is the one

TYPE OF STUDY APPLIED

		Literary/critical	Socio-cultural
AESTHETIC QUALITY	High	Yes	Only as a supporting study
	Low	No	Yes

Figure 2

which even a radical critic like Goldmann defers to, when he claims that it is not his business to *discriminate* amongst literary texts but only to analyse them for ideological significance, so that, the discriminations having already been conveniently made, the works traditionally regarded as 'great' are those in which he finds evidence of a 'world view'. It is this easy identification of the 'literary' with traditional criticism and the 'popular' with both low worth and socio-cultural analysis that is challenged by Tony Bennett in a difficult but stimulating essay.[2]

Bennett's argument sorrowfully recognises the dominance of the third sense of 'popular' given above: 'The concept of popular fiction conveys – beyond the notion of numerical appeal – nothing so much as that it is *not* literature.' Even Marxist literary criticism has shown itself to be at heart a 'bourgeois enterprise' by failing to confront this distinction: Lukács does not even consider popular fiction, while Althusser and Goldmann are forced in the end to fall back on the division between 'authentic art' and that of an average or mediocre level. The Marxists are guilty of having 'patted on the back [bourgeois criticism] for having recognised which works are truly great and taken [it] to task for having misrecognised the reasons for their greatness.' (p. 141)

Since even radical critics conform in the end to traditional assumptions about literary value, Bennett suggests that the question of value itself must be reformulated. The study of 'valued works', he proposes, should be replaced by a study of 'the ideological conditions of the contestation of value'. Since 'value' is clearly not an intrinsic property of the text itself, but a quality attributed to the text by its readers, the radical critic will devote his attention to the question of *why* particular readers value certain texts at particular periods and in particular social environments. Reformulating the role of value makes it possible to dispense with the distinction between literary texts which 'have value' (conceived of as some timeless quality) and are therefore examined using the methods of literary criticism and 'popular' texts which are approached in a sociological spirit.

Although Bennett admits the shortage of information available to a study of readership, he stresses that the way forward is to concentrate less on the origins of the text (its authorship) and more on its consumption – avoiding, however, the complacent assumption that the 'implied reader' is the critic himself. An example of a study of which he might well approve is Janice Radway's *Reading the Romance* (1984). In identifying a group of women in the mid-Western United States who read Harlequin romances (resembling the British Mills and Boon) Radway not only elicited the formula on which most of the novels were based (as highly structured and uniform as that of the Bond novels) but also accounted for the expectations which the readers brought to these novels and the gratifications they took from them. She applied her information, taken from questionnaire and interview, to an analysis of this formula so as to produce a description of the ideology behind it: a patriarchal perspective on the world which enabled these married women of a certain age to 'make sense of' their conditions of existence.

Clearly the dead readers of past authors are not available for this kind of investigation, though their current counterparts are and it is interesting to speculate on whether the readerships for Scott and Jane Austen, say, would be found to be as distinct now as at the time of their first impact. There is no reason either why the consumption of the works of Samuel Beckett and John Fowles for example should not be analysed and its ideological significance discussed as it might be for more popular authors. Bennett expresses the underlying idea in jaw-breaking Marxese: 'It is . . . in the interface between the formation of subjects within the text and the (diverse and plural) formation of subjects outside the text that the (diverse and plural) effects of literary texts are located.' (ibid., p. 164) This may be translated as: 'Just as the text in a sense *creates* its own readers by providing an ideological framework for the economic and social conditions of certain individuals, so the readers create their own text by bringing to it their pre-existent ideological "set". The "effect" is in the reinforcing influence of one on the other.'

Bennett concludes his essay with a declaration that would be ringing if it were less esoteric: 'In order to engage with such issues the very notion of textual analysis needs to be jettisoned in favour of an approach which will *reinscribe* the text within, and theorise its action in relation to, modes of articulation which comprise specific and determinate moments or types of hegemony.' (ibid., p. 164) Is it hopelessly crude to interpret this as: 'Let's see what the text contributes to the maintenance of the economic and social status quo, *how* it does it, and to what extent this is in complicity with its readers, author and the prevailing institutional context or cuts across them?' As this does not in fact seem too shameful a project even for non-Marxists to attempt, it will be reconsidered in the conclusion to this book.

8. Conclusion

(In the form of a trilogue)

The scene is a seminar room.

JOHN: Well that's the end of the last lecture. You'll be relieved to know that this is the last you'll see of me for a while. Phil will be coming in next week to start a five-week block: 'The Novel and Psychoanalysis: Laclos to Lacan'. Then Jenny will be doing five weeks on 'Feminist Approaches to Fiction'. Male students will be expected to serve tea and biscuits. (*Clatter of class leaving.*) In the meantime if you need any help with the assignment, you know where to find me. Don't forget it's due in on the 25th.

What's the matter with you two? No homes to go to?

THOMAS: Patience and I were just wondering about the assignment title. . . . You've asked us to 'Assess the value of the socio-cultural approach to fiction, illustrating your answer by reference to no more than two novels'.

JOHN: That's right.

THOMAS: Would the best way of tackling it be to give a run-down on some of the main theories first?

JOHN: To deal with the topic adequately you'll have to describe the leading theoretical work. . . .

THOMAS: And go through that model of communication you gave us at the beginning?

JOHN: If I were you I'd start by summarising the various elements of the model – such as readership, mode of consumption and so on. That makes up one branch of the socio-cultural approach. Then you need to deal with all the writers who've attempted to construct theories of fiction and society . . . .

THOMAS: *All* of them?

JOHN: Well – *select*. I referred to de Staël, Taine, Marx and Engels and their followers, Leavis, Lukács, Goldmann, Williams, Eagleton, and the reception-theorists. That should be enough to choose from!

PATIENCE: I think that's the trouble really. It's rather a long list. And . . . well, I found them interesting – but didn't you rather bring out the weak points in their theories? I found there were so many flaws that none of the theories seemed to get us much further forward. Is there much point in elaborating some theory, only to knock it down immediately afterwards?

JOHN: Don't forget that these are critics who've had a certain influence in their time and more recent writers often refer to them. . . .

THOMAS: Take Goldmann as an example –

JOHN: An extreme example, perhaps.

THOMAS: Maybe! But my point is that you described his ideas of 'genetic structuralism' and 'world vision' and then hardly referred to them again afterwards. You certainly didn't *apply* either idea to the novels we looked at in detail.

JOHN: That's partly because I was dealing with English novels – or rather British, to take account of Scott. Most of Goldmann's studies are of French literature.

THOMAS: That's exactly my point! It isn't easy to see how Goldmann's theories can be *reapplied* to novels other than the ones he bases the theory on. The whole business is riddled with circular reasoning –

PATIENCE: That's a geometric impossibility!

THOMAS: You know what I mean! But it isn't just Goldmann either. The same applies to most of the other theorists we've looked at. I think there's a huge gap between the approach as you describe it in the abstract and what it actually amounts to when we come to look at specific novels.

PATIENCE: That's not completely fair, Thomas. He did show how important the mode of publication was; Dickens wouldn't have written in the way he did if he wasn't under pressure because of serialisation –

THOMAS: Oh, yeah, yeah, I accept that. All the information about readership and authors and publication – I can see that's relevant. But I reckon John would have to admit that there's nothing new or revolutionary about that stuff – some of it's been around a very long time. What he did in the lectures was to group it together and label it. In my opinion the crux of the matter is to find a theory that will *explain* the relationship between fiction and society. John said himself it must be specific to given novels – and ideally not just the ones that were used to illustrate the original proposition of the theory. The theories we've heard about don't seem to measure up to that criterion – or at least I'd like to hear John show how they do.

JOHN: Wait a minute, it's half-past four on a Friday afternoon.

THOMAS: Well, at least some suggestions – some pointers on how it might be done.

JOHN: I admit I did say when I started that I'd try to assess the current state of the art as far as this sort of literary criticism is concerned – but somehow I didn't leave myself time to get round to it. Would you be prepared to accept it now?

PATIENCE: *Anything* that helps at all with the assignment. The title asked us to 'assess' the socio-cultural approach. I don't think it's fair to leave all the work to us.

JOHN: Here goes then. First of all, it's not true that I didn't mention *any* of the theorists again. I referred to Williams and Eagleton on several occasions – in relation to Dickens, Hardy and Lawrence for example.

PATIENCE: Yes, we noticed that. But some of the critics didn't make another appearance. Was there much point in including them?

JOHN: I did feel I ought to summarise the work of critics who've had influence in their time and also stimulated others. For example Leavis long ago had an influence on Williams, who was once referred to as a 'left-Leavisite'. Williams's refusal to accept the simple base/superstructure distinction might be put down to that.

Secondly there's no knowing when some of these ideas won't be taken up, expanded and *applied* by later critics, now or in the future. They aren't like outdated scientific concepts – phlogiston, say – which are dead once they're disproved. Indeed you might be forgiven for thinking that Leavis's theories were totally discredited – but they do show an amazing inability to lie down and die. Who knows – someone might seize on Goldmann's genetic structuralist method and apply it convincingly to some British fiction.

A third reason for looking at so many theorists is that they have obviously gone up some culs-de-sac – Taine's attachment to climate for example. We need to be aware of that sort of mistake so that we don't commit it ourselves. One difficulty they all have – it's almost an occupational disease – is how to relate aesthetic value to whatever explanatory processes they have developed.

THOMAS: That's one thing I wanted more discussion on! You keep bringing it up, but then you leave the argument in mid-air. Is there any work being done at the moment that looks as if it's going to solve some of these problems?

JOHN: I don't think they'll ever be *solved* in the sense in which the mystery of the genetic code was solved in biology. Each generation looks at the novels of the past in a different way, in the light of its own concerns; hence it will raise new problems as quickly as the old ones look like being dealt with. But if you want my opinion, it seems to me that aesthetic *appreciation* and socio-cultural *explanation* are two unrelated processes, even though much literary criticism mingles them. The only critics likely to claim that the two were identical are those naïve Marxists who regard as unacceptable any work that doesn't support the Revolution. In a sense the most honest approach is Goldmann's (there, I've mentioned him again!) when he says that others have already identified great works of art; his job is to relate them through a study of their structure to the world-vision of the social group that produced them.

PATIENCE: Doesn't the notion of 'ideology' give us any help here?

JOHN: Well, it ought to, particularly as Eagleton uses it; the idea of literature as 'the production of ideology' is a useful and interesting one, which Holderness draws on for his analysis of Lawrence. I'm still not clear, however, what Eagleton is saying about aesthetic value; is the aesthetic pleasure in observing this process of production, or is it relegated to the untutored reader while we more sophisticated souls who are let into the secret of the 'significant absences' are left with the cold intellectual satisfaction of seeing capitalism shored up by its imaginative forms of expression?

PATIENCE: Or failing to be shored up?

JOHN: Yes. Eagleton implicates most writers in the business of implementing middle-class hegemony but then lets the worthwhile ones off the hook by claiming that they are 'in contradiction' with it. Nevertheless Eagleton's model is a productive one –

PATIENCE: So you think it might have some offspring?

JOHN: Holderness's book seems to be one. Also Lovell's essay on Jane Austen and the gentry is sophisticated, in that she manages to make a plausible connection between Austen's supposed ideology and a typology of characters in her novels – the latter would stand alone as a worthwhile piece of criticism. The same is true of a book on Dickens by Steven Connor published in 1985[1] which shows how certain novels (e.g. *Great Expectations* and *Our Mutual Friend*) are ideological reflections of an effort in the 1860s and 1870s to incorporate the more skilled members of the working classes into middle-class dominated society – to extend hegemony in fact and smooth over ideological contradictions. As with Lovell the socio-cultural material and the literary analysis are both convincing enough in themselves; if they can also be plausibly related (as they are in these two cases) the result is a very powerful piece of criticism.

THOMAS: Should we be on the look-out for more studies of individual texts and authors then? Rather than wholesale theories?

JOHN: I hope there will be a lot more specific studies, if only to test whether the existing theories are valuable or not. As far as Eagleton's model is concerned there's an interesting critique of it in a book by Bernard Sharratt, *Reading Relations*.[2]

PATIENCE: *Reading Relations*?

JOHN: The title is quite a complicated pun on (among other things) 'social relations' (in the Marxist sense) and also on the relationship (if any) between reading literature and the practicalities of everyday living. I won't go into too much detail, but – briefly – Sharratt poses some interesting questions about Eagleton's categories of ideology, one of which is why 'ideology' should be attributed to the author only. Why shouldn't there be a Reader's Ideology (ReI) to partner

Eagleton's Authorial Ideology and if so shouldn't there be another set of relations involving revolving round ReI, AI and GI, just as AuI is related to AI and GI?

This argument seems totally logical to me and it expresses in a different way a point I have made several times, that all literature relies on an *interaction* between reader and writer, though it doesn't have to be symmetrical in character or strength. Sharratt's ReI can easily be compared to Jauss's 'horizon of expectation'. What readers *expect* and the image which writers and publishers have of those expectations forms the *overlap of values*, which Iser calls the repertoire.

Too little overlap means that there is no possibility of communication through fiction at all. Too much leads to propaganda or what Jauss calls 'culinary art' – the art of the stereotype. Perhaps Iser is right in claiming that the most successful novels are those that challenge but rely on the repertoire.

PATIENCE: So are you saying that we need more studies of readers?

JOHN: That might be one way forward. Terry Eagleton talks about a 'science of the ideological conditions of the production of value' and Tony Bennett laments the fact that there are 'as yet no serious readership studies'. They seem to be going in the same direction as each other and also as Sharratt – at least that is the impression non-Marxists might take away.

PATIENCE: Would that mean doing the same sort of thing for serious fiction as has already been done for popular novels?

JOHN: One reason for looking at popular fiction in a discussion on the novel is to blow a breath of fresh air into some pretty stale controversies. An example of a 'serious readership study' that might get Bennett's approval is Janice Radway's *Reading the Romance*. Although Bennett warns against 'simple-minded questionnaire technique' Radway's approach combines questionnaires and interviews – I don't see frankly how else you can gather accurate information about readers. Furthermore she relates these findings to an analysis of the formula behind the romances (which turns out to be as all-pervading as Eco's formula is in the Bond books) and then, drawing on feminist theory, shows how these novels serve a particular patriarchal ideology for the mid-Western middle-aged women who read them.

THOMAS: But?

JOHN: You're quick to recognise a note of doubt. The advantage for Radway, writing about current fiction, is of course that all the readers are alive and at least in theory available for interview. We couldn't do the same for Lawrence, much less Defoe or Richardson – unless we confine ourselves to present-day readers. And that opens up the whole matter of whether there's *one* readership for a novel or a series of them and at what point one turns into another – when did Scott become the hero of schoolboys rather than literary lions and when did Jane Austen become reading fare for Marxists as well as girls' grammar schools?

Maybe the reason why there has been much more concentration on authorship rather than readership is that dead authors can be identified and even characterised much more easily than long-dead readers. This is a pity as it could be argued that rather than looking particularly at the class and other characteristics of the writer it may be more productive to look at the interaction between writer and reader. Cases like those of Dickens and Mrs Gaskell are informative and revealing from this point of view; in one case there is the situation of serial publication, in the other the demands and expectations of the publisher created a context which exposed the interactive to a more than usual degree. . . .

PATIENCE: Should we be writing this down?

JOHN: It's a start anyway. What I can't do for you is to outline some all-embracing theory that will resolve all the contradictions in one go and offer a complete explanation of the relationship between fiction and the society which produces it.

PATIENCE: Interaction is the name of the game then?

JOHN: I think there's a lot of mileage in concepts like 'the horizon of expectation'. That doesn't necessarily mean that we need to jettison all our existing suppositions about the middle-class writer and his or her ideological constraints. I would be careful to stress however (that's if I were writing your assignment) that in a novel it's not only the ideology of the author speaking. Communication is a two-way process and never more so than in a market-dominated society where it is necessary to go out to attract an audience in order to 'communicate' at all. The cases of Dickens and Mrs Gaskell suggest, though we can never prove it, that the 'withdrawal of sympathy' which Raymond Williams notices in their account of the victims of poverty and exploitation might have been forced on them as part of an unspoken compromise which allowed the authors to say what they did. Hardy and Lawrence have told us they wanted to say more than contemporary conventions allowed.

Is that a help?

PATIENCE: I'll go and think about it.

THOMAS: At least it gives me something to pull to pieces.

JOHN: Well, in a sense that was the whole point of what I was doing. I never claimed to have any definite solutions. If you can find one that suits you – good luck! In the meantime, there's nothing to be ashamed of in enjoying reading the novels.

Notes

1. INTRODUCTION

1. The term is used by W. H. Bruford, 'Literary criticism and sociology' in J. Strelka (ed.), *Literary Criticism and Sociology* (Pennsylvania State University Press, 1973).

2. F. R. Leavis, *The Great Tradition* (Penguin edn, 1972), represents this approach taken to extremes. However, all higher education courses in literature assume a 'canon' of accepted texts; Raymond Williams discusses this 'selecting out' process in *Writing and Society* (Verso, 1984), pp. 193–4.

3. The standard 'communication model' is based on one developed by the mathematicians Claude Shannon and Warren Weaver. It is described in detail in David Berlo, *The Process of Communication* (Holt, Rinehart and Winston, 1967).

4. The identity of B. Traven, author of *The Treasure of the Sierra Madre*, was not revealed as Herman Feige until ten years after his death in 1969.

2. THEORETICAL APPROACHES

1. Rene Wellek, *A History of Modern Criticism* (Jonathan Cape, 1955), vol. 1, summarises the work of Herder and refers to one or two writers prior to him who interested themselves in the social origins of literature.

2. The original statements of Leavis's theory can be found in F. R. Leavis and Denys Thompson, *Culture and Environment* (Chatto and Windus, 1933) and later in Leavis's *Mass Civilisation and Minority Culture* (Chatto and Windus, 1943) and *Education and the University* (Chatto and Windus, 1948).

3. Plekhanov's work is summarised in Peter Demetz, *Marx, Engels and the Poets* (University of Chicago Press, 1967) and also discussed in Raymond Williams, *Marxism and Literature* (Oxford University Press, 1977), p. 80.

3. THE NOVEL NEW: DEFOE AND RICHARDSON

1. See John J. Richetti, *Popular Fiction before Richardson* (Oxford University Press, 1969), p. 1.

2. For a historical account see Dorothy George, *England in Transition* (Penguin edn, 1953), particularly the Appendix, and Chapter 2 of Roy Porter, *English Society in the Eighteenth Century* (Penguin edn, 1982).

4.   SCOTT AND JANE AUSTEN: VARIETIES OF CONSERVATIVE IDEOLOGY

1. Richard L. Stein, 'Historical fiction and the implied reader: Scott and Iser', *Novel* (Spring 1981) (pp. 213–231). This article examines – but rejects – the application of Iser's theory to Scott's novels.

2. See Elaine Jordan, 'The management of Scott's novels' in the 1985 volume of *The Proceedings of the Essex Conference on the Sociology of Literature* (University of Essex, 1985) pp. 146–61.

3. See Chapter II of Graham McMaster, *Scott and Society* (Cambridge University Press, 1982).

5.   THE NOVELIST IN THE MARKET PLACE: DICKENS AND MRS GASKELL

1. Eric Hobsbawm, *Industry and Empire* (Penguin edn, 1969), p. 84.

2. J. F. C. Harrison, *The Early Victorians* (Weidenfeld and Nicolson, 1971), p. 113.

3. See Kathleen Tillotson, *Novels of the 1840s* (Oxford University Press, 1961) and also Gillian Beer, 'Carlyle and *Mary Barton*, problems of utterance' in *The Sociology of Literature: 1848* (University of Essex, 1978) pp. 242–55.

4. Andrew Blake, 'The place of fiction in Victorian literary culture' *Literature and History* (Autumn 1985), pp. 203–16.

5. Burton M. Wheeler, 'The text and plan of *Oliver Twist*', *Dickens Studies Annual*, 12 (AMS Press, 1983), pp. 41–63.

6. See J. A. V. Chapple and A. Pollard (eds), *The Letters of Mrs Gaskell* (Manchester University Press, 1966), p. 250.

7. David Musselwhite, 'The novel as narcotic', in *The Sociology of Literature: 1848* (University of Essex, 1978), pp. 207–24.

6.   THE NOVELIST ON THE MARGINS: HARDY AND LAWRENCE

1. Gareth Stedman Jones, *Languages of Class* (Cambridge University Press, 1983); see also Louis James, *Fiction for the Working Man* (Penguin edn, 1974), p. 125.

2. See Richard Altick, *The English Common Reader* (University of Chicago Press, 1957), p. 383 for sales figures of bestsellers between 1813 and 1900.

3. See J. A. Sutherland, *Fiction and the Fiction Industry* (Athlone Press, 1978), pp. 12–13.

4. See Chris Baldick, *The Social Mission of English Literature* (Oxford University Press, 1983).

5. Richard Altick, 'The sociology of authorship', *Bulletin of the New York Public Library* (June 1962).

6. See Colin Holmes, 'A study of D. H. Lawrence's social origins', *Literature and History* (Spring 1980) pp. 82–94 and also C. P. Griffin, 'The social origins of D. H. Lawrence: some further evidence', ibid., (Spring 1981): pp. 223–227.

7. This account of the various versions of *Tess* is based on three books: Mary Ellen Chase, *Thomas Hardy: from Serial to Novel* (Russell and Russell,

1964); Richard Purdy, *Thomas Hardy: A Bibliographical Study* (Oxford University Press, 1954); J. T. Laird, *The Shaping of Tess of the d'Urbervilles* (Oxford University Press, 1975).

7.   THE CHALLENGE OF THE POPULAR

1. For a further discussion of the nature of genre see the introduction to Christopher Pawling (ed.), *Popular Fiction and Social Change* (Macmillan, 1984).

2. Tony Bennett, 'Marxism and Popular Fiction', *Literature and History* (Autumn 1981).

8.   CONCLUSION

1. Steven Connor, *Charles Dickens* (Basil Blackwell, 1985).

2. Bernard Sharratt, *Reading Relations* (Harvester Press, 1982).

Bibliography

This bibliography lists all the books referred to or quoted in the text as well as some others which have relevance. It is split into two sections – a list of theoretical and general literary/critical works, plus historical works quoted for context, and books which specifically relate to the key texts examined in detail. The references to the texts themselves are to the easily accessible Penguin editions, except for *Clarissa* (Everyman edition, 1965) and *Thunderball* (Triad/Panther, 1978). For ease of reference a book is listed twice when it seemed particularly relevant in both sections.

General and Theoretical

Walter Allen, *The English Novel* (Phoenix House, 1954)

Richard Altick, *The English Common Reader* (University of Chicago Press, 1957)

—— 'The sociology of authorship', *Bulletin of the New York Public Library* (June 1962)

Chris Baldick, *The Social Mission of English Literature* (Oxford University Press, 1983)

Honoré de Balzac, *The Chouans*, trs. Crawford, (Penguin, 1972)

Tony Bennett, 'Marxism and popular fiction', *Literature and History* (Autumn 1981)

Walter Besant, *The Pen and the Book* (Burleigh, 1899)

Morroe Berger, *Real and Imagined Worlds* (Harvard University Press, 1977)

David Berlo, *The Process of Communication* (Holt, Rinehart and Winston, 1967)

Andrew Blake, 'The place of fiction in Victorian literary culture', *Literature and History* (Autumn 1985)

Victor Bonham-Carter, *Authors by Profession* (Society of Authors, 1978)

Malcolm Bradbury, *The Social Context of Modern English Literature* (Basil Blackwell, 1971)

W. H. Bruford, 'Literary criticism and sociology', in J. Strelka (ed.), *Literary Criticism and Sociology* (Pennsylvania State University Press, 1973)

David Craig, 'Towards laws of literary development', in D. Craig (ed.), *Marxists on Literature* (Penguin, 1975)

Peter Demetz, *Marx, Engels and the Poets* (University of Chicago Press, 1967)

Terry Eagleton, *Criticism and Ideology* (New Left Books, 1976)

—— *Walter Benjamin or Towards a Revolutionary Criticism* (Verso, 1982)

Terry Eagleton, *The Function of Criticism* (Verso, 1984)
Dorothy George, *England in Transition* (Penguin, 1953)
George Gissing, *New Grub Street* (Penguin, 1979)
Lucien Goldmann, *Towards a Sociology of the Novel* (Tavistock, 1976)
—— *Method in the Sociology of Literature* (Blackwell, 1981)
Robert Graves and Alan Hodge, *The Long Weekend* (Faber, 1941)
John Hall, *The Sociology of Literature* (Longmans, 1979)
J. F. C. Harrison, *The Early Victorians* (Weidenfeld & Nicolson, 1971)
James Hepburn, *The Author's Empty Purse* (Oxford University Press, 1965)
Eric Hobsbawm, *The Age of Revolution* (Mentor Books, 1962)
—— *Industry and Empire* (Penguin, 1969)
Richard Holub, *Reception Theory* (Methuen, 1984)
Wolfgang Iser, *The Implied Reader* (Routledge & Kegan Paul, 1974)
—— *The Act of Reading* (Routledge & Kegan Paul, 1978)
Louis James, *Fiction for the Working Man* (Penguin, 1974)
Robert Jauss, *Toward an Aesthetic of Reception* (University of Minnesota Press, 1982)
Diana Laurenson, 'A sociological study of authorship', *British Journal of Sociology*, 20 (1969)
—— (ed.), *The Sociology of Literature, vol. 2, Applied Studies* (University of Keele, 1978)
—— and Alan Swingewood, *The Sociology of Literature* (Paladin, 1972)
F. R. Leavis, *Mass Civilisation and Minority Culture* (Chatto & Windus, 1943)
—— *Education and the University* (Chatto & Windus, 1948)
—— *The Common Pursuit* (Penguin, 1962)
—— *The Great Tradition* (Penguin, 1972)
—— and Denys Thompson, *Culture and Environment* (Chatto & Windus, 1933)
Q. D. Leavis, *Fiction and the Reading Public* (Chatto & Windus, 1932)
Leo Lowenthal, *Literature, Popular Culture and Society* (Pacific Books, 1961)
Georg Lukács, *Realism in Our Time* (Harper & Row, 1964)
—— *Studies in European Realism* (Merlin Press, 1964)
—— *The Historical Novel* (Penguin, 1969)
A. V. Lunacharsky, *On Literature and Art* (Progress Publishers, 1973)
Pierre Machery, *A Theory of Literary Production* (Routledge & Kegan Paul, 1978)
Karl Marx, *The Critique of Political Economy* (1857–9)
Karl Marx and Frederick Engels, *The German Ideology*, (1846)
Robert Mayo, *The English Novel in the Magazines 1740–1815* (Oxford University Press, 1962)
Victor Neuburg, *Popular Literature: A History and Guide* (Penguin, 1977)
Christopher Pawling (ed.), *Popular Fiction and Social Change* (Macmillan, 1984)
Roy Porter, *English Society in the Eighteenth Century* (Penguin, 1982)
John Prebble, *Culloden* (Penguin, 1967)
Janice Radway, *Reading the Romance* (University of North Carolina Press, 1984)

Joan Rockwell, *Fact in Fiction* (Routledge & Kegan Paul, 1974)
Jane Routh and Janet Wolff, *The Sociology of Literature: Theoretical Approaches* (University of Keele, 1977)
Bernard Sharratt, *Reading Relations* (Harvester Press, 1982)
Diana Spearman, *The Novel and Society* (Routledge & Kegan Paul, 1966)
Mme de Staël, *De la Littérature* (1800)
Gareth Stedman Jones, *Languages of Class* (Cambridge University Press, 1983)
George Steiner, 'Marxism and the literary critic', in T. and E. Burns (eds), *The Sociology of Literature and Drama* (Penguin, 1973)
―――― *On Difficulty* (Oxford University Press, 1978)
J. A. Sutherland, *Fiction and the Fiction Industry* (Athlone Press, 1978)
Darko Suvin, 'The social addressees of Victorian fiction', *Literature and History* (Spring 1982)
Alan Swingewood, *The Novel and Revolution* (Macmillan, 1975)
Hippolyte Taine, *History of English Literature* (1872)
―――― *Nouveaux Essais* (1865)
R. H. Tawney, *Religion and the Rise of Capitalism* (Penguin, 1964)
R. C. Terry, *Victorian Popular Fiction* (Macmillan, 1983)
Kathleen Tillotson, *Novels of the 1840s* (Oxford University Press, 1961)
Rene Wellek, *A History of Modern Criticism* (Jonathan Cape, 1955)
―――― and Austin Warren, *A Theory of Literature* (Penguin, 1963)
Raymond Williams, *Culture and Society* (Penguin, 1961)
―――― *The Long Revolution* (Penguin, 1965)
―――― *The English Novel from Dickens to Lawrence* (Paladin, 1974)
―――― *Marxism and Literature* (Oxford University Press, 1977)
―――― *Writing and Society* (Verso, 1984)

Defoe and Richardson

Terry Eagleton, *The Rape of Clarissa* (Basil Blackwell, 1982)
Christopher Hill, 'Clarissa Harlowe and her times', in J. Carroll (ed.), *Richardson: Twentieth Century Views* (Prentice Hall, 1969)
Ruth Perry, *Women, Letters and the Novel* (AMS Press, 1980)
John J. Richetti, *Popular Fiction before Richardson* (Oxford University Press, 1969)
Pat Rogers, *Robinson Crusoe* (Allen & Unwin, 1979)
Mark Shinagel, *Daniel Defoe and Middle Class Gentility* (Harvard University Press, 1968)
Diana Spearman, *The Novel and Society* (Routledge & Kegan Paul, 1966)
Ian Watt, *The Rise of the Novel* (Peregrine, 1983)

Scott

David Craig, *Scottish Literature and the Scottish People 1680–1830* (Chatto & Windus, 1961)

Donald Davie, 'Waverley' in D. Devlin (ed.), *Walter Scott* (Macmillan, 1968)
James Hillhouse, *The Waverley Novels and their Critics* (University of Minneapolis Press, 1936)
Elaine Jordan, 'The management of Scott's novels', in *Proceedings of the Essex Conference on the Sociology of Literature: Europe and its Others*, vol. 2 (University of Essex, 1985)
Georg Lukács, *The Historical Novel* (Peregrine, 1969)
Graham McMaster, *Scott and Society* (Cambridge University Press, 1982)
John Prebble, *Culloden* (Penguin, 1967)
John Henry Raleigh, 'What Scott meant to the Victorians', *Victorian Studies* (September 1963)
Sir Walter Scott, *Letters*, ed. Grigson (Constable, 1932)
Richard L. Stein, 'Historical fiction and the implied reader: Scott and Iser', *Novel* (Spring 1981)

Austen

J. Gornall, 'Marriage, property and romance in Jane Austen's novels', *History Today* 17 (1967)
Terry Lovell, 'Jane Austen and gentry society', in D. Laurenson (ed.), *The Sociology of Literature*, vol. 2, *Applied Studies* (University of Keele, 1978)

Dickens

John Butt and Kathleen Tillotson, *Dickens at Work* (Methuen, 1958)
Steven Connor, *Charles Dickens* (Basil Blackwell, 1985)
Archibald Coolidge, *Dickens as a Serial Novelist* (Iowa State Press, 1967)
Edgar Johnson, *Charles Dickens: His Tragedy and Triumph* (Penguin, 1977)
Guinevere L. Griest, *Mudie's Circulating Library and the Victorian Novel* (David and Charles, 1970)
John Lucas, *The Melancholy Man* (Methuen, 1970)
Steven Marcus, *Dickens from Pickwick to Dombey* (Chatto & Windus, 1965)
Lance Schachtele, '*Oliver Twist* and its serial predecessors', *Dickens Studies Annual 3* (AMS Press, 1980)
Kathleen Tillotson, *Novels of the 1840s* (Oxford University Press, 1961)
Burton M. Wheeler, 'The text and plan of *Oliver Twist*', *Dickens Studies Annual 12* (AMS Press, 1983)

Gaskell

Gillian Beer, 'Carlyle and Mary Barton: problems of utterance', in *The Sociology of Literature' 1848* (University of Essex, 1978)
The Letters of Mrs Gaskell, ed. J. A. V. Chapple and A. Pollard (Manchester University Press, 1966)
David Musselwhite, 'The novel as narcotic', in *The Sociology of Literature*

1848 (University of Essex, 1978)

Edgar Wright, *Mrs Gaskell: The Basis for Re-assessment* (Oxford University Press, 1965)

Hardy

Mary Ellen Chase, *Thomas Hardy: From Serial to Novel* (Russell & Russell, 1964)

Robert Gittings, *The Young Thomas Hardy* (Penguin, 1975)

____ *The Older Hardy* (Penguin, 1980)

Thomas Hardy, 'Candour in fiction', in *Life and Art* (Greenberg, 1925)

John Holmstrom and Laurence Lerner (eds), *Thomas Hardy and his Readers* (Bodley Head, 1968)

Arnold Kettle, *An Introduction to the English Novel*, vol. II (Hutchinson, 1967)

J. T. Laird, *The Shaping of Tess of the d'Urbervilles* (Oxford University Press, 1975)

Richard Purdy, *Thomas Hardy: A Bibliographical Study* (Oxford University Press, 1954)

Merryn Williams, *Thomas Hardy and Rural England* (Macmillan, 1972)

Lawrence

Terry Eagleton *Exiles and Emigrés* (Chatto & Windus, 1970)

C. P. Griffin, 'The social origins of D. H. Lawrence: some further evidence', *Literature and History* (Spring 1981)

Graham Holderness, *D. H. Lawrence: History, Ideology and Fiction* (Gill & Macmillan, 1982)

Colin Holmes, 'A study of D. H. Lawrence's social origins', *Literature and History* (Spring 1980)

F. R. Leavis, *D. H. Lawrence: Novelist* (Chatto & Windus, 1962)

Marvin Mudrick, 'The originality of *The Rainbow*', in *D. H. Lawrence: Twentieth Century Views* (Prentice Hall, 1963)

Harry T. Moore, *The Priest of Love* (Penguin, 1974)

W. W. Robson, 'D. H. Lawrence and *Women in Love*', in Boris Ford (ed.), *The Pelican Guide to English Literature* (Penguin, 1964)

Fleming and Popular Fiction

Tony Bennett ' Marxism and popular fiction', *Literature and History* (Autumn 1981)

____ 'James Bond as popular hero', in *Politics, Ideology and Popular Culture* (Open University U203, Unit 21, 1982)

____ 'Text and social process: The case of James Bond', *Screen Education* (Winter/Spring, 1982)

Umberto Eco, *The Role of the Reader* (Hutchinson, 1981)

Q. D. Leavis, *Fiction and the Reading Public* (Chatto & Windus, 1932)

Christopher Pawling (ed.), *Popular Fiction and Social Change* (Macr 1984)

J. Palmer, *Thrillers* (Arnold, 1978)

Janice Radway, *Reading the Romance* (University of North Carolina 1984)

Joan Rockwell, *Fact in Fiction* (Routledge & Kegan Paul, 1974)

Lars Ole Sauerberg, *Secret Agents in Fiction* (Macmillan, 1984)

J. A. Sutherland, *Fiction and the Fiction Industry* (Athlone Press, 1978)

—— *Bestsellers* (Routledge & Kegan Paul, 1981)

R. C. Terry, *Victorian Popular Fiction* (Macmillan, 1983)

Index